PC-Ⅱ-339

the urban land nexus and the State

Research in Planning and Design

Series editor   Allen J Scott

1 Place and placelessness   E Relph
2 Environmentalism   T O'Riordan
3 The 'new' urban economics   H W Richardson
4 The automated architect   N Cross
5 Meaning in the urban environment   M Krampen
6 Feedback from tomorrow   A J Dakin
7 Birds in egg/Eggs in bird   G Olsson
8 The urban land nexus and the State   A J Scott

p Pion Limited, 207 Brondesbury Park, London NW2 5JN

the urban land nexus and the State

A J Scott

Pion Limited, 207 Brondesbury Park, London NW2 5JN

© 1980 Pion Limited

All rights reserved. No part of this book may be reproduced in any form by photostat microfilm or any other means without written permission from the publishers.

ISBN 0 85086 079 2

Printed in Great Britain by Page Bros (Norwich) Limited

Preface

In this book, I have tried to establish the main guidelines of a determinate analysis of the phenomena of urbanization and planning. I have set about this task in two principal stages. First, I have attempted to identify something of the broad social structure and logic within which these phenomena are embedded, and from which they ultimately draw their character. Second, I have then attempted to discover in detail the ways in which these phenomena appear within society, assume a specific internal order, and change through time.

The point of departure of the book, as laid out in the introductory chapters, consists in the historical materialist conception (as I understand it) of the capitalist mode of production. On this basis, and through a series of analytical derivations, a specifically *urban* theory is proposed in the form of a set of statements about the production, appropriation, development, use, and evolution of urban space and structure. In this book, I argue that urban space and structure can only be meaningfully theorized in terms of the coalescent issues of land, land use, and the land-contingent (or locational) effects of dense social and economic activity. I further argue that it is *these* issues that properly constitute the urban instance as such. As a corollary, the loose notion of *urbanization* is here consistently referred to and conceptualized within the more focussed term, the *urban land nexus*. This latter term already carries with it a very distinctive analytical connotation in that it evokes at once the idea of the city as a seamless garment of land uses forming a compact polarized agglomeration of spatially interdependent events. Whatever their disparate internal nature, these events are identifiable as being *land-contingent* in the highly specific sense that they occur on land, and their concomitant external locational relationships create and re-create the use values of urban land. These relationships represent the very stuff from which the urban land nexus is composed. As already intimated, it is precisely out of the peculiar logic and dynamics of the urban land nexus as an assembly of dense, polarized, land-contingent events that the urban question *par excellence* arises.

The present book seeks to address and to resolve this question via the expansion of a series of concurrent themes, and the argument moves backwards and forwards from theme to theme as a basic conceptual apparatus is progressively built up. For this reason, the arrangement of chapters may at first appear to be a little odd, if only in the sense that it does not conform to any directly discoverable linear order, although, on further scrutiny, this arrangement may be seen in fact to constitute a rather intricate structured pattern. The main thematic lines of argument that are developed below are concerned with (a) the logic of (capitalist) society as a whole, (b) the concomitant structure and outcomes of the behaviour of individual firms and households in urban space, (c) the structure and outcomes of collective urban intervention, that is, urban planning, and (d) the dynamics of the urban land nexus as a total system.

In addition, interwoven through these four main themes is a rather insistent critique of mainstream theories of urbanization and planning. These various issues are addressed in a sequence of twelve chapters, and these chapters are now briefly summarized in turn. It is hoped that this ordered overview of the main contents of the book will provide the reader with an initial broad cognitive map of the staging of the argument as a whole.

Chapter 1, "The urban question in context", seeks to pin down the urban question as having its origins essentially in the spatial (and crisis-prone) momentum of the urban land nexus. It is affirmed that this momentum is derived, through successive intermediations, out of the momentum of capitalist society at large.

Chapter 2, "Mode of production, capitalism, and the State", lays down the principal conceptual foundations for all that follows. It is argued that all social analysis must be rooted (however implicitly) within the concept of a mode of production. Some of the main outlines of the capitalist mode of production and its central core—commodity production—are described. In particular, Sraffa's neo-Ricardian theory of production, pricing, and distribution of the surplus is developed at some length. A brief statement on the nature of the capitalist State is then appended by way of raising in a preliminary way some of the main issues that must be addressed in any viable theory of urban planning in capitalist society.

Chapter 3, "Commodity production and the structuring of geographical space", picks up on the theory of commodity production developed in chapter 2 and shows how it can be manipulated in such a way as to generate a spatially determinate system of land uses and land rents within some finite polarized space. The model of commodity production and land use developed here may be seen as a primitive first approximation to a theory of the urban land nexus. As subsequent chapters unfold, the severely restrictive simplifying assumptions under which this model is developed are progressively relaxed.

Chapter 4, "Urbanization and planning: a brief record of some recent problems and policies", is an attempt to motivate the explicitly urban analysis that follows by making a simple catalogue of some of the major problems that have affected cities in this century and of the major types of policy instruments that have been developed to counter them. It is shown that the human occupation of land in dense polarized spaces is in practice fraught with political predicaments.

Chapter 5, "Mainstream approaches to urban theory", now moves resolutely into the domain of the urban, and attempts to discover how the analysis of complex urban systems has been broadly tackled in the literature hitherto. Three major approaches are described and criticized in the light of what has been transacted in chapters 1-4. These approaches may be generally designated as (1) the Chicago School of urban sociology and its derivatives, (2) neoclassical urban economics, and (3) a revival of a species of nineteenth-century proudhonism that is dubbed in this account 'manipulated-city theory'.

Chapter 6, "Urban patterns 1: production space", is the first part of a two-part description of the formation of urban space as such. In conformity with the methodological and analytical apparatus developed at an earlier stage in the proceedings, this description begins with the topic of production in cities. Then, in conformity with the broad theory of commodity production and land use as set out in chapter 3, an investigation is carried through of the mechanisms governing the geographical distribution of manufacturing, office, and retail firms in the city. A major urban dynamic is deduced out of the fundamental process of the substitution of capital for labour in the sphere of production.

Chapter 7, "Urban patterns 2: reproduction and circulation space", is the second part of the description of the formation of urban space initiated in the previous chapter. The structure of urban residential activity is described, and it is suggested that the sociospatial differentiation of urban neighbourhoods can only be analyzed in the context of the norms and pressures of commodity-producing society. It is suggested, in particular, that the social geography of the city is above all an outcome of the social division of labour. The chapter ends with a discussion of the urban transport system and with a detailed analysis of the impact of urban transport on the distribution of the surplus into profits, wages, and rents.

Chapter 8, "The urban land nexus and the State", rounds out the argument set in motion in chapter 3. In contradistinction to the simple classical model of spatial equilibrium as developed in chapter 3, the present chapter shows in analytical terms that the urban land nexus is in fact susceptible to a multitude of internal dissonances, failures, and conflicts. It is demonstrated how these problems (which threaten the continued viability of commodity-producing society) emanate directly out of the qualities of the urban land nexus as a complex system of land-contingent events. Urban planning is briefly characterized as a historically determinate response to these problems.

Chapter 9, "The origins and character of urban planning", grows out of the ideas developed in chapter 8. A detailed description is undertaken of the emergence of urban planning as a collective political reaction to the innate predicaments of the urban land nexus. Planning is shown, at the same time, to be an intrinsic component element of the capitalist State. It is accordingly argued that the specific content, biases, and limitations of urban planning in practice are understandable only in the context of a problematization of urban planning as (a) a remedial means of dealing with the breakdowns of the urban land nexus, and (b) a definite formation within the total capitalist State apparatus.

Chapter 10, "Urban development and planning intervention: five illustrative sketches", is an attempt to exemplify and highlight the preceding theoretical analyses by means of five simple case studies of urban development and planning intervention. These case studies are drawn from a broad historical and geographical spectrum.

Chapter 11, "Planning ideologies", reviews and criticizes mainstream planning theory in the light of the arguments developed in chapters 9 and 10. Mainstream planning theory is shown to be characterized by two major sophisms, namely voluntarism and idealism, and, as a corollary, to be divorced from an effective comprehension of planning as a concrete social event.

Chapter 12, "Urban problems and urban planning today", briefly summarizes the tenor of much of the earlier discussion by insisting once again that the human occupation of dense polarized spaces creates innumerable predicaments. As urban planning seeks to deal with these burgeoning predicaments so it tends to become increasingly politicized and increasingly a matter of national (as opposed to purely local) concern. Some of the possible lessons of these observations for urban reform and planning practice are then briefly discussed.

The general project summarized above represents a complex, but, I believe, a compelling programme of investigation into the phenomena of urbanization and planning. In it I have tried to catch and to rework, according to my own lights, something of the new urban theory that is currently emerging in Europe and North America along the lines of enquiry originally pioneered by such seminal writers as Castells and Harvey (though it will rapidly become apparent to the reader that my own thinking differs in quite significant ways from that of both of these authors). I must add at once that my object in this book has been less to review and rehearse a mass of previously published statements than to pursue, on their own terms, whatever conceptual and theoretical lines of argument might appear in view. Wherever I have felt a particularly heavy intellectual debt to an author I have been at pains to provide an appropriate reference; similarly, I have made an attempt to provide the reader with some bibliographic signposts where I have been critical of a body of literature or where an important domain of enquiry seems to me to be especially well treated elsewhere. However, I have made absolutely no systematic effort to refer to every author whose published work intersects with mine. I feel it incumbent to make my excuses in this regard since it seems currently to be more or less obligatory in this sort of enterprise to refer directly and doggedly to a vast and disparate mass of literature. I consider this in most cases to produce an effect that varies between the deadening and the hilarious, and in spite of prevailing academic convention I have resisted this particular mode of argument and presentation here. The reader should remark, in passing, that where I have quoted from French-language authors, the translations are without exception my own.

This book has its origins in a graduate course that I taught jointly with my good friend and colleague Shoukry Roweis in the Department of Urban and Regional Planning at the University of Toronto in the academic

Preface

years 1975-1976 and 1976-1977. In one way and another, the fruits of this collaboration are discernible in virtually every page that follows. I want to express my gratitude to Professor Roweis for the warmth of his companionship and for the stimulus of his unstinting intellectual support which so often over the years has resulted in his pointing out to me significant lines of enquiry that I could never have hoped to discover for myself. I also owe Professor Roweis my thanks for his unhesitating willingness to allow me to reproduce freely material from two papers (Scott and Roweis, 1977; Roweis and Scott, 1978) that we wrote together on the basis of our joint teaching endeavour. It was in the latter of these two papers that we first developed the concept of the urban land nexus. Only I, of course, bear the responsibility for what is said, and not said, in the pages that follow. In addition, I owe a particular debt of gratitude to M Boddy, T A Broadbent, and H W Richardson for their detailed critical comments on an early draft of this book. Again, however, I must exonerate these individuals from any complicity in the final result.

Finally, I would like to thank the Social Sciences and Humanities Research Council of Canada for its generosity in awarding me a leave fellowship that allowed me to take the year 1977-1978 off from my teaching duties at the University of Toronto, and to prepare the greater part of this book in the most agreeable intellectual and cultural environment of Paris. At moments when I despaired of making any progress on the manuscript, it was enough for me to look up from my typewriter and to contemplate the view through the window of my apartment close to the Boulevard Saint Germain; it was a view that took in the jumbled roofs of the Latin Quarter and the Ile de la Cité and, in the distance, the spire of the Sainte Chapelle; that view, and the sense of an enduring urban civilization that it evoked, always fully reconfirmed my belief that not only is the urban experience worth writing about, but emphatically worth living too.

Allen J Scott
Toronto, October 1979

Acknowledgements

The author and publishers are grateful to the following organizations and individuals for their permission to reproduce copyright material.

Fraser Institute, Vancouver, British Columbia, and D Nowlan:
    table 8.1 from Nowlan, 1977, in L B Smith, M Walker (Eds) *Public Property?*
Harvard University Press, Cambridge, Massachusetts, and E M Hoover:
    table 6.1 from Hoover and Vernon, 1959 *Anatomy of a Metropolis*
Longman Group Limited, Harlow, Essex:
    figure 10.1 from Stewart, 1952 *A Prospect of Cities* page 159
Macmillan Limited, London:
    figure 7.1 from Clark, 1968 *Population Growth and Land Use* page 344
Presses Universitaires de France, Paris, and P Lavedan:
    figure 10.3 from Lavedan, 1960 *Histoire de Paris*
D Rose:
    table 10.1 from Rose, 1978 *Housing Policy, Urbanisation and the Reproduction of Labour-power in Mid-to-late Nineteenth Century Britain* Department of Geography, University of Toronto
Toronto City Planning Board:
    table 6.4 from City of Toronto Core Area Task Force, 1974 *Report and Recommendations*
Viollet Collection:
    figure 10.2

For N T N

Contents

1	**The urban question in context**	
1.1	Introduction	1
	Some elements of the question	1
	The structure of a general response	2
1.2	The question of the urban land nexus	3
1.3	Critical versus empiricist approaches to the urban question	7
2	**Mode of production, capitalism and the State: a general framework of analysis**	
2.1	Mode of production	10
2.2	The capitalist mode of production	15
2.3	A macroeconomic model of capitalist production relations	18
2.4	The capitalist State	23
3	**Commodity production and the structuring of geographical space**	
3.1	The general role of land within the system of commodity production	28
3.2	Commodity production and land use: analytical foundations	31
	Some definitions	31
3.3	Elaboration of the basic spatial model	35
	The determination of total output	35
	Central prices and differential rents	36
	Scarcity rent	38
3.4	A general solution	40
3.5	Commodity production and the dynamics of land-use differentiation	41
	The process of intensive land-use change	42
	The process of extensive land-use change	47
3.6	A general synthesis of the dynamic process	51
3.7	Concluding remarks	53
4	**Urbanization and planning: a brief record of some recent problems and policies**	
4.1	Urban problems	55
4.2	Urban policy instruments	61
	Fiscal policies	61
	Land regulation policies	63
	Development policies	64
5	**Mainstream approaches to urban theory**	
5.1	The city as an ecology of communities	66
5.2	The city as a system of exchange relations	73
5.3	The manipulated city	82

6	**Urban patterns 1: production space**	
6.1	Introduction	86
6.2	Production space in general	87
6.3	Industrial activities	88
	Some preliminaries	88
	The foundations of commodity production in the modern metropolis	89
	A short analytical history of manufacturing activity in the modern metropolis	95
	Systematic development of some conjectures and hypotheses	99
	An empirical test of the Heckscher–Ohlin theorem in large metropolitan areas	102
	A back-up test	106
	The general role of industry in the urban land nexus	108
6.4	Office activities	109
6.5	Retail and service activities	114
7	**Urban patterns 2: reproduction and circulation space**	
7.1	Urban population distribution	117
7.2	The internal differentiation of urban residential space	119
	Urban residential space observed	119
	Socialization and reproduction problems in nineteenth-century cities	121
	The role of urban neighbourhoods	124
7.3	Reproduction space: the problem as a whole	127
7.4	Circulation space	128
8	**The urban land nexus and the State**	
8.1	Urbanization in capitalist society	135
	The production of the urban land nexus	136
	Private and public decisionmaking in the urban land nexus	137
8.2	Production in the noncommodity form: extraurban imperatives and intraurban consequences	141
	The management of production and reproduction relations	141
	The case of breakdowns in the production of urban equipment and services	143
	The case of breakdowns in the consumption of land-contingent goods and services	145
	Towards urban planning	147
8.3	Static land-use problems	148
	Simple externalities	148
	Negative spillovers in the urban land nexus	149
	Land development bottlenecks	155
	The free-rider problem	158
8.4	Dynamic land-use problems	159
	The slow convertibility of the urban land nexus	160
	Development decisions: timing and choice of land use	161
	The temporal myopia of private locational activity	165

8.5	The private–public interface in the urban land nexus	168
	The private component in the urban land nexus	169
	The public component in the urban land nexus	170
	The private–public interface	172
9	**The origins and character of urban planning**	**175**
9.1	The tasks and qualities of a viable theory of planning	176
9.2	Urban planning and the State	179
	The capitalist State: a brief recapitulation	180
	The situation of urban planning within the State apparatus	184
9.3	The dynamics of urban planning	186
	Urban land problems and the genesis of urban planning	186
	The limits of urban planning	187
	The opposed imperatives of private versus collective action in the urban land nexus	189
9.4	A concluding comment on planning theory	191
10	**Urban development and planning intervention: five illustrative sketches**	
10.1	Introduction	193
10.2	Reproduction and urbanization in Britain in the second half of the nineteenth century	194
10.3	Baron Haussmann and the reconstruction of central Paris	204
10.4	The origins and consequences of land-use zoning in North American municipalities	209
10.5	The US urban renewal programme, 1949–1961	212
10.6	Transport problems and policies in Metropolitan Toronto from 1953 to the mid-1970s	217
10.7	Reprise	226
11	**Planning ideologies**	**228**
11.1	The foundations and biases of mainstream planning theory	229
	A brief description of mainstream planning theory	229
	The failure of mainstream planning theory	231
11.2	The imperfect negation	234
11.3	The idealist–utopian origins of mainstream planning theory	236
11.4	The impasse of mainstream planning theory	238
12	**Urban problems and urban planning today**	**239**
References		**244**
Appendix		**249**
Index		**251**

The urban question in context

1.1 Introduction
Some elements of the question
Early in 1978 in response to the growing crisis of central city areas in the United States, the Carter administration put forward a new national urban policy as outlined by the President's Urban and Regional Policy Group (1978). The main provisions of this policy represent a remarkable change of emphasis in comparison with the main urban policy guidelines that had gradually evolved in the United States in the period following the Second World War. The proposed new urban policy is designed to attack on a broad front the chronic problem of the physical, economic, and social deterioration of central city areas. It seeks to make central cities attractive places to live, to reverse the persistent erosion of their basic economic arrangements, and to help alleviate the crisis of municipal finance that in the mid-1970s brought the city of New York, for example, to the verge of bankruptcy. As a corollary, the policy also seeks to bolster central city redevelopment by attempting to stem in a variety of ways the tide of rapid outward urban expansion that in the last four or five decades has absolutely dominated the process of urbanization in North America. Of course, intimations of this emerging new trend in federal US urban policy have been discernible in prior urban legislation and programmes of aid to central cities. They are discernible, for example, in the urban renewal policies of the 1950s and 1960s, in the model cities programme, in the 1968 Housing Act, and so on. The new policy, however (and whether or not it is ultimately successful in the specific version outlined in the report of the President's Urban and Regional Policy Group), seems to mark a quite definite break with previous federal programmes, which, on balance, tended strongly to favour suburban expansion at the final expense of the central cities. Certainly, it is directed at what has probably become the most critical urban problem in the United States at the present time, and not simply in the United States, for in various ways it is also apparent in Canada and in parts of Western Europe, most notably perhaps in the large British conurbations.

But what, we may ask, brought so many contemporary cities to this particular conjuncture of events? Why in fact have inner cities over the decades steadily lost jobs and population to the urban periphery? Why was this process of decentralization formerly actually encouraged by official policy? Why does that policy now haltingly but unmistakably begin to reverse itself? Why could these problems of inner city areas not have been foreseen and provided for in earlier policies? What new and as yet unforeseen problems will emerge as the new policy begins to run its course? Could these not be anticipated and the new policy modified accordingly? What, in general, is the relationship between spontaneous urban change on the one hand, and public policy and planning on the other hand? Do planners control the urban system? Or does the developmental structure of the urban system preempt the decisions and actions of planners? Are there discoverable 'laws of motion' linking spontaneous urban change and public policy and planning together?

The structure of a general response
It is the aim of this book to establish a general urban problematic within which the elements of a response to all such questions can in principle be discovered. The book represents an attempt to set up a broad theoretical framework that identifies the location of the urbanization process within society as a whole, and that reveals the origins, dynamics, and internal order of urban spaces and systems. In brief, it seeks to illuminate and to render coherent all those apparently disparate and disjointed social events that can be categorized as being in one way or another urban phenomena. The book seeks to achieve this end by addressing four major interrelated levels of analysis, all of which cluster around the central theme of *land contingency*, which, as will be shown below, is taken here to identify a unified basic concept of the urbanization process. More particularly, the theme of land contingency represents a means of rendering intelligible the properties and mutual interactions of all social incidents as they emerge out of a global system of human relationships and are mediated through urban space. Let us briefly consider the main content and orientation of each of these levels of analysis in turn.

The first major level of analysis to which this book is addressed concerns the overall problem of situating the urban system within some wider social context. Here, especial attention is paid to the genesis of the urbanization process within one particular historical totality: the capitalist mode of production. It is shown how this totality is constituted out of a set of primary social entities and relationships comprising, for example, commodity production, the social surplus, social classes, the State, and so on, and how contemporary urbanization, as a secondary social event, is of necessity a derivation out of these phenomena. It is demonstrated, in particular, how the specifically *urban* (land-contingent) functions and rationality of firms and households on the one hand, and planners on the other hand, emerge through a succession of mediations out of the broad structure of capitalist society. In line with this initial orientation, a general attempt is made in chapter 2 to scrutinize the logic and dynamics of capitalism as a whole.

The second major level of analysis is then concerned with a detailed examination of the aggregate behaviour of firms and households as they make their appearance in urban space. This phase of the argument represents an attempt to discover the mainsprings of urban form and development in the logic of private decisionmaking within capitalist civil society, and it is shown, further, how this logic is structurally enveloped within a network of social and property relationships that is built up around the institution and functional imperatives of commodity production. As it manifests itself in urban space, this logic leads endemically to the eruption of obstinate urban problems and predicaments that in turn call urgently for planning intervention.

The third major level of analysis is focussed around a description of the origins and character of urban planning as a (land-contingent) process of public (or collective) intervention in capitalist cities. This third phase of the argument consists in an effort to describe urban planning as a specialized administrative formation within the total apparatus of the State, while, at the same time, demonstrating also that the existence of urban planning is immediately predicated upon the very problems and predicaments brought into existence as a result of the wayward locational logic of private firms and households in urban space. Hence, as will be shown, the nature of urban planning in capitalist society is stamped both by the general properties of the State at large, and by the specific character of the urban problems and predicaments with which the State must actively deal.

The fourth major level of analysis to which the book is addressed represents a tentative theoretical description of the process whereby urban civil society on the one hand and the urban planning system on the other hand combine to form an organically integrated entity designated here the *urban land nexus.* It is then demonstrated how this entity evolves through time in a series of land-use interactions which, through varying surface outcomes, reflects an unvarying structural dynamic that generates one urban problem after another while shackling the ability of planners either to deal effectively with specific symptoms or to readjust in meaningful ways the fundamental social mechanisms that generate those symptoms.

In addition to these four main analytical modules there is a persistent attempt throughout the book to evaluate and to criticize alternative discourses about the city and about the role and significance of collective urban intervention in capitalist society.

1.2 The question of the urban land nexus

From the above brief outline of the main argument that is to follow, it will be already apparent to the reader that the notion of the urban land nexus is highly derivative: it represents a sort of by-product of a prior theoretical analysis of the structure and meaning of capitalist society generally. However, it must be added at once that while the urban land nexus cannot be understood outside of the context of capitalist social and property relations, neither can it simply be conjured away as a purely *a posteriori* category. On the contrary, it possesses, as a concept, a high degree of internal peculiarity which is, in turn, an intellectual echo of its very specific material manifestations. Hence, in its immediate phenomenal appearance, the urban land nexus takes on the form of a *land-use system* consisting of interpenetrating private and public spaces. These spaces are outcomes of the (historically determinate) *locational logics* of various actors in urban space. As a corollary, the urban land nexus may be seen in somewhat more analytical terms as a structured assemblage of *dense polarized differential locational advantages* through which the broad social and property relations of capitalism are intermediated. It represents, in a word, a socially embedded collection of land uses or locations, all of which depend functionally upon one another across a focussed geographical space. It is precisely this characteristic locational integration within the urban land nexus as a geographical unit which raises it to the status of a definite puzzle within social theory as a whole. As will be shown continually throughout the remainder of this book, the urban land nexus posits itself (via the general analytical idea of land contingency) as *the* specific object of enquiry to which any really coherent urban question must be addressed; and this assertion is based in turn upon the observation that the specifically *urban* (as opposed to economic, psychological, cultural, etc) logic and effects of any social event are in the end decipherable only via an analysis of the intraurban system of differential locational advantages.

Something like this identification of the phenomenon of land contingency with the urban question is already implicitly affirmed in all those existing approaches to a general theory of the city that are founded on such thematic issues as urban spatial organization, urban space and structure, the geography of urban patterns, and all the rest. In the present discussion, the urban question is similarly pinned down to these sorts of thematic issues, and to a problematization of the complex relationships that they contain. Here, however, the generic notional expression of those issues, that is, the urban land nexus, is never reified (as it is in much mainstream work) into a self-sufficient and analytically autonomous discourse. On the one hand, the idea of the urban land nexus is indeed taken here to identify, to problematize, and to make coherent all that is innately urban about urban events and phenomena, in the sense that urbanization as such can never be represented by the incommensurable and heterogeneous *things* that are to be found in urban areas, but only by the web of connections that combines those things into a coherent whole, that is, their mutual interdependence via the system of intraurban differential locational advantages. Yet, on the other hand, the conceptual status of the urban land nexus is quite definitely dependent on and derived out of certain more basic mental constructs. In this book, all discourse about the city (the urban land nexus) is taken to be ultimately referrable back to the historical materialist conception of a mode of production in general, and the capitalist mode of production in particular. Within this wider universe of discourse, however, it will be made increasingly evident that *the* urban question is the question of the mutual interrelations of all land-contingent phenomena (both private and public) in urban space—in a word, the urban land nexus as the finally unifying idea of the city.

It is clear from all of this that the general method of attack adopted in this book explicitly rejects [along with Castells (1968)] any attempt to take urban phenomena as 'independent variables'. In view of the pervasive attempt in the ensuing argument always to encapsulate the idea of the urban land nexus within some wider conception of society, and given, by contrast, that the mainstream literature on urban theory and planning falls so frequently into precisely the sophism criticized by Castells, a brief further methodological comment on these matters seems to be in order at this stage, and we may open the argument with the apparently uncontroversial (though often tacitly controverted) assertion that urban occurrences of whatever kind are primarily *concrete social phenomena.* It is important to stress this point for it is commonly denied by implication in much of the literature where the locational patterns of firms and households in urban space are so frequently reduced to the status of simple geometric abstractions, and urban planning is persistently confounded with the purest forms of voluntaristic intervention. On the contrary, both the private and the public dimensions of the urban land nexus are definite social occurrences, connected in complex ways with one another, and with other more general social phenomena. This remark implies at once that urban civil society and urban planning form an intertwined totality constituting the universe of urban reality. And this proposition implies another, running parallel to it, and indeed encompassing it, namely, that there exist connections between this aggregate urban entity and the rest of society such that *this* totalization constitutes the universe of social reality. Two major points need to be developed directly.

First, out of this initial conception, there immediately emerges the question of the manner in which the urban land nexus in general takes its origin in the rest of society. Concomitantly, there emerges the subsidiary question as to the manner in which urban planning (a constituent component of the urban land nexus) takes its origin in both the internal dynamics of the urban land nexus, and the rationality of the capitalist State at large. For we cannot simply make the *a priori* assumption that either an urban land nexus in general, or urban planning in particular, represents an autonomous sphere of activity and development. That is to say, we cannot assume that either the urban land nexus or urban planning emerges, evolves, and acquires its observable qualities in conformity with forces that reside solely within itself. Such an assumption leads inevitably to a metaphysical conception of urban *relata* as systems of self-engendering essences. Above all, it leads immediately to those familiar illusions wherein the urban land nexus is reified into an abstract idealist conception of intraurban space, and urban planning is turned into a transhistorical mechanism of administrative rationality, both of them divorced from any more fundamental roots, and in fact effectively structurally divorced from one another. Nonetheless, acknowledgement of the necessary existence of a complex hierarchy of interconnections running between the various phenomena of society as a whole (civil society and the State), the urban land nexus, and the institution of urban planning, in no way, in and of itself suggests any particular clues as to the nature and substantive content of these interconnections. Only some prior theoretical position can provide such clues. What this acknowledgement does, however, is to affirm by implication that, whatever general theoretical framework we may ultimately adopt, it must be unambiguously capable of illuminating these interconnections.

Second, the urban land nexus in general, and urban planning in particular, are manifestly changeable phenomena, marked as they are by frequent short-run episodes and variations of trend. The opening paragraphs of this chapter are sufficient testimony to this state of affairs. From this it follows that any theory of urban occurrences generally that does not seek to root such changeable and ephemeral phenomena in an understanding of those more enduring social structures to which they are demonstrably related can only produce trivial and/or erroneous statements and predictions. A really viable analytical attack on these phenomena must be capable of *anchoring* them in more deeply rooted and more stable social processes and dynamics. In short, a viable theory of the urban land nexus in general and of urban planning in particular must grow out of a conceptual structure that explicitly reveals the intrinsic social embeddedness of these phenomena.

The significance of these two general points becomes all the more understandable and emphatic when it is recalled that much of the existing literature on urban matters, ignoring precisely these cautionary observations, tends to generate in large quantities various disparate and incommensurable 'points of view', and these points of view fall constantly and predictably into disrepute as mere fashions and whims as the urban system moves rapidly from one conjuncture to the next, and as one specific urban problem succeeds another. If urban theory is to move beyond this sort of eclecticism and incoherence, then it must certainly be underpinned by a conceptual scaffolding that at least meets the two requirements discussed above. In the present study, a concerted effort is made to achieve this goal by adducing a chain of conceptual relations such that, first, the logic of the urban land nexus is derived out of the interdependent logics of private and public decisionmaking in urban space, second, the logics of private and public decisionmaking in urban space are derived out of the logics of civil society and the State, respectively, and, third, the logics of civil society and the State are derived out of the logic of the capitalist mode of production at large (an ultimately durable and indeed, in conceptual turns, irreducible phenomenon). At the same time, it must be pointed out that the complex intermediations that occur as a mode of production finally manifests itself in the urban land nexus are never simply and uniquely unidirectional. Rather, as less durable events and structures arise out of more durable events and structures so there is a process of backward transformation such that the more durable is definitely modified and in part restructured by the less durable. In this way, the urban land nexus never simply dissolves away, via analysis, into its conceptual contexts, but rather retains a definite status as an object of theoretical enquiry, that is, as a *question* that provokes coherent and socially meaningful responses.

It goes without saying that the practicability of the entire intellectual project proposed here is to a very large degree dependent upon a clear demonstration that its major focus of attention—the urban land nexus— does indeed constitute a legitimate and conceptually fertile object of theoretical enquiry. Any final verdict on this matter must obviously be postponed until the major arguments of this book have been fully deployed. However, it is apparent, even at this stage in the proceedings, that the idea of the urban land nexus (in its combined private and public dimensions) does in fact raise a scientifically and practically significant question. It is a question that is addressed to the *uniquely problematical* manner in which land-contingent phenomena behave within the city, interact with one another, arrange themselves across urban space, evolve as an integrated geographical entity through time, create problems and conflicts, call for policy responses, and concomitantly induce idiosyncratic forms of political action and intervention. It is a question, as already indicated above, that resides within the wider problem of the meaning and structure of human society as a whole, and yet it cannot be assimilated without a correspondingly vast loss of information and insights into that wider problem, just as it cannot be simply broken down into a succession of more detailed problems. The pessimistic view of Castells (1977, page 62), who asserts that "urbanization is neither a specific real object nor a scientific object", is simply an evasion of the problem once it is seen that the phenomenon of urbanization does indeed take on concrete form and meaning *qua* the structure and development of the urban land nexus. In short, the scientific authenticity of the notion of the urban land nexus is discernible at once in the distinctive, though perplexing, interrelations of all land-contingent occurrences as such with the urban system. This latter proposition is in no way weakened or invalidated by the necessary addendum that the peculiarly urban qualities of these occurrences are derived out of more global nonurban processes and structures.

1.3 Critical versus empiricist approaches to the urban question

It is now clearly evident that the principal object of theoretical enquiry (the urban land nexus) to which this book is addressed is produced by a process of successive intellectual transmutations out of the prior concept of a mode of production, and, as a corollary, out of the entire machinery of critical analysis that inevitably accompanies this concept. In contradistinction to the empiricist epistemologies (whether of the narrative or abstract varieties) that manifestly dominate urban analysis and theory at the present time, the approach adopted here seeks as an initial point of departure to establish a universe of discourse that reveals, even prior to the examination of particular urban data and situations, those general social categories and relationships (commodity production, the social surplus, class society, the State, and so on) that represent the fountainhead of all specifically urban instances. Here, the city as such is situated within an intellectual apparatus that begins with a philosophical abstraction (the historical materialist notion of a mode of production), moves progressively via a hierarchy of concepts to an examination of the world of concrete urban objects and relationships (the central business district, residential neighbourhoods, locational behaviour, land-use zoning, transport planning, and so on), then turns back upon itself in a critical scrutiny of the world of lived and practical urban reality. A prime objective of this exercise is, of course, to comprehend and clarify the nature of the contemporary city in some way. However, the notions of comprehension and clarification are understood here as going beyond the simple establishment of some logical and internally coherent discourse about the origins and structure of urban space; they are also, and more importantly, taken to signify the achievement of an urban theory that goes some way in the direction of providing the bases for an understanding of and a confrontation with the *current urban situation*, to adapt an expression of Hindess and Hirst (1975). Such a theory is one that attempts explicitly to recognize human purposes and lived predicaments for what they are, in terms of their sociohistorical roots and significance, and that is therefore capable of elucidating and contributing to the course of urban policy in a way that is scientifically rigorous and responsible and yet does not shrink from seeking to actualize itself in advocacy and action.

By contrast, empiricist approaches to urban analysis begin and end with the heterogeneous data of urban life. Nor do they escape from this predicament even when they are cast in terms of the apparently unifying mainstream framework that emerges out of the abstract formal conception of urban space as an independent geographical entity. On the contrary, they are condemned by their own theoretical shortsightedness to permanent mystification and constriction. On the other hand, they are incapable of getting at the deep structural mechanisms that underlie direct urban appearances and hence they can achieve no other kind of generalization than formalistic or statistical abstraction of urban spatial relationships (a kind of generalization of which urban factorial ecology is perhaps the most notorious example). On the other hand, they suffer endemically from eclecticism, artificial disjunction of problems, and dependence on ephemeral current 'issues' as the only way of justifying the social significance of research questions. Thus, empiricist discourses about the city range over an extraordinary gamut of topics from the architectural symbolism of built forms, through the dynamics of street gangs, to the land-use impacts of public investments, but without ever effectively transcending the perennial intellectual inertia, disconnectedness, and faddishness that are intrinsic to such discourses. In the same way, empiricist urban analysis resists meaningful policy deductions (in the sense of deductions as to effective political choices and action) except perhaps in the form of theoretically disengaged 'opinions' appended as afterthoughts to each specific project of enquiry. However, to echo a familiar Weberian theme, a *question* (whether urban or otherwise) in any rich and conceptually productive sense of the term can never be constructed merely by the juxtaposition of classes of events that happen to share a common historical or geographical situation; an *urban question* in particular can only be constructed out of the interdependent notional connections that link together the elements of a definite urban problematic in the context of some wider theory of society as a total structure. Nevertheless, it is precisely in this latter sense that an urban question *can* be identified, that is, as an expression of the complex internal relationships of the urban land nexus, as this phenomenon in turn is situated within the capitalist mode of production. This is ultimately the same as saying that, of all the problems that occur *in* cities, the present account is concerned (via its focus on the urban land nexus) with problems *of* cities.

In conformity with the general project of enquiry discussed above, the present book is an attempt to explain the internal workings of the urban land nexus, and, as a corollary, to clarify the origins and character of modern urban planning. Ultimately, a major purpose of this book is to move once and for all beyond the massive and artificial split that exists in the literature between 'social theory', 'urban theory', and 'planning theory'. A start is now made on this task in the ensuing chapter by considering the interrelated issues of mode of production, capitalism, and the State, as a way of laying the principal foundations for all that follows.

2

Mode of production, capitalism and the State: a general framework of analysis

2.1 Mode of production

The classic notion of a mode of production as originally sketched out by Marx (1859; 1970 edition) is of a society conceived as a *unified total structure*, existing as a definite historical entity, and moving forward through time on the basis of some central and fundamental economic process. The internal logic of any such entity is determined by what Althusser and Balibar (1973) have called "structural causality", which is to say that a mode of production operates via sets of interrelationships that are purely internal to itself. A mode of production, then, represents an essentially closed system, reproducing in a self-determinate manner the conditions of its own existence and dissolution.

The origins of any mode of production are decipherable, as Marx continually pointed out, in the initial and predominant imperative of all human existence: the imperative of securing the material requirements of life. In pursuit of this imperative, humans join together in various ways so as to ensure the production and reproduction of their own physical being. In this way, the production of the material requirements of life becomes a *social* process as marked by its most basic characteristic, the social division of labour. By the same token, the production process acquires definite durability and persistence, for once it becomes institutionalized within some specific social formation the articulations of that process are in no circumstances renegotiated at the start of each day, but are frozen into customary and habitual forms. They acquire an ordered and systematically reproducible existence that transcends by far the volition of the various individuals caught up within them. Or, rather, they take on the character of a stubborn nucleus of socioeconomic connections that is changeable, in any fundamental sense, only at the cost of arduous struggles against entrenched norms and relationships. In one formulation, these articulations are identified as a confluent combination of *forces of production* and *relations of production*, structured by the dominance of the latter (Hindess and Hirst, 1975). Here, the notion of forces of production signifies a work process in which materials and equipment are manipulated by live labour so as to bring forth objects of human use; and the notion of relations of production signifies an ensemble of social institutions that circumscribes the work process as such and determines the various channels through which the output of that process circulates and is appropriated.

However complex and elaborate the social relations of production may be in practice, they are invariably reducible in the final analysis to a binary split between two social classes, generically identifiable as a class of nonlabourers on the one hand and a class of labourers on the other hand. These two

classes confront and oppose one another via their specific relationships to
the work process in general and to the means of production in particular.
The class of nonlabourers plays some dominant and determining role in
the ordering of the work process, and in its own interests, however these
may be defined historically, extracts surplus labour from the class of
labourers. The class of labourers acts directly on the means of production
so as to create physical use values, and in the same process it yields up
surplus labour. This surplus takes on the concrete form of an incremental
product above and beyond what is needed to reconstitute the work process
in some subsequent round of production. In line with these observations,
Hindess and Hirst (1975, page 68) suggest an especially compact definition
of the notion of a mode of production:

> "Mode of production is a fundamental concept of historical materialism
> in which the economic level is defined by the articulation of a mode of
> appropriation of surplus value (relations of production) and a mode of
> real appropriation (forces of production). The concept of the economic
> level is the concept of a determinate articulated combination of relations
> and forces of production."

And within this concept (though at several removes) are to be found the
origins of the entire discourse on urbanization and urban planning that
follows. Admittedly, in a recent autocritique Hindess and Hirst (1977)
have called for a more open and flexible conception of basic social
structure than is to be found in their earlier work. In their autocritique,
Hindess and Hirst have specifically denied any role of determination in the
last instance either to the forces of production, or (the more usual position
in Marxian theory) to the relations of production. Instead, they call for an
examination of the mutual interdependence of the forces and relations of
production within a "single structure of social relations" and for a clear
definition of the conditions of existence of the diverse elements of that
structure. Hindess and Hirst identify this modified conception as a theory
of social formations (that is, specific societies existing as concrete historical
entities) though it might more accurately be described as a reformulated
theory of modes of production since (like the latter theory) it persists
with a central concern for such general matters as the labour process, class
positions, the appropriation of the surplus, the associated category of
consciousness and so on. Thus, in the account that follows (and without
going too far against the spirit of Hindess and Hirst's undoubtedly major
contribution to the historical materialist analysis of human societies) these
same matters will continue to be referred to under the general rubric of
modes of production. While this account evades many of the subtleties
and controversies in the current debate, it does establish some basic
generalized ideas about the elements of social structure, and it thus
provides a stable point of departure for a further enquiry into capitalism
generally and capitalist urbanization phenomena in particular. It must be

added that there is quite definitely no attempt in this procedure to assume away the problem of social formations (as concrete historical entities) and all the more so as any really discriminating analysis of specific urban conditions must surely pay close attention to the actual social systems that envelop them: for even within particular modes of production, there remain immense variations of urban form and structure from one realized set of social relationships to the next. This point will be taken up again in chapter 9 where an attempt is made to describe some of the peculiarities of urbanization and planning in different places and at different historical moments within capitalism.

A mode of production, then, can be seen as a basal structure that emerges out of the intertwined combination of the forces and relations of production. In any such structure, the class of nonlabourers appropriates via the relations of production a social surplus produced by means of the labour of the class of labourers. These relations of production contain an intrinsically antagonistic element, for any increase in the amount of surplus appropriated by the class of nonlabourers must (for any given level of economic activity) entail a corresponding diminution of the material returns that the class of labourers is able to secure for itself; and, in precisely the same way, any increase in material returns to the class of labourers must (again, for any given level of economic activity) reduce the magnitude of the surplus appropriated by the class of nonlabourers. This antagonism between the labourer and the nonlabourer is thus structural; whether it is merely latent in consciousness or expressed in open social conflict, it rests upon an endemic collision of interests that grows directly out of the given relations of production. This collision of interests is not merely, however, the result of competing claims on the part of the nonlabourer and the labourer for mutually exclusive shares in the material fruits of production. More importantly, perhaps, it also rests upon the inherently exploitative and oppressive relationship within which the nonlabourer confronts the labourer. This relationship is one in which the positions of the nonlabourer and the labourer represent, respectively, authority and subordination in the work process: the nonlabourer commands that process and defines its purposes while the labourer must defer to the decisions and interests of the former. As a corollary, the economic surplus appropriated by the nonlabourer consists of surplus labour extracted from the labourer in a work process that the labourer endures grudgingly at best. Furthermore, the hallmark of a *class* society, in the strict sense, is that these positions of authority and subordination are mutually and organically interdependent. Thus, the nonlabourer is dependent on the labourer since the surplus product generated by the latter secures and furthers the historically determinate interests of the former (for example, in feudal society, the maintenance of a hierarchical system of hereditary power; in capitalist society, the process of accumulation).

And the labourer is dependent on the nonlabourer in the specific sense that the nonlabourer plays some critical and determining role in the organization of economic production. Thus, in capitalism, the capitalist secures the means of production, organizes and oversees the internal structure of the firm, hires labour, sells off the output of the work process, and so on. On the basis of such broad relationships as these, the main configurations of a mode of production and some concomitant social formation are established.

At the same time, in any given social formation, a constellation of subsidiary strata, fractions, and groups invariably develops around the central functional core as represented by the antagonistic but interdependent relations between two fundamental social classes. Hence in modern capitalist society, landowners (to take an example that is particularly apposite to the main theme of this book) represent a definite social contingent, that cannot, however, be designated a *class* in the very specific meaning of that term as developed above. To be more accurate, specific *types* of landowners (for example, traditional landed property, landowning commodity producers, financial institutions, etc) constitute specific sorts of social fractions depending on their varying functional relationships to land (cf Massey and Catalano, 1978). Further, whereas landowners in contemporary capitalist society bear an ultimately exploitative relationship to workers via their appropriation of surplus product in the guise of land rent, they nevertheless play an entirely passive role with respect to the labour process. For this reason, landowners must be seen as a secondary and essentially derivative phenomenon within the capitalist system. However, like all structurally determined social fractions, owners of land play an active social role that is explicitly keyed to the dynamics of their structural basis; in particular, landowners as a group are variously politically emergent or recessive depending on specific conjunctural events and the varying role of land within those events. It is pertinent to add at this point that the logic of any social class, or of any other social group whose historical existence is structurally determined, is *not* [as Poulantzas (1974) stresses with great clarity] an object of conscious choice or the expression of pure subjective preferences. On the contrary, the logic of social *positions* (in contradistinction to the *individuals* who occupy those positions) is determined by the preestablished logic of some mode of production, and it is a logic that exists independently of any direct volitional component.

This latter proposition requires immediate qualification. The logic of social positions is indeed preordained within a given mode of production, but it is also mediated and brought forward via the expression of innumerable individual human intentions. Nonetheless, human intentions are themselves historically determinate in the sense that the interests they express are also the outcome of the given social positions occupied by specific individuals; in other words intentionally acting human agents, in pursuit of their own interests, select *opportunities* which are created by—

objectively given by—historical circumstances. This latter assertion is in no sense intended to signify that the relationship between material historical conditions and human action is one of simple mechanical causation. On the contrary, human consciousness, which interposes itself between historical conditions and human action, reserves to itself the freedom to accept or reject whatever concrete choices may present themselves to the individual human actor. It need hardly be added that there remain significant problems (concerning such matters as rationality, self-awareness, social and psychological conditioning, and so on) as to just how this process works out in practice. Many of these problems were raised over four decades ago by Wilhelm Reich in his courageous enquiries (in face of violent opposition from both left and right) into psychoanalytic theory. In spite of Reich's unerring critique of the dogmatic economism that permeated (and still permeates today) much Marxian discourse on the nature of the relationship between social conditions and human action, there has even yet been no really effective attempt to deal with the fundamental problems raised by Reich:

"The Marxist thesis to the effect that originally that which is materialistic (existence) is converted into that which is ideological (in consciousness), and not vice versa, leaves two questions open: (1) how this takes place, what happens in man's brain in this process; and (2) how the consciousness that is formed in this way reacts upon the economic process" (Reich, 1933; 1975 edition, page 50).

With these provisos in mind, it may now be added that human volition, to the degree that it possesses historical efficacity, is, by the same token, produced *somehow* as the expression of a set of concretely achievable projects. These projects are embedded in a given social system, just as individual socialization, roles, and life expectations are also embedded in the same system. Human consciousness, then, emerges as a complex of realized and realizable ideas and norms-in-practice. It is not, as idealist social theory supposes, exterior to, and prior to, the world of concrete social relationships, but is rather organically rooted in those relationships. Even so (and to repeat) consciousness most certainly incorporates an element of intentionality and it is through this intentionality that consciousness mediates social change, firstly, by transposing problems and predicaments generated within the existing system of social and property relations into sociopolitical imperatives of various sorts and, secondly, by converting these imperatives via action into new elements of the social formation. Therefore, and looking ahead to the subsequent discussion, it is not an independent and autonomous system of ideas about urban planning that produces the manifest facts of actual urban planning; it is rather the realities of contemporary urbanization (themselves reflections of the realities of contemporary capitalism) that give rise to urban planning as a necessary social activity. Subsequently, a plethora of theoretical ideas (even if in part mystified and fallacious) is built up around this necessary social activity.

2.2 The capitalist mode of production
The capitalist mode of production is organized around the general social relations of commodity production and exchange. These relations began to take on definite shape over the eighteenth century as the phenomenon of exchange of monetary equivalents came to establish itself as a universal principle regulating all exchanges in human society. This phenomenon was in turn the outcome of a progressive liberation of the basic factors of production—capital, labour, and land—from customary and ascriptive constraints on their utilization, and of their reorganization within the framework of free market systems. Capital, labour, and land thus steadily were transformed into simple commercial values within the general process of commodity production and exchange, each commanding a universal price established in the process of multiple market dealings. These various developments were in turn echoed in the ideological revolutions that accompanied the emergence of a full-blown capitalist system and that insistently expressed themselves in the call for individual responsibilities, equality, and rights. These developments were also associated with immense scientific and technological advances, fuelled by the burgeoning imperatives of capital accumulation, *and with an entirely new mode and tempo of urbanization* (cf Roweis, 1975).

As capitalist society emerged, it took on a quality that was at once progressive, rational, and full of human potential in comparison with the society that had preceded it. But the emerging new society possessed, in addition, a side that was regressive, irrational, and predatory. Beneath the surface patina of freedom of contract and exchange there lay the class character of the new society as embodied in the structural domination by capital of labour. On the one side, capitalists possessed the means of production, organized the labour process, and, of course, appropriated a profit out of the total revenues yielded by the work process. On the other side, workers had no viable option but to hire themselves out to capitalists through a competitive labour market for a wage. Exploitation and oppression are inherent in these circumstances, for in selling their labour to capitalists, workers enthrall themselves within a labour process that dispenses with and suppresses that which is human, personal, and idiosyncratic—actually or potentially—in the worker, seeks out only that which is generally and abstractly work-creating, and channels this capacity into servitude of the process of blind accumulation. But, in addition, the oppression of the worker by the capitalist is compounded by the fact that the magnitude of the profits (or surplus labour) accumulated by capitalists is directly dependent on the degree to which capitalists are successful in holding back and restricting the wage demands of workers. Moreover, as each of these two classes seeks to expand the basis of its material existence,

that is, as capitalists seek to augment the mass of profits by squeezing
wages, and as workers seek to increase wages by making incursions on the
total surplus, so the irrevocable class character of capitalist society breaks
out into various forms and expressions of conflict: work stoppages,
sabotage of industrial plant and equipment, strikes, and, in recent decades,
clashes with the State apparatus on the part of the representatives of capital
and labour.

In its double manifestation as a society governed at once by market
exchanges and by class relations, capitalist society presents an apparent
paradox in the sense that equivalence and nonequivalence exist side by
side within a single domain of reality. The paradox disappears, however,
in any analysis of the interdependent and intermediated reflections whereby
these two moments of social reality confront one another. On the one side,
class relations depend on the smooth functioning of market institutions,
and above all on the unhindered rotation of exchange transactions in
commodities and labour. On the other side, market institutions, so far
from eliminating, that is, dissolving, class relations, merely *register* through
the pricing system, the events of the central class conflict of capitalist
society. Not surprisingly, continued stable functioning of this two-faceted
system of social relations is possible only in circumstances where there
exists some generalized power (the State) that is capable of sustaining the
tense social balance that exists between capital and labour over the division
of the surplus generated within the labour process. From these perspectives,
the neoclassical doctrine that free market exchange leads to equilibrium
via an efficient (if not just) distribution of the economic surplus by
rewarding each factor of production according to its marginal productivity,
is essentially a theoretical and ideological diversion. In fact, as the work
of the so-called Cambridge School has shown (cf Sraffa, 1960), market
prices (the very essence of exchange relations) are themselves nothing but
the observable results of the central class conflict of capitalist society.
For, as will appear more rigorously in the succeeding argument, commodities
cannot be priced *before* the distribution of profits and wages is known,
and this distribution is itself directly an echo of the existing balance of
power between capital and labour at any specific moment in time. Prices,
in short, are analytically subsequent to profits and wages; and profits and
wages are in turn dependent on the deep structure of capitalist social and
property relations. Clearly, a scientific and hence useful political economy
(and, concomitantly, a scientific and hence useful urban theory) must start
out on the basis of those historically given social and property relations
that underlie and shape observable patterns of exchange.

In line with the above remarks, the emergence—both historically and
analytically—of a specifically capitalist society can now be clarified in
terms of three major conditions. First, the emergence of capitalist society
presupposes that humans have achieved a stage of technical productivity
such that they can produce an economic surplus over and above what is

needed for simple self-replacement of the economic system in some new round of production. Second, it presupposes that production has become sufficiently advanced and articulated to allow for the emergence of specialized commodity producers in the form of capitalist firms. Third, it presupposes that wage-labour involving the exchange of labour-power for monetary wages determined on a labour market has become the customary mode of organizing the recruitment of workers. Given these conditions, capitalist commodity production emerges in the manifest overall form as depicted schematically in figure 2.1. Capitalist firms hire wage-labour to work on materials and equipment (capital) in the sphere of production. The commodities thus produced are then exchanged for money prices, representing, in aggregate, *gross income*. Gross income is then spent in part to replace materials and equipment used up in the production process. Whatever is left (let us designate it here *net income*) after these payments have been made is split between firms in the form of profits (surplus labour) and workers in the form of wages. Wages are spent upon consumption items necessary for the reproduction of the labour force; and these expenditures ensure that the cycle of commodity production and exchange

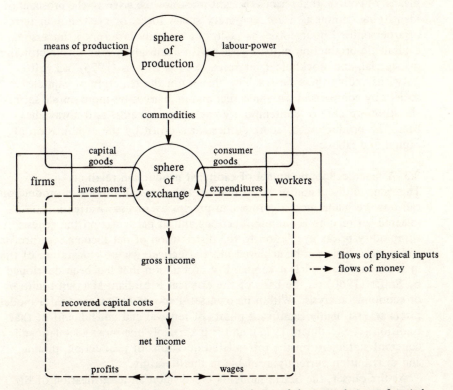

Figure 2.1. Commodity production: a simple schema of the interrelations of capital and labour.

as a whole is closed and sustained. Under the relentless competition among firms to preserve and augment their market capacity, profits are reinvested so as to enlarge the sphere of production, thereby driving the whole system forward through various phases of economic growth and development. Thus, in its most bare and skeletal form, proceeds commodity production, and with it, the historically specific process of the accumulation of capital.

As the dynamics of accumulation come into play, so the system of commodity production (even at this rudimentary level of definition) goes through various mutations of structure and appearance. Thus, in comparison with early *laissez-faire* capitalism, contemporary capitalist society has tended to develop within itself such radically novel phenomena as the trend to monopoly over whole branches of production; the emergence of massive trades unions; the extension of the wages system to include not only direct monetary remuneration, but also health benefits, education, unemployment insurance, etc; the gradual disappearance of the individual capitalist as owner-entrepreneur; and the rise of the impersonal capitalist firm managed by a salaried white-collar stratum. This latter observation means, of course, that serious thought must now be given to the prospect of identifying capital as a contemporary social force, or class, not in terms of a personified bourgeoisie, as such, but basically in terms of impersonal capitalistic production units together with a subsidiary web of directorial, managerial, and stockholder interests. Yet as Roweis (1975) has written, notwithstanding these far-reaching changes in the structure of capitalist society by comparison with an earlier and in many ways more simple society, the stubborn core of contemporary capitalism remains, as it always has been, the production of commodities for a profit by the combination of capital and labour.

2.3 A macroeconomic model of capitalist production relations

This general discussion of the structure of the capitalist mode of production can now be made more rigorous and precise by focussing attention on a selected set of core economic functions and in particular on the genesis of commodity prices in relation to the distribution of net income into profits and wages. This can be achieved most effectively via an elucidation of the macroeconomic model of commodity production that has been developed by Sraffa (1960) on the basis of the classical Ricardian-Marxian tradition of economic analysis. Within its own self-imposed limits, the Sraffa model offers several highly significant points of renewal and amendment of that tradition (cf Steedman, 1977), and it is certainly the most adequate and coherent statement on the interrelated questions of production, pricing, and distribution currently available in the literature.

At the outset, the Sraffa model is based upon an identification of the mechanics of commodity production as a general input-output process.

Prices and the social relations of production are then built into and expressed through this input-output process. In this way, the Sraffa model renders explicit the important role of the distribution of net income into profits and wages in the determination of commodity prices, and it also reveals with total clarity the endemically antagonistic nature of the structural relations between profits (capital) and wages (labour). Hence, while the Sraffa model in its primary form is silent on the sociopolitical significance of these structural relations, it nonetheless leads directly on to this particular issue; and through the Sraffa model there ultimately reappears, once more, that central political question in capitalist society of the human uses, purposes, and meaning of society as a whole. It should be indicated, in passing, that the Sraffa model is rejected out of hand by certain Marxian theorists (cf Amin, 1977), largely, it appears, because it stands apart from that blunt interpretation of the labour theory of value that dogmatically (if not doggedly) insists on rigidly counting out all economic quantities in terms of simple labour hours. However, as Steedman (1977) has demonstrated, the labour theory in this simplistic and mechanical interpretation is superfluous when set alongside the Sraffa model, which fully identifies in its own terms all the necessary and sufficient conditions for the determination of production prices and profits. Not only does the Sraffa model provide a coherent and determinate account of prices and profits, but, as will be made evident in the next chapter, it can also be applied in such a way as to yield some remarkable insights into the role of land and land rent within the system of commodity production.

With these preliminary remarks in mind, the Sraffa model may now be built up analytically on the foundation of a simple input-output model. Assume that there is given a commodity-production system comprising n different branches or sectors of production. The total physical output of the jth branch is given symbolically as the quantity $\bar{X}_j$, which includes both final consumption of commodity j and all intermediate inputs from branch j to all other branches. The individual physical inputs from branch j to branches $1, 2, ..., n$ are written, respectively, $X_{j1}, X_{j2}, ..., X_{jn}$. The total amount of labour employed in the jth branch is given as L_j. Then, a global input-output system expressing the purely physical relations of production can be written simply and generally as the set of n transformation functions,

$$\left. \begin{array}{l} f_1(X_{11}, X_{21}, ..., X_{n1}, L_1) \rightarrow \bar{X}_1 \ , \\ f_2(X_{12}, X_{22}, ..., X_{n2}, L_2) \rightarrow \bar{X}_2 \ , \\ \vdots \\ f_n(X_{1n}, X_{2n}, ..., X_{nn}, L_n) \rightarrow \bar{X}_n \ , \end{array} \right\} \quad (2.1)$$

where, if the system is at least physically self-replacing, the following condition must obviously hold:

$$X_{j1} + X_{j2} + ... + X_{jn} \leq \bar{X}_j \qquad (j = 1, 2, ..., n) \ . \qquad (2.2)$$

Remark that all physical quantities identified above (namely X_{ij}, L_j, and $\bar{X}_j$) are taken to be constant and their values given exogenously.

This physical system is now complemented by a set of social relationships expressing the price system and the structure of distribution. Accordingly, let p_j represent the production price of the jth commodity; let ρ symbolize the normal rate of profit on capital; and let w symbolize the general and invariant rate of wages (though in fact differentiated wage rates may be incorporated into the model without the slightest difficulty). Combining the input-output system described above with these new quantities (production prices, the rate of profit, and the rate of wages) yields the basic macroeconomic model of production, prices, and distribution as proposed by Sraffa:

$$\left.\begin{aligned}(X_{11}p_1 + X_{21}p_2 + ... + X_{n1}p_n)(1+\rho) + L_1 w &= \bar{X}_1 p_1 \ , \\ (X_{12}p_1 + X_{22}p_2 + ... + X_{n2}p_n)(1+\rho) + L_2 w &= \bar{X}_2 p_2 \ , \\ &\vdots \\ (X_{1n}p_1 + X_{2n}p_2 + ... + X_{nn}p_n)(1+\rho) + L_n w &= \bar{X}_n p_n \ . \end{aligned}\right\} \quad (2.3)$$

In verbal terms, the jth equation of this model signifies that total revenue, $\bar{X}_j p_j$, in branch j, is equal at equilibrium to the sum of (a) aggregate capital advanced by firms in branch j, namely, $X_{1j}p_1 + X_{2j}p_2 + ... + X_{nj}p_n$, plus (b) a normal profit on all capital advanced, namely, $(X_{1j}p_1 + X_{2j}p_2 + ... + X_{nj}p_n)\rho$, plus (c) the total wages bill, namely, $L_j w$. Observe that in a perfect capital market the rate of profit ρ will be constant over all branches of production, for any adventitious change (up or down) in ρ in any specific branch will always be counteracted by a corresponding flow of capital (in or out), thus tending to equalize rates of profit over all branches. In the equation system (2.3), the n production prices, $p_1, p_2, ..., p_n$, and the rate of profit, ρ, represent unknown variables whose magnitudes remain to be determined. By contrast, the value of w is given exogenously to the model and is in practice, in modern capitalism, determined very largely as the outcome of the differential social power of management and unions in fixing the terms of labour contracts. At the same time, the Sraffa equations are expressed in such a way that no profits are earned on the actual wages bill, and this is a reflection of the usual situation in capitalist society, where it is workers who advance their labour to firms, rather than firms that advance wages to workers.

All that remains to be accomplished now is to close off the model by fixing the aggregate level of profits and wages (net income) in some way. Net income is by definition equal to aggregate gross revenues from commodity production less the total cost of all intermediate physical inputs (excluding labour costs). If we set net income equal to any arbitrarily chosen numeraire (say unity), it can be identified in symbolic terms as

$$\sum_{j=1}^{n} \bar{X}_j p_j - \sum_{i=1}^{n} \sum_{j=1}^{n} X_{ij} p_i = 1 \ . \tag{2.4}$$

Expressed in this way, net income is also designated by Sraffa the *composite commodity*. This composite commodity fixes the absolute monetary level of production prices, though whatever its value—and this is the important point—all price ratios remain constant. Care must now be taken to ensure that the exogenously given rate, w, is expressed in units that are commensurable with this numeraire; and this commensurability may be most effectively accomplished in two stages as follows. First, define w as that *fraction* ($0 \leq w \leq 1$) of total net income that is paid out to labour in the form of wages. Second, for consistency, normalize all labour inputs to commodity production such that $L_1 + L_2 + ... + L_n = 1$, [hence $(L_1 + L_2 + ... + L_n)w = w$]. In this manner, w is transformed into a simple variate that measures directly the overall relations of distribution (or, in another vocabulary, the class struggle). Simple algebraic manipulation of the Sraffa equation system (2.3) and the numeraire (2.4) reveals that total profits and total wages are indeed equal (as they must be) to total net income, that is

$$\sum_{i=1}^{n} \sum_{j=1}^{n} X_{ij} p_i \rho + \sum_{j=1}^{n} L_j w = \sum_{j=1}^{n} \bar{X}_j p_j - \sum_{i=1}^{n} \sum_{j=1}^{n} X_{ij} p_i = 1 \ . \tag{2.5}$$

From this latter equation it is at once evident that since total wages (defined equivalently as $\sum_{j=1}^{n} L_j w$ or as w) are equal to a fraction of net income, then total profits must be equal to the residual fraction of net income, namely $1 - w$. In other words, any change in total wages must produce a corresponding inverse change in total profits (and *vice versa*) for any given level of net income (cf figure 2.2). This relationship makes it abundantly clear that the direct material interests of capital and labour must exist in permanent structural collision with one another in any system of capitalist commodity production.

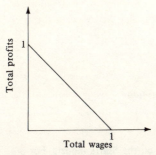

Figure 2.2. The relationship of total profits to total wages in a commodity-production system.

As stated earlier, the unknown variables of the Sraffa model are the production prices, $p_1, p_2, ..., p_n$, and the rate of profit, ρ. A numerical determination of the values of these $n+1$ variables is at this stage obtainable by solution of the simultaneous equation system represented by the n equations of the basic Sraffa system [equation (2.3)] together with the numeraire as defined by equation (2.4). The very fact such a numerical determination is possible signifies immediately that the state of technology (as represented by the physical relations of production) and the parameters of distribution (as represented by the given proportional assignment of net income to profits and wages) suffice to define prices of production and the *rate* of profit on capital. From this it follows, as already indicated above, that any theory of value whose main concern is simply to translate all economic quantities into equivalent labour hours must be at best redundant in fixing the level of these variables (Steedman, 1977). Note that this remark does not seek to question the origins of capitalistic profits in surplus labour, in that profits represent goods and services foregone within the established political structure of distribution by those whose alienated life-force has been channelled into the production process. It must also be pointed out forthwith that it is not prices that determine the rate of profit, nor supply and demand (as they are conventionally described in neoclassical theory) that determine production prices; to repeat, and as the Sraffa model demonstrates without equivocation, it is a given technical structure of production in the overall context of the prevailing conflict between capital and labour over the issue of distribution that ultimately fixes both the level of all production prices and the rate of profit on capital.

Now, these latter assertions do not deny the significance of an interplay of supply and demand processes within the system of capitalist exchange relations. On the contrary, supply and demand (that is, a market mechanism) are necessary and integral moments in the total structure of commodity-producing society. Without a consistent set of market transactions

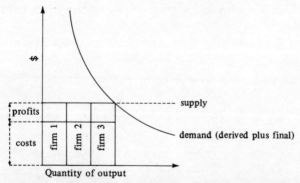

Figure 2.3. A supply-demand system superimposed on the Sraffa model. For simplicity, total output is here assumed to be produced by three firms, each with identical technologies and constant returns to scale in the production process.

sensitive on both the supply side and the demand side to price signals, the commodity system *à la* Sraffa simply could not exist. But in any equilibrium situation, it is also the case that those price signals are in practice mediations out of the deep structure of production (cf figure 2.3) and are not, as neoclassical theory asserts, the unadulterated expression of pure exchange relations. Depending on the vagaries of supply and demand, *market* prices may well temporarily deviate from production prices, but in any long-run equilibrium situation they will always return to the level of production prices. Furthermore, in view of the entire preceding discussion, it is now clear that profits and wages can never be what they are claimed to be by neoclassical economists, that is, the neutral and technically defined marginal productivities of capital and labour, respectively. Rather, they are nuclei of explicit human interests, rooted in the dynamics of a continuing social conflict, and pregnant with political significance and tensions. For these reasons, the maintenance and reproduction of those social structures that give rise to profits and wages and to the human concerns that surround them, call immediately for the emergence of a State apparatus in capitalist society. This remark leads directly into a brief survey of the political character of capitalist society and of the dynamics of the capitalist State.

2.4 The capitalist State

Like all other social phenomena, the State is contained within a specific field of historical action. That is, the State is organically rooted in and draws its particular rationality from some final concrete frame of reference in the form of a given mode of production. In commodity-producing society, the State makes its historical appearance in response to the collective imperative of circumventing a potentially cataclysmic gap in the logic of social relations. This gap reflects precisely the peculiar circumstance that capitalist civil society has never had the means of reproducing spontaneously all the conditions necessary for its own existence. Some *political* agency (namely the State) that is at once external to, and yet of necessity rooted in, civil society must come into being in order to close that gap and to ensure the continued viability of commodity production as a whole. The tasks that it must perform in order to secure this function are manifestly of a highly diverse nature though they can in principle be reduced to two interdependent categories of political action: one is to assuage the inflammatory capital–labour relation; concomitantly, the other is to mediate the crisis-ridden process of capital accumulation and growth. However peripheral to these tasks any specific realm of capitalist State intervention (for example, taxation, import–export regulation, regional development, social work, control of environmental quality, urban planning, etc) may at first appear to be, it is in fact invariably an outcome in one way or another of those two fundamental problems of capitalist society. Thus, in both its genesis and its functions, the capitalist State

expresses the specific exigencies and logic of commodity production. At
the same time, the complex relationship that links commodity-producing
civil society and the State into a functioning structured whole expresses
not only the mutual dependence of the one upon the other but also their
mutual opposition, so that it expresses in dialectical form both the unity
and the separation of the civil and the political in capitalist society. On the
one hand, the sphere of civil society is above all a sphere of private property,
decentralized control and personal action, that is, a sphere in which
particular events are motivated above all by *individual* decisionmaking and
behaviour. On the other hand, the State represents a sphere of *collective*
action that comes into existence precisely as a means of resolving vital social
problems that can never be resolved via the privatistic logic of civil society.
However, in capitalist society, collective action is at once antithetical to and
subsidiary to private action. It is antithetical because it curtails and negates
private action; it is subsidiary—despite appearances to the contrary—because
it grows out of and hence reflects the very *lacunae* of private decisionmaking
and action. Hence, as it goes about its historically determinate tasks, the
State inevitably finds its range of potential collective intervention constantly
hemmed in by the selfsame system of social and property relations that
calls for its historical emergence in the first place. This latter proposition
will be reworked at length in subsequent chapters as the basis of a composite
statement about the necessary failures of urban planning in capitalism.
For the present, however, let us pursue in further detail the two broad
politicoadministrative problems alluded to above which the capitalist State
must constantly confront.

In the first place, then, one of the absolutely crucial articulations within
the totality of capitalist society is that moment when net income is divided
into profits on the one side and wages on the other side. For profits and
wages are not simply abstract analytical categories, they also represent
definite modalities of social being. Outwardly, the capital-labour relation
partakes of the law of exchange of equivalents (exchange of a given quantity
of labour-power for a given standard wage), and this circumstance invests it
with an appearance of reasonableness, equitability, and impartiality. More
fundamentally, however, this same relation is also one of exploitation and
nonequivalence (in life expectations, life chances, conditions of material and
psychological existence, and so on), a circumstance which openly and
persistently breaks forth in the form of the attempts of labour, throughout
the history of capitalism, to free itself from or to mitigate in various
ways, the restraints and conditions that this relation imposes on it. Yet these
attempts on the part of labour to ameliorate its social situation threaten
the material bases of capital and, in particular, its central essence, the rate
of profit. As a result, and in contradistinction to the euphoric theories of
universal harmony as posited by conventional economics and sociology,
capitalist society is ever ready to implode in upon itself, and is indeed
inherently autodestructive, for the constant and irrevocable collision of

class interests in that society poses an endemic threat to its basic social and property arrangements. In the absence of some external agency capable of maintaining social balance and cohesion, capitalist society would in fact rapidly disintegrate. However, it is precisely out of the social conflict that exists between the claimants of profits and the claimants of wages that an agent of political integration emerges: the capitalist State, that is, makes its gradual but irreversible historical appearance as the guardian of the brittle social balance that pervades the capital-labour relation, and it establishes itself as a general mechanism of collective social survival. The State performs this function by legitimating (via ideological programmes) and guaranteeing (via its monopoly of legitimate violence, to use an often quoted expression of Weber) the social and property relations of capitalist society. In this process, the State automatically preserves and sustains the specific order of authority and subordination implied by those relations.

In the second place, and in much the same way, a State apparatus is called into existence as a means of collectively mediating the contradictory process of capital accumulation and growth, itself but a further manifestation of the basic capital-labour relation. This process is manifest not simply in the secular booms and slumps that regularly derange business activity, but also in such cognate phenomena as the development of large monopolies and multinational corporations, currency crises, imbalances of foreign trade, unequal regional development, and so on. When critical conjunctural events of these sorts begin to undermine the stability and workability of capitalism, the State will intervene, and (overriding the privileged structures of private decisionmaking and action that pervade the commodity-producing system) it will begin to implement such policy measures as seem likely to secure the survival of society as a whole, though by reason of its very origins and logic it will seek out such measures as promise to be immediately effective while leaving the basic arrangements of civil society maximally intact. To exemplify with a particular case that has had profound implications for the course of urban and regional planning in the recent past: some time in the 1930s, the major capitalist States found themselves having to jettison the remnants of a now discredited and in practice unworkable strategy of economic *laissez-faire*, and to intervene directly and massively in matters of production and reproduction. In North America, this process was manifested in an aggressive new strategy of Welfare Statism. This involved schemes for the planned deployment of underutilized units of capital and labour; it involved considerable public expenditures on urban and regional infrastructures of all kinds, as well as on social overhead capital; it involved schemes for the special encouragement of propulsive branches of production; and it involved an ever escalating burden of administrative, bureaucratic, and legal control. By and large, Welfare Statist policy held back from any fundamental attempt to reform the *internal* structure of commodity production, and instead sought to underpin the future economic viability of capitalism by means of attempts to shore up commodity production from outside via public investments in infrastructure and social overhead capital. For a time, the policy worked very well indeed, although its very success has now brought North American and Western European society forward to a new critical state in the accumulation process that is marked by widespread and endemic stagflation and fiscal demise. This situation, however, points only to the evident deduction that *yet further* initiatives, readjustments, and interventions on the part of the State are essential for the survival of capitalist society at large.

From all of this it follows that the role and functions of the capitalist State emerge directly out of the concrete dissonances and failures of civil society. For this reason, moreover, the State bears a definite and *dependent* relationship to the configuration of capitalist society as a whole: it represents an instrumentality in the form of an articulation of collective activities whereby the forward reproduction of society is ensured. In practice, this means that the State supports the continuing hegemony of capital while engaging in policies that encourage the continued assent of the populace to this hegemony. However, the capitalist State is in no sense the private preserve of capital or a privileged fraction of capital. On the contrary, the State assumes to itself the form of a public institution detached from any direct specific interest. Holloway and Picciotto (1977, page 33) have captured this quality of the State in a passage that echoes many of the basic points already affirmed above:

"The relationship of the individual to the State is thus quite separate from his relation to capital: it is a peculiarity of capitalism that the political status of the citizen is in no way determined by his relationship to production. The essential inequality of the capital relation appears not only as equality in the sphere of exchange but also as equality before the State. The equality of political status enshrines and reinforces the inequality of its essential basis."

We may ask, along with Pašukanis (1970), why is it that the apparatus of the State does *not* constitute itself as the exclusive monopoly of the dominant class? Why does it separate itself from this class and carry out its historically determinate functions as an apparently disinterested and impersonal public power? The answers are already implicit in what has been said earlier about the nature of commodity-producing society: the capitalist State as the contingent creature of capitalist social and property relations must necessarily be detached and impartial to the same degree and in the same senses that those relations are themselves detached and impartial. Thus, even though rigorous analysis reveals that market structures are merely a surface manifestation that masks an immanent social inequality, the formal equivalence of all commercial values (capital, labour, land, etc) represents the immediate tangible appearance and *sine qua non* of capitalist social and property relations. As an instrument of social integration, the State itself is embedded in the society that is bound by the law of exchange of equivalents. Concomitantly, the State, too, takes on an appearance of neutrality and nonpartisanship, though in practice its actions only serve to reinforce that particular condensation of class relationships that emerges in the domination by capital of labour. It is neither necessary nor analytically correct to invoke class conspiracies in order to affirm the class character of political intervention in capitalist society. In late capitalism, of course, the State finds itself compelled to intervene more and more in the affairs of society, so that its actions begin to permeate all dimensions of modern life, and in these circumstances the State's fundamental class-contingent logic becomes increasingly transparent and demystified, and its innate functional relationship to the imperatives of commodity production revealed. The increasingly evident class-contingent logic of collective intervention, nonetheless, is in no sense to be confounded with direct manipulation of the State apparatus by the immediate agents of capital.

However—and in contradistinction to the ideological position of much social science in North America today—neither can State intervention in capitalism be seen as the working out of some inexplicably mysterious reformist Spirit or Idea: as a corollary, the State is *not* that avatar of the eighteenth-century theory of natural rights which produced a conception of political power as the counterpart of the freely chosen self-restraint of equal and independent individual subjects. State intervention in capitalist society can only be understood as a continual flow of responses to the unresolved—and in capitalist society the unresolvable—contradiction between the predominant imperative of private decisionmaking and action (as imposed by the very logic of commodity production and exchange) and the subsidiary imperative of collective action (as imposed by the dictates of continued social cohesion). It is now possible to anticipate part of the subsequent argument, and to assert that that specialized domain of State intervention, *urban planning*, emerges, like all activity of the State, out of a web of concrete historically determinate conflicts and predicaments embedded in the social and property relations of capitalist society generally, and embedded in the process of capitalist urbanization in particular.

Commodity production and the structuring of geographical space

In what has gone before, commodity production was shown to consist of an articulated set of physical and social relationships involving basically an input–output system, a pricing mechanism, and a distributional structure. However, commodity production does not occur in a "wonderland of no dimensions", to borrow a phrase from Isard (1956). In particular, commodity production is delineated in geographical space; *it takes place on land*; and the task of accordingly modifying the macroeconomic model of commodity production as developed in the previous chapter now becomes immediately incumbent. This task involves a demonstration as to how commodity production, as a primary phenomenon, is *mediated through* the dimension of geographical space. It also involves incorporating into the analysis a third fraction of net income in addition to profits and wages, namely, land rent, and a third social force in addition to capital and labour, namely, landowners. For the moment, the question of the State as such will be allowed to recede into the background, and the argument in the present chapter concentrates on showing how a simple basic economic geography (together with its elementary dynamics) emerges out of the general process of commodity production. At a later stage, this economic geography will be shown to be inherently crisis-prone, and it will then be shown how, as a result of this tendency, the State reappears once more as an integral and vital element within the overall structure of society.

3.1 The general role of land within the system of commodity production

Land is naturally endowed with two fundamental use values, the one being fertility, the other being location (relative to other locations). Both of these use values are susceptible to vast enhancement by human activity. The latter use value, in particular, is virtually wholly produced as a historically determinate category, that is, as a *social* relation contained within the wider system of capitalist social relations. It is this specific use value that is of prime concern in the present account, both as the key to any general enquiry into the geographical foundations of political economy and in its specific role as the essential component element of the urban land nexus. Let us at the outset, then, consider the global role of land, *qua* a complex of locations, within the general structure of commodity production.

The overall set of relationships that emerges as land is injected into the structure of commodity production is shown schematically in figure 3.1, which is directly based on and elaborated out of figure 2.1. Any plot of land that has some locational value—in the sense that it provides access to other locations—will command a rent representing a periodic payment to the landowner for the usufruct of that plot of land. Alternatively, the land may be purchased outright by the user at a price that is precisely a direct capitalization of all *future rent* accruing to it. This latter proposition indicates at once (in view of the discussion of production prices undertaken in chapter 2) that land prices are altogether different in their origins and significance from production prices on ordinary commodities. In general, two principle varieties of rent-yielding land are distinguishable. On the one hand there is land used by firms in order to produce commodities; and, on the other hand, there is land used by households for residential purposes. The rent that firms pay for commodity-producing land represents a deduction out of their total profits, and specifically out of their excess profits. The rent that households pay for residential purposes represents a deduction out of total wages. The phenomenon of land rent thus reduces the profitability of firms and the real wages of workers. That is, land rent

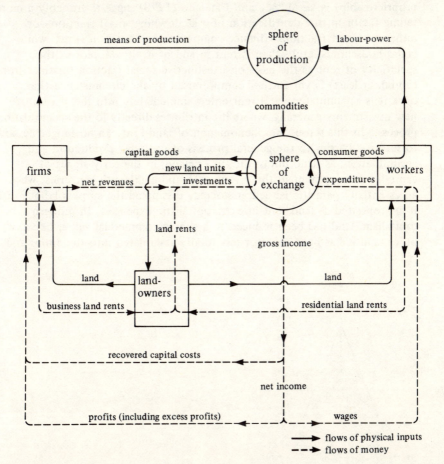

Figure 3.1. Commodity production: a simple schema of the interrelations of capital, labour, and land.

is ultimately a simple proportion of total net income appropriated by landowners, and it stands in inverse relation to both profits and wages just as profits and wages stand in inverse relation to one another (cf figure 3.2). For this reason alone, the land question emerges as a particularly explosive issue at critical conjunctures (for example, during periodic property booms in capitalist cities) when anomalously large quantities of net income begin to be siphoned off as land rent into the hands of landowners. At such moments as these, landowners as a group are likely to find themselves on the defensive not only in relation to labour, but also, in extreme cases, in relation to capital generally. Nevertheless, the land question as a political issue is enormously complicated by the variable role that land plays in the functional orientations of, and conflicts among, different categories of land users.

This factor of land use (and associated differential forms of land proprietorship) is, as Massey and Catalano (1978) suggest, probably a more telling factor in the identification of a landowning social fraction—or, rather, series of fractions (finance companies, construction firms, white-collar households, etc)—than is rent in and of itself. Moreover, the specificity of rent as the basis of a distinctive social fraction (distinct from capital, at least) is yet further compromised by the circumstance that, once it is accumulated, land rent enters immediately into the stream of new investments generally, where it contributes directly to the accumulation process. In this sense, the phenomenon of land rent can no longer be said to set up a barrier to the general process of capitalist production and accumulation, as it no doubt did, in England, in the early stages of capitalist development in the seventeenth and eighteenth centuries, when an essentially parasitic landed aristocracy dissipated the surplus labour that it appropriated as land rent in extracapitalistic expenses. In modern capitalism, land has been reduced to a simple commercial value, like any other, and it has been more or less totally assimilated into the ambit and

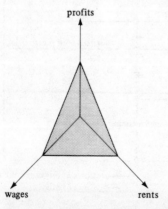

Figure 3.2. The relationship between profits, wages, and rents in a commodity-production system.

logic of commodity-producing society. This suggests, in spite of frequent predictions by Marxian theorists to the contrary, that modern capital and modern landownership are likely to remain firmly allied to one another, except perhaps in circumstances of the most aberrant incursions of the land-rent mechanism on the immediate profitability and viability of commodity production. In addition, as will be made clearly apparent towards the close of this chapter, and in contradistinction to the thesis proposed by Massey and Catalano (1978), land rent (and specifically differential rent) does *not* shackle accumulation by "prematurely" equalizing profit rates at all locations thereby allegedly diverting new investment away from the most efficient and potentially profitable locations. As will be shown, despite the existence of differential rent (or, rather, on account of it), there remain forceful economic mechanisms that tend to encourage new investment at technically efficient locations and to discourage new investment at technically inefficient locations.

With these general introductory comments in mind, let us now consider how the central core of commodity production in capitalist society may be translated into spatial terms, and how, as a consequence, distinctive (but derivative) patterns of productive land use and land rent appear. At a later stage, the argument will turn to a consideration as to how residential land use may be accommodated within this scheme.

3.2 Commodity production and land use: analytical foundations

We will consider here, by way of an entry point into the general problem of the geographical structure of commodity production, a relatively simple and tractable case. This case involves taking on the one hand the Sraffa model of production, prices, and distribution, and integrating it with a classical von Thünen model of land use and land rent. The ultimate function of this analysis is to serve as the basis for a discussion of the economic geography of the contemporary city; however, for the present and for ease of exposition, the argument may perhaps be thought of as being most relevant to the analysis of a simple agricultural situation.

Some definitions

For purposes of immediate discussion let us take it, in accordance with the usual von Thünen assumptions, that there exists a single central market on a perfectly uniform plain over which transport is ubiquitously available. Three commodities (or, in this deliberately simplified initial case, crops), labelled a, b, and c, are produced on this plain under conditions of perfect competition. The process whereby these commodities are produced is understood to be describable in terms of the Sraffa system as discussed in the previous chapter. For simplicity, joint production possibilities are eliminated from the analysis and capitalist firms (or farms) are assumed variously to specialize in the production of some single commodity. All commodity producers have equal access to a given set of production technologies. In the simplest case, competition and economic rationality then impose the result that commodity producers in any one branch will all adopt a common optimal technology such that every firm will consume the same amount of land and will produce the same total output as every other firm in the same branch. In due course, it will be shown how a much more elaborate and complex case than this may emerge. Let us identify the standard land area of firms of types a, b, and c as A_a, A_b, and A_c, respectively. Total output of each of the three types of firms is identified as $\bar{x}_a$, $\bar{x}_b$, and $\bar{x}_c$ respectively.

Now commodity producers will compete among each other for the sale of their output at the central market; this will bring into being a set of unified market prices for each commodity. Firms will also compete among each other for the use of the best land, that is, in the present context, land that is most accessible to the central market; this will bring into being a set of spatially variable land rents. This latter process will also be associated with the emergence of a geographically disaggregated pattern of production, such that each commodity occupies a distinctive annulus or *von Thünen ring* around the central market. The emergence of these rings is also in part related to the rent-maximizing propensities of landlords. Thus land at any given location is ceded only to producers of that commodity that can pay the highest rent at that location. Without any loss of generality, we may assume for the purposes of the present analysis that commodity a occupies the entire ring extending from the central market out to a radius of d_α distance units from the market; that commodity b occupies all land in the ring defined by $d_\beta - d_\alpha$ (where $d_\beta > d_\alpha$); and that commodity c occupies all land in the ring defined by $d_\gamma - d_\beta$ (where $d_\gamma > d_\beta$) (cf figure 3.3). The values of d_α, d_β, and d_γ are all ultimately determined endogenously to the analysis. For the moment, it may be taken that the residences of the labour force engaged in production are distributed in conformity with the distribution of production itself; this assumption will be corrected at a later stage in the argument.

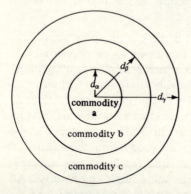

Figure 3.3. The spatial structure of production.

A nonspatial three-sector Sraffa system

In order to fix ideas, let us first consider this three-sector production system independently of its geographical foundations. The physical core of this system is of course an input–output process as discussed in chapter 2, but now in addition disaggregated down to a firm-by-firm process. Thus, for each firm of type a, input–output relations are definable as

$$f_a(x_{aa}, x_{ba}, x_{ca}, l_a) \rightarrow \bar{x}_a \ . \tag{3.1}$$

For each firm of type b, input–output relations are

$$f_b(x_{ab}, x_{bb}, x_{cb}, l_b) \rightarrow \bar{x}_b \ . \tag{3.2}$$

And for each firm of type c

$$f_c(x_{ac}, x_{bc}, x_{cc}, l_c) \rightarrow \bar{x}_c \ , \tag{3.3}$$

where $\{x_{aa}, x_{ba}, x_{ca}\}$, $\{x_{ab}, x_{bb}, x_{cb}\}$, and $\{x_{ac}, x_{bc}, x_{cc}\}$ represent sets of inputs of commodities a, b, and c used in producing the output of firms of types a, b, and c respectively, and l_a, l_b, and l_c represent labour inputs to firms of types a, b, and c respectively. Production prices for each type of output are, as usual, p_a, p_b, and p_c. A composite Sraffa model for this simple nonspatial three-sector model can now be written directly in terms of a series of three equations, where each equation identifies the general production relations for the typical firm in some specific branch, that is

$$(x_{aa}p_a + x_{ba}p_b + x_{ca}p_c)(1+\rho) + l_a w = \bar{x}_a p_a \ , \tag{3.4}$$

$$(x_{ab}p_a + x_{bb}p_b + x_{cb}p_c)(1+\rho) + l_b w = \bar{x}_b p_b \ , \tag{3.5}$$

$$(x_{ac}p_a + x_{bc}p_b + x_{cc}p_c)(1+\rho) + l_c w = \bar{x}_c p_c \ . \tag{3.6}$$

We may now simply append some numeraire to this system say, for simplicity,

$$f(p_a, p_b, p_c) = 1 \ , \tag{3.7}$$

[cf equation (2.4)] and the numerical values of the four unknown variables consisting of the production prices, p_a, p_b, p_c, and the normal rate of profit, ρ, can be deduced immediately. In order to identify total output in any branch of production, we simply multiply output per firm by the number of firms in that branch.

The Sraffa model in spatial context

Mention has already been made of the fact that extension of the Sraffa model to a spatial context involves the introduction of a third social force in addition to capital and labour, in other words, landowners, who, through their appropriation of land rent, absorb a quantity of net income that would otherwise be converted into profits or wages. We must also introduce an additional technical process in the form of a transport system, though in the present chapter this transport system is taken as a purely exogenous sector of economic activity.

Recall that all exchange of commodities occurs at the central market. We must therefore clearly distinguish between f.o.b. prices at the point of production, and c.i.f. price at the market. More explicitly, we must distinguish, on the one hand, price at the point of production not only before payment of the costs of transport to the central market, but also before payment of land rent; and on the other hand, price at the central market after payment of both transport costs and rent. This accounting convention is important in establishing the basic structure of the Sraffa model in spatial context. In the first place, it reflects the evident circumstance that transport costs can only be imputed to that part of total production that passes through the market, and not to that part that is held back for subsequent use in the production process. And in the second place, it is simply convenient here for notational purposes to impute rent only to that part of total production that passes through the central market. With respect to this latter statement, it is in fact a matter of indifference as to whether a firm accounts for its own inputs to itself net of rent or inclusive of rent. For under either circumstance, the residue (rent) that is left over after subtracting all true costs (evaluated at the normal rate of profit where applicable) from total revenues (as determined in relation to prices at the market) is always a constant value. It should be added that any part of any firm's output that is retained for use in the next round of production must always be fully accounted for at its real production price (so that it generates a concomitant normal profit), for it does indeed represent immobilized capital. With these various comments in mind, let us now identify production prices before payment of transport costs and rent as p_a, p_b, and p_c for commodities a, b, and c respectively; and let us identify delivered prices at the central market after payment of transport costs and rent as p_a^{π}, p_b^{π}, and p_c^{π}.

With these various definitions in mind, we can write the equations of the first stage of a spatialized Sraffa model as follows:

$$(x_{aa} p_a + x_{ba} p_b^{\pi} + x_{ca} p_c^{\pi})(1+\rho) + l_a w = \bar{x}_a p_a , \qquad (3.8)$$

$$(x_{ab} p_a^{\pi} + x_{bb} p_b + x_{cb} p_c^{\pi})(1+\rho) + l_b w = \bar{x}_b p_b , \qquad (3.9)$$

$$(x_{ac} p_a^{\pi} + x_{bc} p_b^{\pi} + x_{cc} p_c)(1+\rho) + l_c w = \bar{x}_c p_c , \qquad (3.10)$$

and

$$f(p_a, p_b, p_c, p_a^{\pi}, p_b^{\pi}, p_c^{\pi}) = 1 . \qquad (3.11)$$

In this model, the intermediate inputs from any firm to itself are, in accordance with the discussion in the preceding paragraph, priced at their production price net of transport costs and rent. All other intermediate inputs are priced at their central market price. The question remains: how can the price of these latter inputs be fixed at a constant level given that commodity producers must transport them *back* from the central market to the various and scattered locations where they will be used in the production process? The answer to this question is readily apparent. Firms must indeed defray the differential costs of transporting commodities back from the market. However, a differential rent on land will emerge in perfect inverse proportion to the costs of the backward journey, and such that the sum of those costs plus rent will be constant at every location in any given land-use ring. To facilitate the analysis that follows (and without any loss of generality) this constant will henceforth simply be tacitly assimilated into the analysis by assuming that all transport costs and all land rents on all commodities are paid *in toto* at the end of each production period.

In the ensuing discussion, the detailed components and extensions of this model will be elaborated at some length.

3.3 Elaboration of the basic spatial model
The determination of total output

Total demand for each of the commodities a, b, and c is composed of two main categories: direct replacements for used-up materials and equipment (capital inputs), and final consumption items. In this initial static model, accumulation of profits and rents is simply for the moment, assumed away. It is, of course, also assumed that all physical inputs to any firm are fully exhausted within the duration of a single production period. The demand per firm for replacements for used-up materials and equipment is determined in relation to the input–output conditions (3.1), (3.2), and (3.3). Overall demand for intermediate capital inputs in any branch can be obtained simply by multiplying demand per firm by the total number of firms in that branch. In addition, let us suppose that total final consumption can be expressed simply as the given quantities F_a, F_b, and F_c for commodities a, b, and c, respectively. At equilibrium, total demand for each commodity can be written as the aggregate of derived demand for capital inputs plus final consumption, that is,

$$x_{aa}\frac{\pi d_\alpha^2}{A_a} + x_{ab}\frac{\pi(d_\beta^2 - d_\alpha^2)}{A_b} + x_{ac}\frac{\pi(d_\gamma^2 - d_\beta^2)}{A_c} + F_a = \bar{X}_a \;, \quad (3.12)$$

$$x_{ba}\frac{\pi d_\alpha^2}{A_a} + x_{bb}\frac{\pi(d_\beta^2 - d_\alpha^2)}{A_b} + x_{bc}\frac{\pi(d_\gamma^2 - d_\beta^2)}{A_c} + F_b = \bar{X}_b \;, \quad (3.13)$$

$$x_{ca}\frac{\pi d_\alpha^2}{A_a} + x_{cb}\frac{\pi(d_\beta^2 - d_\alpha^2)}{A_b} + x_{cc}\frac{\pi(d_\gamma^2 - d_\beta^2)}{A_c} + F_c = \bar{X}_c \;, \quad (3.14)$$

where $\bar{X}_a$, $\bar{X}_b$, $\bar{X}_c$ represent endogenously determined total demands for the outputs of branches a, b, and c, respectively, and where the expressions d_α^2/A_a, $(d_\beta^2 - d_\alpha^2)/A_b$, and $(d_\gamma^2 - d_\beta^2)/A_c$ identify the total numbers of firms of types a, b, and c, respectively.

In addition, the total production or supply of any one commodity is governed by the total geographical area devoted to the production of that commodity. Thus, the following supply conditions must also apply to the model

$$\frac{\pi d_\alpha^2}{A_a} \bar{x}_a = \bar{X}_a \ , \tag{3.15}$$

$$\frac{\pi(d_\beta^2 - d_\alpha^2)}{A_b} \bar{x}_b = \bar{X}_b \ , \tag{3.16}$$

$$\frac{\pi(d_\gamma^2 - d_\beta^2)}{A_c} \bar{x}_c = \bar{X}_c \ . \tag{3.17}$$

Evidently, demand and supply must be equated via the variables $\bar{X}_a$, $\bar{X}_b$, and $\bar{X}_c$. Recall, in addition, that d_α, d_β, and d_γ, are endogenous variables in this model, so that the relations defined by equations (3.12)-(3.17) are all fully interdependent.

Central prices and differential rents

In a competitive economic market, prices are always fixed by the price at which the least competitive, or marginal, firm can sell its product. Within the frame of reference set up in this chapter, the marginal firm, or rather firms, with respect to the central market are producers of commodity c located along the outer limits of production at radius d_γ from the centre. These firms are marginal in the sense that, because of their location, they would always be the first producers to be eliminated from the market in any economic downturn. Furthermore, so long as the supply of commodity c is perfectly elastic then competition at the central market will prevent producers of commodity c at distance d_γ from earning any excess profit beyond the normal rate of profit. That is,

$$r_c(d_\gamma) = 0 \ , \tag{3.18}$$

where r stands for excess profit (or differential rent) per unit of output. Similarly let t stand for transport cost, and in such a way that $t_c(d_\gamma)$, for example, represents the total cost involved in transporting one unit of commodity c over the distance d_γ to the central market. Then, a *first approximation* to a determination of the central market price of commodity c is given by the expression

$$p_c^\pi = p_c + t_c(d_\gamma) \ . \tag{3.19}$$

This expression represents the total final market cost (including a normal profit) of one unit of commodity c produced at distance d_γ from the centre, and then transported to the market. Moreover, p_c^π as defined above now fixes the general price of commodity c on the central market. Intramarginal producers of commodity c will now sell at the same price, thus earning an excess profit due to their better accessibility to the market.

At distance d_δ from the central market, this excess profit per unit of output of commodity c is determined in conformity with the rule

$$r_c(d_\delta) = p_c^\pi - p_c - t_c(d_\delta) = t_c(d_\gamma) - t_c(d_\delta) , \qquad d_\beta \leq d_\delta \leq d_\gamma , \qquad (3.20)$$

so that excess profit, in the present instance, is purely a function of transport cost differentials.

Now, at β and inwards towards the market, commodity b replaces commodity c on the economic landscape. Moreover, economic competition and rationality will obviously fix the location of the boundary between commodity b and commodity c in such a way that excess profit (rent) per unit area earned on crop b at the boundary will exactly equal excess profit per unit area earned on crop c at the boundary; in short, the overall land-rent surface, under conditions of a competitive land market, will form a continuous and unbroken integument. This proposition means that at distance d_β from the market the condition must hold,

$$\frac{\bar{x}_b - x_{bb}}{A_b} r_b(d_\beta) = \frac{\bar{x}_c - x_{cc}}{A_c} r_c(d_\beta) , \qquad (3.21)$$

where $\bar{x}_b - x_{bb}$ represents the total amount of commodity b per firm that is actually marketed at the central point, and $\bar{x}_c - x_{cc}$ represents the total amount of commodity c per firm that is marketed. Recall that, in accordance with an earlier argument, excess profit is imputable only to that part of total production that passes through the central market.

At the same time, producers of commodity b along the boundary at β are themselves marginal with respect to all other producers of commodity b. Thus, with excess profit on commodity b at distance d_β identified as in equation (3.21), we can write the market price of commodity b as

$$p_b^\pi = p_b + t_b(d_\beta) + r_b(d_\beta) . \qquad (3.22)$$

And excess profit on commodity b earned by nonmarginal producers at distance d_δ from the market is

$$r_b(d_\delta) = p_b^\pi - p_b - t_b(d_\delta) = t_b(d_\beta) + r_b(d_\beta) - t_b(d_\delta) , \qquad d_\alpha \leq d_\delta < d_\beta . \qquad (3.23)$$

Precisely the same structural relations exist between producers of commodities a and b as exist between producers of commodities b and c. Thus, excess profit on commodity a at the inner land-use boundary at d_α distance units from the centre is given by the equation

$$\frac{\bar{x}_a - x_{aa}}{A_a} r_a(d_\alpha) = \frac{\bar{x}_b - x_{bb}}{A_b} r_b(d_\alpha) . \qquad (3.24)$$

The market price of commodity a is therefore

$$p_a^\pi = p_a + t_a(d_\alpha) + r_a(d_\alpha) . \qquad (3.25)$$

Lastly, excess profit on commodity a earned by nonmarginal producers at distance d_δ from the market is equal to

$$r_a(d_\delta) = p_a^\pi - p_a - t_a(d_\delta) = t_a(d_\alpha) + r_a(d_\alpha) - t_a(d_\delta), \quad 0 \leqslant d_\delta \leqslant d_\alpha . \quad (3.26)$$

Of course, the excess profits, r, do not remain in the hands of capitalist firms but disappear immediately in the form of differential rent. More explicitly, since these excess profits result in the first place from the differential economic advantages of various locations in relation to the geographical situation of the central market, they are directly bid away by commodity producers in mutual competition with one another for rights to the usufruct of those locations. The resulting price of these rights is not a consequence of any positive role that landowners as such play in the process of commodity production, but only an expression of the juridical power of private property to tax away a proportion of total surplus labour (net income) in the form of rent.

We need at this stage to consider a second and less familiar type of land rent.

Scarcity rent

Under certain conditions, a *scarcity rent* will appear on land in addition to ordinary differential rent. Such a scarcity rent corresponds to a levy, extracted out of total net income, and imposed by landlords as a function of the absolute scarcity of land.

From a purely formal point of view, scarcity rent bears some resemblance to the Marxian category of absolute rent, a category that is, however—and for reasons that need not detain us here—analytically suspect [cf Scott (1976) for a critique of the concept of absolute rent]. In terms of its function and genesis, scarcity rent is more clearly identifiable in terms of the Walrasian theory of rent. This theory characterizes rent as an increment to the price of a naturally scarce resource, and this increment then functions in such a way as to dampen the demand for that resource down to the available limited supply. Samuelson (1959), in an examination of Ricardian theory, describes a somewhat analogous rent as "residual rent". In the present context, under the assumption that the uniform plain is now strictly bounded in some manner, this proposition translates into the equivalent idea that scarcity rent (on land) represents in some sense an increment to the market prices of commodities a, b, and c, and with the consequence that consumption of those commodities is thereby reduced to a level consistent with the given restricted production possibilities of the land base.

Thus let us now suppose that the outer boundary of production at distance d_γ from the central market is strictly limited by some barrier, such as a seacoast, or a belt of relatively infertile soil, or some administratively imposed restriction such as a political boundary or a zoning limit. Let us imagine that production of commodity c has extended up to this barrier, but that even at the market price $p_c^\pi = p_c + t_c(d_\gamma)$ there still exists some excess demand for commodity c. In this case, there is bound to be an increase in the price of commodity c as consumers compete against each other to secure a portion of the restricted total supply. This increase is really a rent on the absolute scarcity of land and, as such, it is appropriated by landowners rather than by firms.

Let us designate s as this scarcity rent on land *per unit area*. Clearly if the rent s forms on land-producing commodity c, then, in a competitive land market, it must also form on land producing commodities a and b. Concomitantly, the general scarcity rent, s, translates into specific rents *per unit of centrally marketed output* by the following operations:

$$s_a = \frac{A_a s}{(\bar{x}_a - x_{aa})},\tag{3.27}$$

$$s_b = \frac{A_b s}{(\bar{x}_b - x_{bb})},\tag{3.28}$$

$$s_c = \frac{A_c s}{(\bar{x}_c - x_{cc})}.\tag{3.29}$$

The expressions (3.27), (3.28), and (3.29) now imply that market prices can be fully and finally defined as follows:

$$p_a^\pi = p_a + t_a(d_\alpha) + r_a(d_\alpha) + s_a,\tag{3.30}$$

$$p_b^\pi = p_b + t_b(d_\beta) + r_b(d_\beta) + s_b,\tag{3.31}$$

$$p_c^\pi = p_c + t_c(d_\gamma) + s_c.\tag{3.32}$$

Observe that, if a scarcity rent exists, then even marginal producers at distance d_γ from the market will pay a positive rent for land. However, if land is so abundant that d_γ is effectively unrestricted, then the scarcity rent s cannot be sustained at a positive level, for it would be driven down to zero by the action of landlords competing among themselves to rent their land along the elastic margins of production. The final equilibrium value of s is thus determined in conformity with the rules,

$$s \geqslant 0 \text{ if land is scarce},\tag{3.33}$$

$$s = 0 \text{ if land is abundant}.\tag{3.34}$$

These conditions mean, further, that s and d_γ are mutually exclusive variables in the overall model. Thus, if land is scarce, then d_γ is fixed exogenously accordingly, and s is determined endogenously. If land is abundant, however, then s is directly equated to zero, and the numerical value of d_γ is determined as an endogenous variable.

3.4 A general solution

The various interrelationships between prices, rents, and transport costs as described above are demonstrated graphically in figure 3.4.

The model sketched out above is now seen to represent a perfectly interdependent structure. This model contains the nineteen variables p_a, p_b, p_c, p_a^π, p_b^π, p_c^π, ρ, $\bar{X}_a$, $\bar{X}_b$, $\bar{X}_c$, $r_a(d_\alpha)$, $r_b(d_\beta)$, s, s_a, s_b, s_c, d_α, d_β, and d_γ in the eighteen equations, (3.8)–(3.17), (3.21), (3.24), and (3.27)–(3.32). However, since s and d_γ are mutually exclusive elements of the model, there are, in practice, only eighteen variables (in eighteen equations) so the model is fully determinate. The full interdependence of the Sraffa and von Thünen systems is now, in addition, fully apparent. The production prices p_a, p_b, and p_c first appear as the outcome of a general process of commodity production; then they translate via the spatial system into the market prices p_a^π, p_b^π, and p_c^π; the latter prices in turn enter into the production process, thus determining the values of p_a, p_b, and p_c; and so on *ad infinitum*.

It is now also possible to relax the initial assumption that the spatial ordering of all land-use rings must be known in advance. If it is required

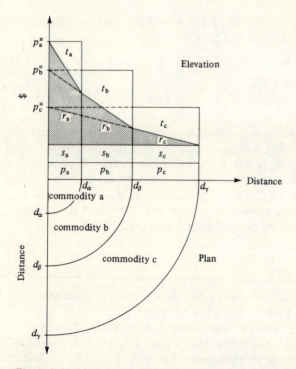

Figure 3.4. Land rents, prices, and transport costs on the uniform plain. For simplicity in constructing this figure it is assumed that the conditions of production are such that $p_a = p_b = p_c$, $s_a = s_b = s_c$, $r_a(d_\alpha) = r_b(d_\alpha)$ and $r_b(d_\beta) = r_c(d_\beta)$. The shaded area represents differential rent.

to determine this ordering as an endogenous output of the model, then an extended model can be established, analogous to the model developed above, but with the added feature that production of each commodity is initially permitted at each and every location. The competitive equilibrium solution is then simply determined by maximizing total land rent subject to the Sraffa-von Thünen conditions as established here. In fact, figure 3.4 finally clarifies the role and function of land rent as a sorter and arranger of land uses, for each individual location within the geographical interval $\{0, d_\gamma\}$ is clearly uniquely occupied by that commodity that can pay the highest aggregate rent at that location under competitive market conditions.

3.5 Commodity production and the dynamics of land-use differentiation

A particular shortcoming of the model of commodity production and land use as described above is that it is purely static; it provides an overview of a given economic-cum-geographic situation in which, however, all processes of temporal development have been suppressed. This is a doubly untoward state of affairs. In the first place, the process of commodity production is interpenetrated in its deepest structure by the dynamic process of capital accumulation. In the second place, and as a concomitant, actual land-use patterns, most especially in the contemporary city, are observably in a continuous ferment of flux and readjustment as the economic system moves forward through time. Nevertheless, it is now possible to begin responding to certain of these issues and, building upon the analysis as it has developed thus far, to identify at least in part some basic dynamic processes. Thus, in what follows, a significant and fundamental mechanism of land-use change is now described as an outcome of the central process of accumulation and technical change. It is shown here how a very basic process of land-use change is rooted, not so much in changes in the external environment of commodity production, but in the whole phenomenon of internal transformations in the technical structure of production.

In order to initiate this phase of the analysis, let us begin by focussing attention on a single branch of production. Let us at the outset assume that all firms in this branch make use of a single dominant production technique. The total set of firms will form a single continuous land-use zone surrounding the central market, and we will take it that the outer limits of this zone are fixed at d_β distance units from the centre, (cf figure 3.5). If (again for simplicity) scarcity rent is assumed to be zero, then market price is given by the equation

$$p^\pi = p + t(d_\beta) \tag{3.35}$$

and differential rent per unit of output at distance d_δ from the centre will be, directly,

$$r(d_\delta) = p^\pi - p - t(d_\delta), \qquad 0 \leq d_\delta \leq d_\beta. \tag{3.36}$$

Bearing these definitions in mind, let us now consider, first, two very simple mechanisms of land-use change (designated here *intensive* and *extensive* land-use change) and then, second, generalizing out of this analysis, the mechanism of land-use change at large. These mechanisms of land-use change essentially represent *switching processes* defined over geographical space.

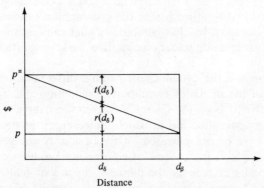

Figure 3.5. Prices, transport costs, and differential rents as a function of distance from the central market in a simple one-commodity economy.

The process of intensive land-use change

Let us suppose that some technical innovation in the production process becomes available, such that it is now possible for firms (within the specific branch of production under examination here) that switch to the new technique to increase their total physical output, though only at the expense of some corresponding increase in production costs (that is, an increase in total capital and/or labour costs). Specifically, let us suppose that any firm that adopts the new technique of production is able to increase its aggregate output from $\bar{x}$ to $\bar{x} + \Delta \bar{x}$ while its production price rises from p to $p + \Delta p$. [In passing remark that the cases where (a) output falls but production price rises, and (b) output rises but production price falls, are both trivial; in the former case, the new technique is uncompetitive in relation to the old technique and, in the latter case, the new technique simply everywhere replaces the old technique.] We will take it here in order to simplify the ensuing argument (though without any loss of generality) that any firm that switches to the new technique consumes precisely the same amount of land after conversion as it did before. We may also take it that the new production price, $p + \Delta p$, reflects any fixed costs involved in converting from the old to the new technique. Given that the total land area consumed by any converted firm remains unchanged after conversion, it is evident that a process of capital and/or labour intensification has gone on in relation to land inputs; and, in what follows, this process will be consistently referred to as a process of *land-use intensification*.

At the outset, and so long as only a few firms have switched to the new intensive technique, central market price, p^π, will remain stable. This means (on the assumption that all output is carried directly to the central market and none is held back for use in the next production round) that each converted firm will earn a total revenue of $(\bar{x}+\Delta\bar{x})p^\pi$. For each such firm, aggregate production price will be $(\bar{x}+\Delta\bar{x})(p+\Delta p)$; total transport costs to the central market will be $(\bar{x}+\Delta\bar{x})t(d_\delta)$ (for a firm located at d_δ distance units from the market); and total land rent will be simply $\bar{x}r(d_\delta)$. Just as market price will remain stable at the outset, so land rent will remain unchanged after conversion to the new technique; for, so long as conversion to the new technique is quite limited there will be as yet little or no added competition in the land market sufficient to drive land rents upwards. Moreover, if the total rent paid by any firm that adopts the new technique remains at the level $\bar{x}r(d_\delta)$, then, as a corollary, rent per unit of output will fall to the level $\bar{x}r(d_\delta)/(\bar{x}+\Delta\bar{x})$.

In these various circumstances, then, any converted firm at distance d_δ from the central market will be able to bring its output to the market at the minimum cost per unit of output identified by the cost function $c(d_\delta)$ as follows,

$$p+\Delta p+t(d_\delta)+\frac{\bar{x}}{\bar{x}+\Delta\bar{x}}r(d_\delta) = c(d_\delta) \ . \tag{3.37}$$

Given the relation between $t(d_\delta)$ and $r(d_\delta)$ as defined by equation (3.36) it is clear that the function $c(d_\delta)$ must diminish in value as d_δ diminishes. Furthermore, if the new technique is economically competitive in relation to the old technique at distance d_δ from the central market then the condition must hold,

$$c(d_\delta) \leq p^\pi \ , \tag{3.38}$$

that is, total cost at the market for those firms that switch to the new intensive technique must not exceed current market price. From equation (3.37) it is evident that this condition is most likely to be satisfied by firms that occupy locations where land rents are already relatively high (see also figures 3.6 and 3.7); at such locations, the discount (due to land-use intensification) on land rent per unit of output will be at a maximum, thus offsetting the increase, Δp, in production price. In addition, wherever the condition (3.38) is satisfied, any intensified firm will be able to appropriate an excess profit on each unit of output. Let us designate this excess profit as the function of distance $\Delta r(d_\delta)$; it can be defined explicitly as

$$\Delta r(d_\delta) = p^\pi - c(d_\delta) \ ; \tag{3.39}$$

or, substituting the expression (3.36) for p^π and the expression (3.37) for $c(d_\delta)$, and simplifying,

$$\Delta r(d_\delta) = -\Delta p + \frac{\Delta \bar{x}}{\bar{x} + \Delta \bar{x}} r(d_\delta) \ . \tag{3.40}$$

Simple algebraic manipulation of this last equation reveals that excess profit falls to zero where land rent falls to the value of

$$r(d_\alpha) = \left(\frac{\bar{x}}{\Delta \bar{x}} + 1\right) \Delta p \ , \tag{3.41}$$

where d_α designates the critical distance from the central market such that the new intensive technique is economically viable at all locations where $d_\delta \leq d_\alpha$ and nonviable at all locations where $d_\delta > d_\alpha$.

Obviously, from equation (3.40) excess profits due to land-use intensification will be at a maximum at the centre of the land-use system and will diminish with distance outwards until they disappear to zero at distance d_α from the centre. This means that if the new technique is adopted sequentially by firms over a period of time (and given conditions of a free capital market) then it is most likely to be adopted first at

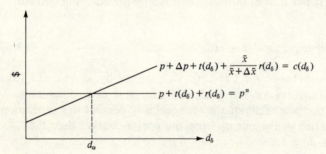

Figure 3.6. Prices and costs as a function of d_δ. The new intensive technique is economically competitive where $d_\delta \leq d_\alpha$ and uncompetitive where $d_\delta > d_\alpha$.

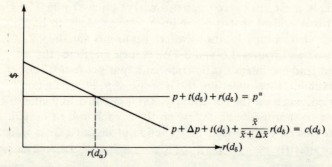

Figure 3.7. Prices and costs as a function of $r(d_\delta)$. The new intensive technique is economically competitive where $r(d_\delta) \geq r(d_\alpha)$ and uncompetitive where $r(d_\delta) < r(d_\alpha)$.

locations close to the centre and subsequently to diffuse through the land-use system in a regular pattern outwards until it is finally arrested at distance d_α from the centre. But as this process continues, so increasing competition among adopters of the technique for accessible locations will progressively transform any excess profit, $\Delta r(d_\delta)$, into land rent. In fact, once the new intensive technique has attained to its maximum outer geographical limit, competition in the land market will have become such that all excess profits will have been bid away from the pockets of landowners thus reducing the profits of all intensified firms back to the normal level as determined by the normal rate of profit ρ. As a result, the land-rent surface within the geographical interval $\{0, d_\beta\}$ will become internally articulated as shown in figure 3.8. Land rents paid per firm (land rents per standard unit land area) will now be established in accordance with the functions

$$R(d_\delta) = \bar{x} r(d_\delta) + (\bar{x} + \Delta \bar{x}) \Delta r(d_\delta) , \qquad 0 \leqslant d_\delta \leqslant d_\alpha , \qquad (3.42)$$

$$R(d_\delta) = \bar{x} r(d_\delta) , \qquad d_\alpha \leqslant d_\delta \leqslant d_\beta , \qquad (3.43)$$

where $R(d_\delta)$ is total land rent per firm at distance d_δ from the central market.

At the same time, while the new technique is in the process of diffusing through the land-use system, and as total production expands accordingly, so firms located at the geographical margin of production will be steadily eliminated from the central market. This means, first, that the geographical margin of production will shrink progressively inwards as more and more firms intensify their use of land and, second, that the market price, p^π, will fall [in conformity with the relationship established in equation (3.35)]. Concomitantly, there will be complex changes in the global pattern of land rents. At the waning perimeter of land use, rents will tend universally to decrease. Towards the centre of the land-use system, however, rents will tend first of all to increase as the land-use intensification process gets

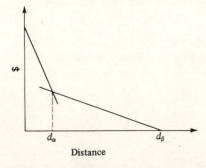

Figure 3.8. Land rent per unit area within a land-use zone differentiated into two subzones on the basis of a relatively intensive production technique in the geographical interval $\{0, d_\alpha\}$, and a (preexisting) relatively extensive production technique in the geographical interval $\{d_\alpha, d_\beta\}$.

under way, but then they will tend to fall (especially if demand is relatively price inelastic) as the boundary of production moves steadily inwards and as p^π continues its relentless descent. Nevertheless, judging by empirical events in contemporary cities, the overall process of urban growth and expansion is likely in fact to override and to swamp these tendencies, so that in practice real land-use systems appear everywhere to be characterized by rising prices and rising land rents.

These various findings are now generalizable to the case where not just one but several different land-use-intensive techniques become available. Consider, for example, the case of three different technical innovations labelled T′, T″, T‴, so that they are ordered from most to least land-use intensive in the specific sense that $\Delta p' > \Delta p'' > \Delta p'''$ and $\Delta \bar{x}' > \Delta \bar{x}'' > \Delta \bar{x}'''$. Let us take it that each technique is economically competitive within some limited geographical range; this implies in particular that $c'(d_\delta)$ is lower than $c''(d_\delta)$, $c'''(d_\delta)$, or p^π in the geographical interval $\{0, d_{\alpha'}\}$; that $c''(d_\delta)$ is lower than $c'(d_\delta)$, $c'''(d_\delta)$, or p^π in the geographical interval $\{d_{\alpha'}, d_{\alpha''}\}$; and that $c'''(d_\delta)$ is lower than $c'(d_\delta)$, $c''(d_\delta)$, or p^π in the geographical interval $\{d_{\alpha''}, d_{\alpha'''}\}$ where $d_{\alpha'} < d_{\alpha''} < d_{\alpha'''} < d_\beta$. The general situation described by these conditions is depicted schematically in figure 3.9. It is now evident that any single von Thünen zone may be indefinitely differentiated into multiple subzones on the basis of a proliferation of (spatially determinate) switching possibilities among different commodity-production techniques with varying degrees of associated land-use intensiveness. This remark implies, further, that where several different techniques of production are already in use within a given land-use system then the possibility always exists of an additional technique

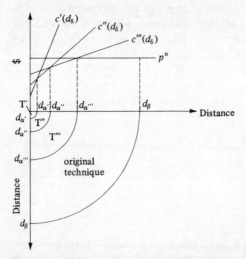

Figure 3.9. A land-use zone differentiated into four subzones on the basis of an original production technique and three relatively intensive techniques, T′, T″, T‴.

being introduced not only at the extreme land-use-intensive (and, as will be shown, at the extreme land-use-extensive) margin of production, but also, under the right conditions (as implied by the analysis of the techniques T', T'', and T''' above), at some intermediate location within the whole land-use system.

The process of extensive land-use change

The method developed above to demonstrate the process of land-use intensification contains within itself a dual process of extensive land-use change. Of course, extensive outward development of any land-use zone will invariably occur where transport costs are reduced or where there are upward shifts in the demand curve. Here, however, attention is focussed only on land-use changes that are related to the phenomenon of the switching of techniques within the commodity-production process.

Let us consider, as before, the simple case of a homogeneous land-use type that is initially dominated by a single technique of production. Let us suppose that some technical innovation becomes available such that any firm that adopts the new technique is able to reduce its capital and/or labour inputs in relation to land, though with the countervailing disadvantage that it must also reduce its total output, either absolutely or per unit of land. To simplify matters (though again without compromising generality) let us continue to assume that any firm that converts to the new technique will consume precisely the same amount of land after conversion as it did before. After conversion, then, production price will fall from p to $p - \Delta p$, and output will fall absolutely (in this simplified case) from $\bar{x}$ to $\bar{x} - \Delta \bar{x}$. Then, this new technique is *land-use extensive* in relation to the original technique of production in the sense that it requires a lower total of capital and labour inputs per unit of land and yields a correspondingly lower output per unit of land. As will be shown below, this new extensive technique also generates an outward expansion of land use.

Any firm at distance d_δ from the central market that adopts this new technique can now bring its output to the market for a total minimum cost, $c(d_\delta)$, per unit of output that is equal to a production price plus a transport cost plus a land rent as in the case of equation (3.37) above. However, the explicit functional form identifying this cost is rather more complex than it was in the case of the intensive technique, and, in particular, it possesses two major different phases. A first phase is identified as existing within the geographical interval $\{d_\alpha, d_\beta\}$ where d_α defines the inner boundary of the new extensive technique; a second phase is identified as existing within the geographical interval $\{d_\beta, d_\gamma\}$ where d_γ defines the outer boundary of the new technique. Notice that if it is economically competitive in relation to the existing land-use situation then the new extensive technique will be introduced in a subzone that straddles both sides of the current land-use boundary at d_β distance units from the central market.

Then, the first phase of the function $c(d_\delta)$ can be written

$$p - \Delta p + t(d_\delta) + \frac{\bar{x}}{\bar{x} - \Delta \bar{x}} r(d_\delta) = c(d_\delta) , \qquad d_\alpha \leq d_\delta \leq d_\beta , \qquad (3.44)$$

which, as shown in figure 3.10, decreases as d_δ increases. And the second phase can be written

$$p - \Delta p + t(d_\delta) = c(d_\delta) , \qquad d_\beta \leq d_\delta \leq d_\gamma , \qquad (3.45)$$

which, as shown in figure 3.10, increases as d_δ increases. In point of fact, functions (3.44) and (3.45) are equivalent given that $r(d_\delta)$ is everywhere null for values of d_δ that are greater than or equal to d_β.

Now, if the new extensive technique is economically competitive in relation to the preexisting dominant technique over the geographical interval from d_α to d_γ, then the condition (3.38) specified above must hold at locations contained within that interval. Moreover since any firm that converts to the new technique must experience an *inflation* of land rent per unit of output [cf equation (3.44)] then the condition (3.38) is most likely to be satisfied where land rent is already low or zero. This statement confirms the assertion made in the preceding paragraph that the new technique is most likely to be introduced at locations adjacent to the existing geographical margin of production. Furthermore, in relation to the existing market price, adopters of the new technique will now be able to earn an excess profit, $\Delta r(d_\delta)$, defined as

$$\Delta r(d_\delta) = p^\pi - c(d_\delta) . \qquad (3.46)$$

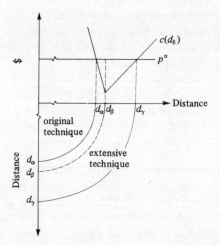

Figure 3.10. Establishment of a land-use subzone comprising a new extensive production technique in the geographical interval $\{d_\alpha, d_\gamma\}$.

More particularly, in the geographical interval $\{d_\alpha, d_\beta\}$ excess profits will be given by the equation

$$\Delta r(d_\delta) = \Delta p - \frac{\Delta \bar{x}}{\bar{x} - \Delta \bar{x}} r(d_\delta) , \qquad d_\alpha \leqslant d_\delta \leqslant d_\beta , \qquad (3.47)$$

and in the geographical interval $\{d_\beta, d_\gamma\}$ excess profits will be given by the equation

$$\Delta r(d_\delta) = \Delta p + t(d_\beta) - t(d_\delta) , \qquad d_\beta \leqslant d_\delta \leqslant d_\gamma , \qquad (3.48)$$

where the latter expression reflects the fact that beyond the preexisting geographical margin of production, market price, p^π, can be most simply written as the spatial constant $p + t(d_\beta)$. From the equation (3.47) it may be deduced that the inner boundary of the new technique at d_α distance units from the central market is defined where

$$r(d_\alpha) = \left(\frac{\bar{x}}{\Delta \bar{x}} - 1\right) \Delta p , \qquad (3.49)$$

and from equation (3.48) it may be deduced that the outer boundary at d_γ distance units from the centre is defined where

$$t(d_\gamma) = \Delta p + t(d_\beta) . \qquad (3.50)$$

Remark that the values of functions $c(d_\delta)$ and $\Delta r(d_\delta)$ will both be asymmetrically distributed with respect to the preexisting margin of production d_β distance units from the market. In short, if transport costs behave in a normal fashion then the cost function $c(d_\delta)$ will slope relatively sharply downwards [so that $\Delta r(d_\delta)$ will slope sharply upwards] in the interval $\{d_\alpha, d_\beta\}$ while $c(d_\delta)$ will slope relatively moderately upwards [so that $\Delta r(d_\delta)$ will slope relatively moderately downwards] in the interval $\{d_\beta, d_\gamma\}$. These relative tendencies will be exaggerated where there is no preexisting land use beyond d_β distance units from the central market, so that conversion costs will be correspondingly reduced in this area.

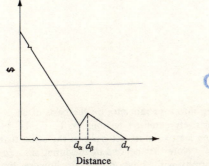

Figure 3.11. Land rent per unit area after full deployment of a new extensive production technique in the geographical interval $\{d_\alpha, d_\gamma\}$.

Once more, all excess profits, $\Delta r(d_\delta)$, will eventually, and in the long run be bid away in the form of land rent. Thus, in the long run, land rents per unit area in the interval $\{d_\alpha, d_\gamma\}$ will take on the values

$$R(d_\delta) = \bar{x} r(d_\delta) + (\bar{x} - \Delta \bar{x})\Delta r(d_\delta) , \qquad d_\alpha \leq d_\delta \leq d_\beta , \qquad (3.51)$$

$$R(d_\delta) = (\bar{x} - \Delta \bar{x})\Delta r(d_\delta) , \qquad d_\beta \leq d_\delta \leq d_\gamma \qquad (3.52)$$

[cf equations (3.42) and (3.43)]. As a consequence, the overall land-rent surface will develop a secondary peak which attains its maximum value at d_β distance units from the central market, as shown in figure 3.11. In spite of the appearance of this secondary peak in the land-rent surface, recall that delivered price, p^u, will remain constant for all producers.

If adoption of the new extensive technique is characterized by a spatiotemporal diffusion process, then (in a free capital market) this process will assume a double-edged motion: the new extensive technique will be initially introduced at the current land-use boundary at d_β distance units from the centre (for at this boundary the excess profit function is at its maximum) and it will diffuse both inwards and outwards at varying velocities depending on the relative rates of slope of the excess-profit function in the geographical intervals $\{d_\alpha, d_\beta\}$ and $\{d_\beta, d_\gamma\}$. This diffusion

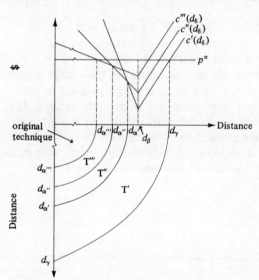

Figure 3.12. A land-use zone differentiated into four subzones on the basis of an original production technique and three relatively extensive techniques, T', T'', T'''. The latter three techniques are ordered from least to most extensive in the sense that $\Delta p' > \Delta p'' > \Delta p'''$ and $\Delta x' > \Delta x'' > \Delta x'''$. Note that beyond d_β the functions $c'(d_\delta)$, $c''(d_\delta)$, and $c'''(d_\delta)$ are all parallel [in conformity with equation (3.45)]; however, in the more general case, to be demonstrated at a later stage, this parallelism no longer necessarily holds true.

process will be finally arrested at its ultimate inner boundary at d_α distance units from the centre, and at its ultimate outer boundary at d_γ distance units from the centre. In addition, if adoption of the new technique entails a net increase in total physical output, then, as in the case of the intensive technique considered earlier, market price, p^π, will fall; and, at the same time, there will be a concomitant inward retraction of the new land-use boundary defined by d_γ. Where several economically competitive extensive techniques become available, several new subzones within the single von Thünen land-use zone will be established as shown in figure 3.12.

3.6 A general synthesis of the dynamic process
Thus far the analysis has been restricted to an examination of switching phenomena in geographical space under conditions where a single homogeneous commodity is produced. But what of the more general case of switching phenomena under conditions where several different commodities are produced, and, in particular, where several different land-use zones exist in some determinate spatial order? A brief global response to this question permits a general synthesis of all that has been transacted up to this stage; and it permits, in addition, a final demonstration of the essential unity of the two processes of intensive and extensive land-use change.

Consider, then, some given general land-use system divided up into a series of individual von Thünen zones, and where each zone produces some specific and distinctive commodity. At any location at distance d_δ from the central market, land rent *per unit standard firm area* is given by the function $R(d_\delta)$. The overall land-rent surface is articulated into sections, each section corresponding to a specific land-use zone. Let it be understood that some new technique of production has become available. To simplify matters, let us combine the intensive and the extensive land-use change processes into a single process by writing $\bar{x} \pm \Delta\bar{x}$ as $\bar{y}$ and $p \pm \Delta p$ as q. Then, the overall unit cost of production (with the use of the new technique) at distance d_δ from the central market, together with the cost of getting output to the market, can be expressed directly as

$$q + t(d_\delta) + \frac{R(d_\delta)}{\bar{y}} = c(d_\delta) \, , \tag{3.53}$$

and this cost function is valid whether the new technique is intensive or extensive. Note that $t(d_\delta)$ is the transport rate appropriate to the commodity produced by the new technique, and it thus has no necessary precise numerical relationship to $R(d_\delta)$ for any arbitrarily given value of d_δ. As usual, the new technique will be introduced at locations wherever $c(d_\delta)$ is less than the prevailing market price (p^π) of the commodity produced by the new technique. If the new technique is land-use intensive (hence associated with relatively high values of both $\bar{y}$ and q) it will tend to generate a cost function that attains its minimum expression at locations lying towards the central market; such a technique is therefore most likely to be adopted at those locations. If the new technique is land-use extensive (hence associated with relatively low values of both $\bar{y}$ and q) it will tend to generate a cost function that attains its minimum expression at locations lying towards the periphery of the land-use system; such a technique is therefore most likely to be adopted at *those* locations.

The behaviour of the cost function, $c(d_\delta)$, however (and hence the pattern of its associated locational outcomes), is of some complexity in a multicommodity land-use system. Depending on the relative numerical values and spatial variation of the transport-cost function, $t(d_\delta)$, and the land-rent function, $R(d_\delta)$, the cost function, $c(d_\delta)$, as described by equation (3.53) is liable to display some wide variations of trend. Recall that $t(d_\delta)$ has a positive slope (is positively correlated with d_δ) while $R(d_\delta)$ has a negative slope (is negatively correlated with d_δ); recall also that $R(d_\delta)$ is likely in any real situation to undergo changes of slope at any land-use boundary. In these circumstances, the behaviour of the function $c(d_\delta)$ may be quite erratic, displaying marked changes and even reversals of slope at each land-use boundary. Specifically, $c(d_\delta)$ will assume a positive slope in land-use zones where $t(d_\Delta) - t(d_\delta) > [R(d_\delta) - R(d_\Delta)]/\bar{y}$, and it will assume a negative slope in land-use zones where $t(d_\Delta) - t(d_\delta) < [R(d_\delta) < [R(d_\Delta)]/\bar{y}$ (where $d_\Delta > d_\delta$). Furthermore, the function $c(d_\delta)$ may undergo *several* alternating reversals of slope in any given land-use system, even where $t(d_\delta)$ and $R(d_\delta)$ are quite well behaved.

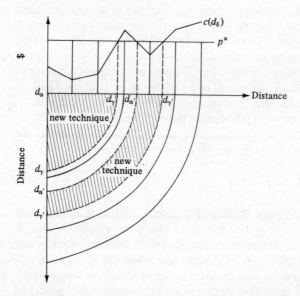

Figure 3.13. A possible configuration of the cost function $c(d_\delta)$ in a multicommodity land-use system. A reswitching phenomenon is apparent: the technique associated with this cost function will be adopted in the geographical interval $\{d_\alpha, d_\gamma\}$ *and* in the geographical interval $\{d_{\alpha'}, d_{\gamma'}\}$.

In order to elucidate the locational consequences of these properties of the function $c(d_\delta)$, let us consider the relatively simple exemplary case demonstrated in figure 3.13. As implied by the situation shown in this figure, there is no necessary reason why adoption of the new technique (producing any given commodity) should be restricted to a land-use zone that already produces the same commodity; in fact, the new technique may be adopted at any location anywhere within the land-use system provided only that $c(d_\delta) \leq p^\pi$ at that location. This implies that any given land-use system may eventually be characterized by spatially recurrent land-use zones, each producing precisely the same commodity (by various techniques) and each separated from the others by different kinds of land-use activities. At the same time, figure 3.13 demonstrates the clear possibility of the appearance of the phenomenon of the spatial reswitching of techniques in a multicommodity land-use system. In other words, as shown in figure 3.13, the interrelations of $c(d_\delta)$ and p^π may be such that the *same* technique may be put to use in two different zones separated geographically from one another by any number of intervening zones. Generalization of these observations to the case of a multiplicity of new techniques proceeds without difficulty along the lines suggested earlier in the individual analyses of the processes of intensive and extensive land-use change. Clearly, where switching and reswitching processes of the sorts described here are in effect, the overall land rent surface is likely to exhibit a complicated series of secondary peaks and articulations.

3.7 Concluding remarks

The entire argument developed above has attempted to show, first, how general land-use systems are propagated by the overall process of commodity production, and second, how the basic mechanisms of land-use change are in fact also intrinsic to the commodity-production process. In accomplishing this second task in particular, it has been shown how any single von Thünen zone may be differentiated into multiple subzones on the basis of a process involving the switching of techniques in geographic space. More generally, it has been shown how the switching (and reswitching) process is potentially capable of producing intricate geographical patterns and recurrences within any given multicommodity land-use system. The phenomenon of the switching of techniques suggests that in any specific land-use zone production densities may diminish in a step function from the inner to the outer margin of that zone. By contrast, where a single production technique prevails over the whole zone, there will be everywhere a constant density of production. In practice, at any given instant (especially no doubt in the contemporary city) the entire land-use system is likely to be typified by a pattern of ongoing and uncompleted rounds of land-use conversions as various technical innovations diffuse through the system.

Finally, the analysis presented here would seem to lend itself not only to the study of the economic geography of commodity production as such, but also to the study of urban residential land-use processes. In this latter case, the constant market price p^π would now be interpreted as the monetary equivalent (the wage) of labour-power as delivered at some central point, or at some aggregate weighted set of urban destinations; that is, p^π would be equal in the first instance to the cost of total personal consumption, plus a transport cost, plus a land rent. Then, given only the mild (and economically rational) choice criterion that, all else being equal, urban residents will prefer to pay lower rather than higher transport costs, it is apparent that the inexorable search for excess profits on the part of housing suppliers would in and of itself (that is, abstracting away from the additional complications of socioeconomic variation) account for the emergence of a relatively high density of housing in inner-city areas, and a relatively low density of housing in suburban areas. Thus, it would seem that there is a real possibility of a reevaluation of the whole theory of urban residential activity on some basis other than pure utility-maximizing principles and the recurrent supposition that urban residential outcomes (and, in particular, spatial variations in housing densities) are nothing more than the unadulterated expression of autarchic subjective tastes. This proposition does not seek to deny the likelihood that consumers make subjectively meaningful residential choices; it questions only the possibility of founding an adequate theory of the formation of residential space on subjective choice criteria alone, and suggests instead that subjectively determined housing choices are subsequent to, rather than prior to, the production of urban space. In any case, in view of the argument developed above, certain openly perverse possibilities contained in consumer sovereignty models of the housing market are now thrown into sharp relief. In particular, if such models are to be believed, then there is always some probability of aberrant and idiosyncratic residential land-use patterns appearing in individual cities, depending on the structure of personal preference functions. The analysis presented here suggests why it is that such a state of affairs is never realized (or realizable) in contemporary city systems.

This discussion now provides a basic point of departure for thinking about some significant issues in the political economy of spatial systems. In what follows, the argument moves forward from the analysis of simple abstract spatial systems as outlined above, to a consideration of complex concrete urban situations. This argument will demonstrate that the human occupation of land can never be effectively coordinated in economic terms alone, but that it also, and necessarily, involves a political dimension of far-reaching human consequence.

Urbanization and planning: a brief record of some recent problems and policies

Up to this point in the argument, attention has been largely focussed on a general theoretical frame of reference as the essential foundation of any putative urban science. In order now to motivate the subsequent discussion, the present chapter offers a brief digression on some of the principal historical developments within the capitalist city over the last several decades, and proposes a categorization of the major types of government policies and programmes that have evolved to cope with those developments. The present chapter thus represents a transition from the rather abstract generalities of the previous chapters to the analysis of the specifically urban logic and dynamics that forms the bulk of what follows. For the moment, the discussion is held to a predominantly descriptive and informational level, and such analytical machinery as may obtrude into the discussion is kept deliberately somewhat restrained.

4.1 Urban problems

In the twentieth century, almost all urban problems in both North America and Western Europe have been contingent in some way upon the global phenomenon of urban growth and expansion consequent upon general economic development. This phenomenon has consistently confronted society with grave problems over the issue of the collective production and utilization of urban land. Already, in the nineteenth century, such problems had been a marked and endemic feature of the whole process of urbanization, and they had made themselves felt, for example, in matters of urban sanitation and public health, the development of streetcar suburbs, the perennial shortage and inferior quality of working-class housing, and so on. They were thus not new problems, though by the beginning of the twentieth century they were starting to take on new forms, just as the economic system itself was starting to take on new forms of structure and organization. The old methods of treating these emergent urban problems were thus becoming increasingly inoperative and outmoded while effective new methods were still in an experimental or prototypical stage of development.

Towards the end of the nineteenth century, one of the most pressing of all the general problems that affected cities in North America was the uncontrolled proliferation of land-use conflicts as a result of the repeated juxtaposition in urban space of incompatible types of social and economic activities. An early but abortive policy response to this problem had made its appearance in the 1890s in the guise of the City Beautiful Movement. However, the protagonists of the City Beautiful Movement were evidently unable to diagnose the essentially economic and political nature of the problem, and, mesmerized as they were by its purely formal symptoms (namely, visual and architectural discord) they proposed an agenda of urban reform based on an aesthetic programme that was as unworkable as it was historically meaningless. During the early years of the present century, then, the City Beautiful Movement inevitably faded gradually away. Nevertheless, in the period following the First World War, a feasible and practical response to the problem of land-use discord in the context of insistent urban growth started to emerge in most North American cities. It was a two-faceted policy involving the rationalization of land uses by zoning, combined with aggressive peripheral urban expansion encouraged and underwritten by government programmes.

From the time of its inception in the city of New York in 1916, zoning spread with notable rapidity across both the United States and Canada. By encouraging the formation of homogeneous land-use districts, thereby reducing many of the negative spillover effects that appear when different sorts of locational activities are allowed to intermingle, zoning helped to augment the functional effectiveness of the city, and thus to stabilize or raise land values and to enlarge the bases of municipal taxation. At the same time, partial rationalization of urban land uses by zoning was facilitated by the release of pressure on intraurban locations as a result of energetic suburban spread. An early wave of outward urban expansion had taken place towards the end of the nineteenth century in the form of streetcar suburbs, that is, compact, dense, and geographically distinct clusters of suburban housing. After the First World War, the private automobile rapidly became a predominant mode of urban transport, and the early pattern of compact suburban expansion now gave way to a new pattern of sprawling interminable low-density suburbs. This was associated with the general widening and paving of county roads, and the outward extension of utilities, particularly trunk sewers, frequently well in advance of actual housing construction. The nineteenth-century arrangement of annexation of peripheral communities as the city grew was steadily abandoned in favour of a system of independent municipal governments in expanding suburbs. And the first intimations of an accelerating flight of economic activity from the central city became apparent as manufacturing firms now began to abandon high-cost downtown locations and to take advantage of new (land-use extensive) production technologies in the suburbs.

As the major cities in North America (and Western Europe) continued to grow so the process of outward urban expansion started to assume new rhythms and modalities. The centrifugal movement of firms and households was compounded by a multiplier effect such that increasing decentralization of firms encouraged yet more suburbanization of households, and yet more suburbanization of households encouraged further decentralization of firms. In this process, the production of new suburban subdivisions evolved from a prevailing pattern of small-scale undertakings to one of massive integrated construction operations over large tracts of land so as to secure economies of scale in the overall land servicing and building process. Thus it now became possible to conceive and to build whole suburban communities at a time, and from the period between the two World Wars, such communities began to appear with increasing frequency on the urban landscape. Many of these new communities were simple physical extensions of the built-up area of the city. However, it was becoming increasingly feasible to reap the full advantages of large-scale methods of producing peripheral housing and associated industrial estates, and to build suburban communities as *new towns* on cheap land well beyond the existing built-up area, though still within the functional orbit of the central city. The British New Towns Policy after 1946 was in effect a direct reflection of this novel form of suburban development, with the additional characteristic that in the British case it was initially also linked to a strategy of slum clearance and urban renewal in inner London. The development of new towns in Britain had the further advantage that it permitted some control over the augmenting problem of urban sprawl around the major conurbations, and new towns programmes in Britain and elsewhere have invariably been developed in harmony with various kinds of greenbelt and farmland preservation policies.

Contrary to much received opinion, this double policy of land-use zoning and aggressive peripheral growth via suburban extension and new towns development was quite successful in dealing with urban problems. It allowed for the provision of ample space for industrial needs; it partly succeeded in helping to rationalize the geographical configuration of urban infrastructure; it encouraged expansion of the supply of housing, whether directly (to high-income families) or indirectly by filtering (to low-income families); and it expedited the takeover of highly accessible downtown locations by retail and office activities. Furthermore, throughout the period stretching from about the beginning of the 1920s to the end of the 1950s, the massive and continuous expansion of serviced peripheral land staved off excessive land hoarding, helped to hold down intraurban land prices, and underpinned the success of zoning policies by encouraging lower densities of central city development than would otherwise have been the case. Ironically, this very success became the prime source of most manifest urban land problems in the 1950s, 1960s, and 1970s.

By the early 1950s, the process of headlong suburban expansion was beginning to meet with a number of problems and dilemmas, many of them connected with various sorts of transport issues. The private car, which in the first instance had sustained the process of outward urban growth, was now starting to encounter real upper limits to its further use and efficiency. The existing network of streets and highways linking the far-flung suburban communities with the central city (where a significant proportion of suburban dwellers continued to work) was inadequate to the increasing demands that were now being put upon it, while at the same time the realized pattern of suburban sprawl and development imposed strict limits on the effectiveness and viability of mass transit as a solution to the burgeoning urban transport problem. Thus, in the United States in particular, a programme of massive intraurban expressway construction was set in motion, thereby encouraging yet further suburban expansion and yet further use of the private car (and producing as a consequence formidable traffic congestion and parking problems in central cities). A syndrome was thus created whereby urban expressways gave rise to the need for yet more urban expressways. So long as public funds were forthcoming in generous quantities, this syndrome seemed to be never ending, and the flight of firms and households from the central cities to the suburbs continued apace, leaving behind a stubborn residue of working-class families (characterized by high levels of poverty and unemployment) living in blighted neighbourhoods distributed around the innermost business core. Despite this latter circumstance, central business districts nevertheless typically retained, and even increased, their hegemony as centres of white-collar employment, and all the more so as urban renewal in US cities in the 1950s and 1960s moved steadily away from its initial main objective of housing rehabilitation, and increasingly emphasized programmes seeking to support and reanimate commercial centres. As a result of all of this, a characteristic and economically wasteful pattern of daily intraurban travel began to make its appearance. On the one hand, white-collar workers commuted from the suburbs to the central business district. On the other hand, low-income blue-collar workers commuted from the central city outwards to the new peripheral industrial belts. Yet more highway links and parking facilities had to be added in the central cities in order to accommodate this wasteful transport pattern. Concomitantly, portions of the already diminishing stock of low-income central city housing were destroyed, a phenomenon exacerbated by the continuous expansion of commercial activities in the core. By the early 1970s, however, even this expansion was beginning to slow down in response to the general climate of stagflation and fiscal crisis that was beginning to pervade the economy at large.

Prior to this recent slowdown, a highly characteristic dynamic pattern of central business district development was evident. So long as the transport access of the central business district was being improved relative to the rest of the urban system in the 1950s and 1960s, so the price of land at central locations escalated steadily upwards. In general, such price escalation results in an apparently contradictory set of outcomes. On the one hand, an insistent intensification of land uses tends to take place; and on the other hand, land hoarding in anticipation of increased gains by delaying development becomes a common phenomenon. By diminishing effective supply, land hoarding drives prices still higher, producing yet more intensification of central land uses. Given that central business district firms tend to be highly labour-intensive, land-use intensification in the core soon compounds existing central city problems by inducing increases in traffic congestion, by exacerbating the scarcity of parking spaces, by helping to create yet more overloads on public transport, and so on. Political momentum thus builds up over the issue of inadequate downtown transport access, and this produces planning intervention in the form of improvements in transport capacity and service. These improvements augment the locational advantages of the central business district, and this in turn leads to still further increases in land prices, and to new rounds of land-use intensification. As a consequence of this process of land-use intensification, two sorts of pressures characteristically come into play in the old residential districts surrounding the core. First, as land prices escalate in the core so pressure mounts to redevelop surrounding low-income residential properties into office and commercial space. Second, as the ratio of white-collar to blue-collar employment in the core rises, so significant numbers of middle- and high-income families are prompted to purchase and renovate old houses in low-income neighbourhoods in close proximity to the core. Both types of pressure threaten to dispossess low-income families of their housing, a situation that is made all the more urgent given the restricted availability of alternative low-income housing elsewhere in the urban system. These pressures then result in political confrontations, in the disruption of old neighbourhoods with a high degree of social cohesion, and in further rises in land and house prices.

Such disruption of old inner city neighbourhoods was a particularly marked phenomenon in Canadian cities in the late 1960s and early 1970s. In Canada, the inner city areas had retained a lively mosaic of densely populated neighbourhoods, for whereas migration of jobs and households out to the periphery had proceeded at a fairly rapid pace in the 1950s and 1960s, this process was nonetheless much less insistent in Canada than it had been in the United States. Thus, in Canada, the urban land development process tended in certain respects to follow rather idiosyncratic lines. In particular, intraurban expressway construction was fairly restricted in Canada by comparison with what occurred in the majority of large US cities, so that there tended to be a lag in the whole process of outward urban expansion[1]. This situation led in turn to an overall inflation of land and housing prices over the entire extent of inner city areas in Canada. In these circumstances, land hoarding became particularly attractive, and large vertically integrated development firms began to acquire considerable reserves of land. The unusually high land prices, together with a persistent land shortage on the urban periphery (due, again, to the restricted public investment in intraurban expressways) made high-rise residential developments feasible and indeed highly profitable, especially in central city areas. However, in the process of assembling land units for the purpose

[1] A recent study by Goldberg (1977) further elucidates this proposition by providing a detailed empirical comparison between the cases of Seattle and Vancouver.

of constructing high-rise apartment blocks, land development companies typically triggered off a series of direct confrontations with neighbourhood groups producing, as a by-product, an especially strong and vocal citizens' movement in Canada towards the end of the 1960s. Members of neighbourhood organizations correctly recognized the destructive impacts of high-rise developments on their communities and they thus tended vehemently to oppose them. By contrast, under conditions of increasing demand pressure on the housing market, combined with rising land prices, it was economically logical for development companies to seek to redevelop central city land at maximum feasible densities. The result was a sharp collision between neighbourhood groups and developers, which also enmeshed various government agencies and planning organizations in difficult and often costly political and administrative dilemmas.

In the United States (as well as in Britain to a somewhat lesser extent) the evacuation of inner city areas was very much more marked than it was in the case of Canada, and this evacuation produced a series of further symptoms. In US and British cities, notwithstanding the highly localized functional success of central business districts proper, inner city areas as a whole in the early 1970s began to show signs of a severe crisis of municipal finance as the steady out-migration of jobs and people provoked a continuing erosion of the local tax base. This phenomenon led inevitably to a deterioration in the basic infrastructure and fabric of the central cities, as well as in their levels of social and community services, and this in its turn produced still further rounds of out-migration to the periphery. Even this long-established process of outward peripheral expansion, however, began to slow down as public funds continued to dry up in the 1970s, not only in the central cities (where the crisis was most extreme) but everywhere. The inefficiencies of suburban expansion relative to the overall functioning of the urban system now became glaringly apparent, particularly as low densities of development mean relatively wasteful expenditures on infrastructural services. Furthermore, each increment of outward suburban expansion costs geometrically more (in terms of total social costs) than the preceding increment. Thus, by about 1970 the hitherto prevailing process of aggressive peripheral expansion was itself being very markedly dampened down by a retraction of public spending on infrastructure in the urban fringe. This slowing down of the process of suburban expansion has also in part been associated with an increasing realization by urban policymakers that the current crisis of central city viability is to a large degree due to the relentless outward urban growth that has taken place over the last two or three decades. In response to these circumstances, urban policy in the United States as well as in Britain is now evolving in the direction of seeking definitely to contain suburban expansion and (contrary to the main drift of previous policy) of seeking to revitalize central city areas by redirecting growth from the urban periphery to the inner city.

Many of the urban land-use conflicts that erupted in major cities in North America and elsewhere in the 1950s and 1960s have tended to subside in recent years as economic conditions have become less and less ebullient and as the urban land market has become more calm and orderly. Even so, in the absence of real structural changes in the nature of contemporary urbanization processes, it is evident that the sorts of conflicts described above have not subsided entirely, but are rather in abeyance, and ready to break forth once more (whatever their specific form) as soon as significant new growth pressures and strains begin to make themselves felt in the urban system. In the long run, moreover, the complex unfolding of the urban process as it is currently constituted diminishes both the economic and the political prospects of more rational urban development in the future. This assertion is based on two general observations. First, the standard planning procedure of making piecemeal increments to existing infrastructure and social overhead capital to cope with bottlenecks as they arise (reactive planning) preempts more general and far-reaching policy options in the future. Second, massive but premature private investment in localized renovation and redevelopment in conformity with a purely private calculus of costs and benefits blocks future possibilities of more socially rational collective redevelopment schemes.

This discussion of urban problems has sought only to outline a number of general tendencies and trends. Of course, particular cities will exhibit particular deviations from the schematic outline presented above. Nevertheless, the problems and predicaments described above are (in one form or another) virtually everywhere observable in North America and Western Europe. In the face of the pervasiveness and seriousness of these problems the question immediately arises: what general types of policy instruments have been developed to counter them?

4.2 Urban policy instruments

Urban governments in North America have in general intervened in urban affairs in three rather different ways: first, by attempting to control certain kinds of monetary variables (fiscal policies); second, by legally restricting private rights to use urban land in certain ways (land-regulation policies); and, third, by directly undertaking urban development and redevelopment projects (development policies). A brief description of each of these major kinds of policies follows directly.

Fiscal policies

The use of fiscal devices by municipalities to control the process of urbanization seems in practice to have been quite eclectic and piecemeal. Such devices include, among others, the property tax, controls on the pricing of certain urban goods and services, and direct government subsidies and grants.

The property tax is ubiquitous in North America. In recent years, in addition, various mutations of the simple property tax, as such, have appeared; these include development levies and taxes, speculation taxes, and taxes on unearned increments to land. But for all their variety, these taxes have one fundamental characteristic in common, namely the fact that they have left intact the operation of those macrostructural forces that determine the private exchange, utilization, and development of urban land. For this reason, property-tax policies have tended to have only a minor impact on the general urban land-use problems discussed above.

Controls on the pricing of urban goods and services include such measures as rent controls, road pricing, legislated limits on housing mortgage rates, and so on. These policies have definite and marked effects on the private use of urban land. However, they tend to be employed in a rather fragmentary way as occasional stopgap measures, independently of any global planning strategy. At the same time, they are frequently applied as a response only to the superficial symptoms of more durable and deeply rooted urban problems. Hence, rent control, for example, is invariably a politically popular but entirely makeshift response to the endemic structural shortage of low-income housing in North American cities. From this perspective, these kinds of controls often in the end only serve to complicate the very problems that they were intended to resolve.

Direct governmental subsidies and grants are represented by a veritable profusion of policy devices, for example, subsidies on mass transit, financing of low-income housing programmes, the provision of grants for community services, industrial location incentives, and so on. Many kinds of urban activities would have been impossible in the absence of such public financial support. Moreover, so long as public revenues were forthcoming in a sufficient quantity to cope with reformist demands, very few individuals with the exception of a small minority of conservatives (cf Banfield, 1973) have seriously questioned this type of urban intervention. Urban intervention via subsidies and grants tends to have a twofold drawback, however. In the first place, it has tended (like controls on the pricing of urban goods and services) to deal with symptoms rather than with the fundamental problems of urban land use. In the second place, urban reform via subsidies and grants tends to be ultimately self-negating. The continued feasibility of such measures requires that, in the long run, aggregate expenditures keep pace with aggregate public revenues. This in turn requires that the demands of revenue-absorbing sectors keep pace with revenue-producing sectors. However, recent experience in North American cities has amply demonstrated that this sort of equilibrium is far from being satisfied. On the contrary, public expenditures have tended in recent decades persistently to outrun public revenues as the State is called upon to an ever-increasing degree to fulfill its role as guarantor of last resort in an unending escalation of urban land problems. Not only do direct subsidies and grants frequently fail to deal with these problems in any fundamental sense, but, again, in some instances they actually exacerbate them. Thus, continued subsidization of inefficient urban services may well only contribute to those services being offered at yet higher levels of inefficiency. Fiscal policy instruments tend in general to be both merely palliative and in the end self-negating.

Land regulation policies
Legal restrictions on the use of urban land include such devices as official plan provisions, zoning ordinances, subdivision controls, construction codes, building height limitations, and so on. They also include certain recent experiments with legal transfers of development rights. These various types of restrictions all possess the *technical potential* of significantly modifying the operation of the urban land market and, as a consequence, the spatial configuration of urban land prices and uses. However, in practice, and for *political* reasons, they have tended to be formulated in such a way that their impacts on the urban land market have been deliberately restrained. It is obvious, for example, that if tight and durable controls were imposed on office building heights at downtown locations then this would eventually depress land prices at these locations, and would in all probability cause an acceleration in the decentralization of central business district activities. But, for this to happen, the controls must indeed be tight and durable. If landowners and developers sense that the controls are liable sooner or later to be modified and diluted, then they will continue to exchange and develop land more or less as if the controls did not exist. Admittedly, there are innumerable cases in which such legal controls have been fairly definite, and they have accordingly exerted some influence on the functioning of the urban land market. In other cases, they have not been able to withstand the political pressures to change them. We may ask: what accounts for the observed tightness and durability of controls in certain cases, and their ephemeral existence in others?

Cases where legal restrictions on land uses have been significantly durable tend to share a common characteristic: they are typically cases where land prices are raised, or at least stabilized, rather than lowered by the restrictions; that is to say, they are cases where those restrictions are meaningful and effective in terms of the fundamental imperatives of capitalist society. Thus land zoned for suburban residential activity, for example, tends to maintain its legal designation over long periods of time precisely because such designation is necessary to preserve the environmental conditions crucial for the reproduction of a privileged stratum of capitalist society, namely, white-collar labour. By contrast, cases where legal restrictions on urban land use have been continually relaxed are typically cases where such restrictions would otherwise threaten the rationality of capitalist urbanization process, and would thus, as a corollary, threaten to depress land prices. Either they threaten to depress land prices generally, or at least they threaten the interests of a politically significant group of property owners. The mutations of planning regulations in the business cores of large metropolitan centres represent an object lesson in this process.

Development policies
The third and last type of policy device to be considered here—direct physical land development or redevelopment by government agencies—has probably had a more widespread general impact on the functioning of urban land markets than the other two. It includes such activities as the provision of various types of urban infrastructure (including transport networks), new towns development, public housing construction, urban renewal, the laying out of industrial estates, land banking, and so on. Through this type of intervention, government plays a key role in producing privately developable land and in shaping the spatial pattern of land prices and land uses. Yet ironically, and despite its crucial role, this type of intervention has remained, by default, virtually incapable of dealing with real urban problems. Publicly serviced land is left to be exchanged and utilized by innumerable private owners and users, all of them following specific individual interests, and oblivious (indeed, necessarily so, in view of their privatistic rationality) to the collective consequences of their actions. This anarchical process leads to uncontrolled, unexpected, and unintended geographical delineations of the urban land nexus, and hence to critical conformations of urban land prices, uses, and problems. Despite the definite potential effectiveness government might have through the deployment of development policies of various sorts, it in fact invariably finds itself participating in the perpetuation of the very problems it seeks to combat.

From this very sketchy review of urban land problems and land policy instruments, three basic conclusions emerge. First, whereas a wide variety of policy instruments has been employed to guide and regulate private rights to the use of urban land, none (especially in North America) has seemed to have had very great and unambiguous long-run effectiveness in subjecting the overall pattern of urban land to socially decided outcomes. Second, whereas governments have assumed a major and rapidly expanding responsibility for the production of developable urban land, the spontaneous utilization of this land is nevertheless largely left to follow its own momentum. Third, control over the urban land market, as such, remains weak and ineffective, and hence the anarchical outcomes of the market process continue to have a predominant impact on the entire urban system. As a consequence of these three circumstances, there remains a large and intractable body of concrete social and political problems around the issue of the urban land nexus. Further, if these various remarks are correct in substance, it is clear that urban policies and programmes have been not so much in control of the urban process as they have themselves been persistently manipulated by historical circumstances; and this means in turn that urban planning has almost certainly been a far less politically progressive and liberating activity than is commonly supposed, particularly in those utopian discourses that pass, in North America, for 'planning theory'. To be sure, considerable progress is currently being made in a number of planning areas, not least with respect to the very specific issue of the recovery of community-created unearned increments on urban land (as witness, for example, the British Community Land Act of 1975). As important and real as this latter issue may be, however, and notwithstanding its pride of place within the sorts of political programmes proposed by urban reformers, it is not *the* urban problem. The urban problem *par excellence* is the problem of how to control and rationalize in some reasonably definitive way, the overall pattern and dynamics of the urban land nexus. The brief discussion in the present chapter has already indicated in a preliminary way that this problem remains largely and effectively unresolved. As it is, contemporary urban land-use patterns are *not* the expression of socially decided purposes. They are the expression of an impersonal and (in human terms) irrational capitalistic logic as mediated through urban space. We are all, moreover, entrapped in a daily life that constantly echoes this fundamental irrationality, whether it be in the increasing separation between home and work, in polluted and blighted urban environments, in the destruction of inner city neighbourhoods, and so on. If it is a relatively easy matter to identify the symptoms of the problem, it is considerably more difficult to discover in any rigorous way root causes, and to pinpoint potential avenues of solution. It goes without saying that any effort to confront these matters must be based on an *urban science* that is indeed worthy of the name.

In the chapter that follows, a number of current paradigms that claim (though fail) to represent just such a science are reviewed and evaluated, and their major shortcomings revealed. The objective of this exercise is to highlight critical issues that must be addressed in any really viable, though as yet prospective, urban science.

Mainstream approaches to urban theory

The point of focus of this book is an elucidation of the structure of the urban land nexus as a specific object of theoretical study situated within the capitalist mode of production. In relation to this point of focus, the various data of contemporary urbanization are interpreted and reinterpreted in terms of a global process involving the intermediation of the logic of commodity-producing society through urban space. It need hardly be pointed out here that this general approach to the investigation of urban phenomena is far from being universally or even widely accepted. On the contrary, a number of other approaches to urban analysis currently compete among one another for intellectual hegemony within academic debate. Before further development of the main theme of the present study, therefore, it is of some importance to review these other approaches, both for the sake of perspective upon the line of attack adopted here, and for the sake of uncovering potentially productive avenues of enquiry. The approaches reviewed in this chapter may be identified as a 'mainstream' in the sense that collectively they constitute a currently dominant universe of discourse about urbanization. They fall into three main conceptual categories representing problematics that can be severally identified in terms of their basic intellectual lineage. The first of these categories is represented predominantly by the work of the former Chicago School of sociology; the second is directly an emanation out of neoclassical economic theory; and the third represents a prevalent 'critical' view of the city that grows by a kind of mechanical negation out of the other two categories, but, by reason of its own analytical failures, is unable to transcend them so that it remains essentially a part of the mainstream as a purely internal critique. These three categories of urban analysis are discussed below under the respective main headings: (1) the city as an ecology of communities; (2) the city as a system of exchange relations; and (3) the manipulated city. In the discussion that ensues the main outlines of these three approaches (together with their planning and policy consequences) are briefly described in turn, and their scientific meaning critically evaluated.

5.1 The city as an ecology of communities

The classical version of the notion of the city as an ecology of communities flourished between the two World Wars in the work of the so-called Chicago School of urban sociology. The essence of the work of this school of thought is contained in a basic conception of urban space as a sort of natural biotic phenomenon governing the overall configuration of urban society. In this work, the city is seen as forming a system of natural regions, or ecologies, each occupying a characteristic locational niche relative to the others, and each with its characteristic complex of sociopsychological qualities. The logic of the city as a whole is then alleged to be decipherable in terms of the natural laws governing the development and interaction of these ecologies.

The immediate geographical expression of these ideas can be found in the familiar schematic model of urban form proposed by Burgess (1925) (cf figures 5.1 and 5.2). The Burgess model is in essence an inductive generalization out of the specific instance of Chicago, a city that constituted the basic laboratory for the intellectual explorations of the early urban ecologists. However, the model is also claimed to represent an archetype of the North American metropolis generally. It distinguishes five principal ecological regions in the metropolis, with each region forming a concentric zone arranged around a single central point. At the core of the metropolis, the model identifies a zone comprising the central business district, the most accessible part of the city and virtually wholly given over to business, commercial, and office functions. Immediately around the central business district lies a zone of transition, containing small industrial and commercial activities, and inhabited by recent immigrants to the city living in generally deteriorated and overcrowded housing; the zone of transition is also typically a locus of such social pathologies as poverty, crime, prostitution, mental illness, alcoholism, and so on. Beyond the zone of transition is to be found a zone of workingmen's houses; these are occupied above all by second-generation immigrants, now well on the way to full assimilation into American society. These second-generation immigrants, in brief, are near to the stage where they (or their children) will finally abandon once

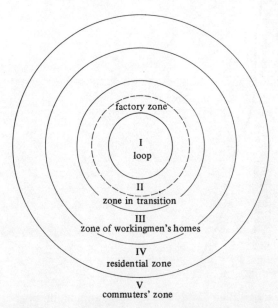

Figure 5.1. Urban areas. Redrawn from the original in Burgess (1925, page 55).

and for all the inner reaches of the city and will move out to one or other of the two outermost zones of the metropolis, comprising (a) the residential suburbs as such, and (b) a ring of scattered commuter dormitory settlements. In addition to these five main zones representing basic urban ecological types, the Burgess model distinguishes at a more finely grained spatial level such detailed ecological entities as 'Chinatown', the 'Black Belt', 'Deutschland', 'Little Sicily', and so on. These more detailed entities are then superimposed on the broad five-zone schema as described above, and the composite formal model thus produced transcribes with some fidelity the social geography of the modern metropolis, as it was, at least, in the quite recent past. Subsequent to Burgess's work, a number of other urban analysts, in particular Hoyt (1939), and Harris and Ullman (1945) have proposed various alternative formal models of the city, though without in any sense attacking (or even addressing, except in the most desultory ways) the basic theoretical apparatus that the Chicago School in general brought to bear on the problem of the structuring of metropolitan space. Lacking as they do any analytical content other than inductive abstraction from given data, these alternative formal models are little more than inert taxonomic devices: simple atheoretical vessels for the containment and codification

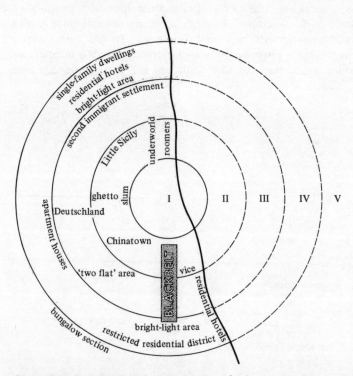

Figure 5.2. Detailed spatial disaggregation of urban areas. Redrawn from the original in Burgess (1925, page 51).

of empirical information. As such, they affirm the socially given while remaining unself-conscious as to their own essentially conservative bias.

The theoretical roots of the Burgess model, by contrast, penetrate deeply into a tangled undergrowth of ideas ranging from natural history through social Darwinism to naked ethnocentrism. These ideas sought to comprehend the city not simply as a static snapshot (as in the graphic version of the Burgess model), but also as an expanding and evolving system. Hence, as the city grows—and in the case of Chicago it grew remarkably from 1·7 million inhabitants in 1900 to 3·4 million in 1930—so the various ecological communities identified in the Burgess model also are seen as going through a number of transmutations. These communities are supposed to represent the basic elements of a total integrated organism—a biotic phenomenon—which like any other natural organism develops through time in dynamic (ecological) equilibrium with itself. The elucidation of the logic and internal order of this organism was proposed by Park (1936, page 15) as the central scientific project of ecological theory:

"Human ecology is fundamentally an attempt to investigate the processes by which the biotic balance and social equilibrium (i) are maintained once they are achieved and (ii) the processes by which, when the biotic balance and social equilibrium are disturbed, the transition is made from one relatively stable order to another."

Then, basing his argument directly on the findings of plant and animal ecology, Park described the city (*qua* a mosaic of communities) as an outcome of the struggle for survival in which each type of community struggles to secure for itself a life-sustaining urban environmental niche. The most powerful social groups seize and dominate the most desirable environments, while weaker social groups must adjust themselves socially and psychologically to what remains. In his 1936 statement, Park went on (with characteristic vagueness, it might be added) to describe these presumed natural processes in the following terms:

"The so-called natural or functional areas of a metropolitan community—for example the slum, the rooming house area, the central shopping section and the banking centre—each and all owe their existence directly to the factor of dominance, and indirectly to competition.

The struggle of industries and commercial institutions for a strategic location determines in the long run the main outlines of the urban community. The distribution of population, as well as the location and limits of the residential areas which they occupy are determined by another similar but subordinate system of forces."

In addition to these processes of ecological dominance and competition, Park also suggested that a process of invasion and succession (itself lifted straight out of plant and animal ecology) is at work in the determination of the spatial pattern of intraurban communities. Thus, according to Park, the process of urban change can be interpreted largely in terms of a phenomenon of invasion of specific territories by alien (but now dominating) ecological types, thereby forcing the original occupants to move on, and hence re-creating the process of invasion elsewhere.

Given the intellectual trajectory of the Chicago School in the 1920s and and 1930s, a grand theoretical statement linking together the processes allegedly governing the formation of urban space and the sociopsychological constitution of metropolitan society could not be long in making its appearance, as it finally did in a seminal statement by Wirth published in 1938. In his statement, Wirth identifies three fundamental ecological factors as being the mainsprings of the geographical differentiation and the dynamics of the modern metropolis. These factors are size, density, and heterogeneity. *Size* is alleged to induce a decay of traditional family and community restraints on individual behaviour; the big city encourages impersonal, transitory, superficial social relations, and these relations are further segmented by the spatial segregation of residential communities; the result is a social vacuum in which feelings of anomie and estrangement prevail. *Density* fosters a spirit of competition and mutual exploitation; it gives rise to frequent close physical contact with others, and this phenomenon, combined with persistent social distance, accentuates each individual's sense of reserve and loneliness. *Heterogeneity* gives rise to a situation in which the individual tends to belong simultaneously to a multiplicity of different groups and social fractions; and this condition breaks down social rigidities, and produces a higher degree of social differentiation in the metropolis than is characteristic of more traditional and integrated kinds of societies. Out of such theoretical prepossessions as these, the Chicago School at large fashioned a general theory of the modern metropolis in which the qualities of impersonality, anonymity, and segmentation of human relationships are viewed on the one hand as producing the delinquent and marginal individuals characteristic of Burgess's zone of transition, while, on the other hand, those same qualities are also viewed as producing the competitive, self-confident, creative, and innovative individuals characteristic of the outer suburban zones of the metropolis. The Darwinist overtones are immediately revealed.

Evidently, then, the urban sociologists of the Chicago School were much preoccupied on the one side by problems of social disorganization, and (to a somewhat lesser extent) on the other side by what was perceived to be the polar opposite of social disorganization, namely suburban life, the latter representing the outcome of a long but asepticizing process of urban evolution. As a corollary, urban ecological theory was dominated by a pervasive (but unspoken) ideological norm, that is, a conception of American suburban middle-class society as the terminal point and the highest expression of modern society. Towards this point all social progress was seen to converge as manifest in an ecological process of socialization involving the slow but sure transmission of generations of people through urban space from the inner zone of immigration and social decay, via a series of intermediate ecological levels, to a definitive end state as represented by the suburban middle-class community.

From all this, it is at once clear that the urban ecologists of the Chicago School and their *epigoni* made the initial and disastrous error of attempting to understand the city as an *a priori* category, that is, as a thing-in-itself whose basic inner logic is discoverable without reference to any wider structure of (historically determinate) relationships. For the classical urban ecologists the city was a closed and self-sufficient entity; and, having made this identification, it was a fairly logical next step for them to attempt to elucidate its inner complexities as though it were an 'organism'. Analogies with plant and animal ecology then inevitably followed. But these analogies were also masks. They imposed an intuitionistic doctrine of 'natural' competition, dominance, invasion, and succession upon a system of urban relationships that is, in fact (like all social phenomena), rooted in a mode of production and some concomitant economicopolitical dynamics (for example, commodity production, the division of labour, market exchange, and so on). Nor is there (nor can there be) in the work of the Chicago School any rigorous disclosure as to how it is and why it is that these presumed natural occurrences come into existence in the first place. In spite of both Park's and Wirth's bravura attempts at a definitive statement, the urban sociologists of the Chicago School failed signally to bridge in any analytically rigorous way the yawning gap between the empirical events that they sought to explain and the largely second-hand theoretical apparatus that they brought to bear on those events. Even so, the work of the classical urban ecologists had a clearly identifiable ideological thrust. It turned city life into an unalterable and naturalistic destiny in which human beings are mechanically caught up, much as the planets are mechanically caught up in their motions around the sun. In this way, then, urban poverty, slums, racial segregation, etc are seen not as *socially imposed* (and therefore mutable) phenomena, but as the inescapable expression of the self-engendered environment of the metropolis. Within this environment, the implacable evolutionary laws of ecological development produce a constant struggle for living space between competing but innately unequal social groups. An inherently political reality is thus transformed in discourse into the expression of a rather depressing fate. However, the notion of an urban ecological struggle for survival (and its ultimate manifestation in the form of a dominant suburban stratum in metropolitan society) only succeeds, in the end, in making clear once and for all the ethnocentric and social Darwinist proclivities of the Chicago School ideology. Ecological theory forever conceals the real mutability of social laws, and hence it also conceals the real possibilities of social change and reform. It leads directly to the sort of passivity and conservatism [explicitly evident in the work of McKenzie (1925), for example] that asserts either that nothing can be done in the face of ineluctable circumstances, or else that any attempt at interference is only likely to disturb the balance of natural forces and thus to make matters a good deal worse than they already are. Sentiments such as these are echoed resoundingly in the modern work of Banfield (1973).

Since the Second World War, urban sociology in the tradition of the Chicago School seems gradually to have lost much of its impetus as a concerted theoretical programme and to have fallen into atrophy. Nevertheless, two definite substreams of thought are still discernible today as carrying on certain aspects of the Chicago School tradition, though in a much modified form. In the first place, one substream, commonly referred to as *factorial ecology* (cf Schwirian, 1974), has developed as a purely inductive and empirical science that has more or less jettisoned the explicit theoretical apparatus of the Chicago School, and that seeks simply to document and record the observable statistical regularities of urban social space. In the second place, another substream has addressed itself to behavioural issues and personal value patterns, and has, in the process, become conflated with modern urban environmental psychology and behavioural theory. This latter substream while acknowledging a certain intellectual debt to the work of the Chicago School tends to set itself apart from this work by criticizing the bluntness of traditional urban ecological analysis and, in particular, by pointing out the real failure of the Chicago School to take into account the subtle interrelations that exist between the fine details of the built environment and individual decisionmaking activity (cf Michelson, 1970). Despite the comparative sophistication of their analyses, the protagonists of this latter substream remain identifiable with the Chicago School tradition by reason of their historically empty attempts to match such social variates as life-style and value systems with urban environmental conditions. Whereas these protagonists eschew any assertion of the existence of mechanical one-way causalities running from the environment to human behaviour and society, they nevertheless tend to see the built environment of the city as a sort of prothesis that can be treated as a control variable within a general programme of social engineering.

Neither the Chicago School of urban sociology nor its various modern derivatives have paid much, if any, attention to the wider questions of political economy and historical theory which—for reasons adduced in earlier sections of this book—must be resolved before a viable *urban* theory can be attained. They have thus persistently failed to discover, if they have not actively occluded, the mainsprings of a noneclectic and politically self-conscious discourse about the city. It seems that little more can be expected in the way of active work from the now almost moribund tradition of the Chicago School, at least in its classical form. And neither factorial ecology, in spite of the useful empirical information that it brings to light, nor environmental psychology, in spite of its unquestionably significant potential contribution to good building design, appears to have the necessary depth, or strength, or intellectual range to carry the tradition much further forward.

5.2 The city as a system of exchange relations

Urban theory in North American academia is quite clearly dominated at the present time by that particular analytical perspective which seeks to identify urban space and structure as the outcomes of a market process. This perspective is grounded in the immensely impressive methodological machinery of neoclassical economics, and it is specifically manifested in a wide variety of mathematical models of urban land and property markets (cf Richardson, 1977, for a thorough review). Notwithstanding the wide formal variety of these models, they are almost all centrally concerned with the single task of attempting to decipher the decisionmaking processes whereby individual firms and households choose locations in urban space and select for themselves quantities of land inputs. By and large, neoclassical urban models proceed with this task on the basis of a general theory of optimum-seeking economic behaviour, and, in particular, of utility-maximizing consumer choice behaviour. A rapid examination of this latter theory and of its immediate applications to the formation of urban space seems, then, to constitute a logical point of departure for the present brief exposition and critique of the neoclassical conception of the city as a system of exchange relations.

Neoclassical urban analysis begins with the assumption that every individual enters into the economic arena after having established in some *a priori* psychological process an ordered preference function consisting of a list of consumption items together with an associated set of utilities. In accordance with their specified preference functions, individuals will then select an actual consumption programme that maximizes individual satisfaction (total utility), subject, of course, to the prior condition that each individual's aggregate level of consumption is limited by some fixed and given level of income. These general ideas are translated into a specifically urban context in the following way: Each individual residing somewhere in urban space is presumed to have a set of tastes and preferences describable in terms of a utility function that comprises three major elements. First, utility is taken in part to be a positive function of the quantity of residential space consumed; second, utility is taken in part to be a negative function of the total distance (or its equivalent in units of time) travelled daily between home and various urban destinations (these destinations being frequently collapsed for analytical simplicity into a single central point); third, utility is taken in part to be a positive function of all other goods and services consumed. Following Alonso (1965), the utility function for any arbitrarily chosen individual can now be written in general as

$$U = U(A, d, z) , \qquad (5.1)$$

where A represents a quantity of residential space consumed, d represents distance travelled daily between home and the city centre, and z is a composite variable representing all other goods and services. Every individual will then seek to maximize this function subject to the budget condition limiting individual expenditures. This budget condition may be written symbolically

$$r(d)A + t(d) + p_z z = y \,, \tag{5.2}$$

where $r(d)$ is rent per unit area at distance d from the city centre, $t(d)$ is the cost of personal transport over the distance d, p_z is the notional price of one unit of all other goods and services, and y is personal income. The budget equation (5.2) thus distributes any individual's income over a set of payments comprising land rent, transport costs, and all other expenditures.

In conformity with this characterization of the nature of economic being in urban space, each individual then sets about the task of acquiring a residential location at which the aggregate utility function (5.1) is maximized. This involves finding an equilibrium location such that total expenditures at that location fully exhaust the quantity of income, y, and such that any other location (or, equivalently, any other reallocation of the budget) will only result in a lowering of the individual's overall level of utility. This situation is described graphically in figure 5.3. Here, a sample of typical indifference curves, or bid-rent curves, is shown in relation to a given urban land-rent surface. With A and z held constant for simplicity, each indifference curve represents a fixed and invariant value of the utility function (5.1) for different values of d. As shown in figure 5.3, these indifference curves have a negative slope with respect to

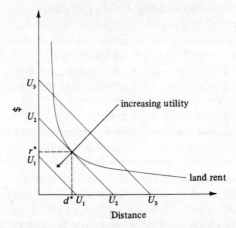

Figure 5.3. The neoclassical interpretation of individual locational equilibrium in urban space. The curves labelled U_1, U_2, U_3 represent sample indifference curves (bid-rent curves) for some specified individual. The individual's optimal location (at a rent of r^*) lies at d^* distance units from the city centre.

distance from the city centre, signifying that as this distance increases so any individual will seek to trade off concomitant increases in transport costs against lower land rent. Thus, for any *given* level of utility, it is possible to deduce from the corresponding indifference curve the rent that any individual is willing to pay (bid rent) at any given location. Clearly, each individual will seek out a combination of a bid rent and a residential location such that (a) the bid *just* secures that location by exactly matching its predetermined rent, and (b) no other bid at any other location can yield a higher level of utility. As shown in figure 5.3, these conditions correspond to a solution represented by the tangential intersection of the given land-rent curve and an associated indifference curve. The tangential intersection of these two curves designates an optimal residential location at distance d^* from the city centre in the sense that it identifies a feasible bid rent at the highest possible level of aggregate utility. Any lower bid at this or any other location would fail to secure a location for the bidder; and any higher bid would automatically reduce total utility. Analytical treatment of consumer choice behaviour with respect to the variable A (hitherto held constant) proceeds in precisely the same spirit. If the amount of space that any individual consumes is allowed to vary, the individual will immediately begin to make utility-enhancing substitutions between choice of location and quantity of residential space rented or bought. In this regard, the basic neoclassical urban model is invariably based on the particular assumption that individuals will desire to substitute accessibility for space at high-rent sites close to the city centre, but will desire to substitute space for accessibility at low-rent sites towards the urban periphery.

The neoclassical urban model as a whole has been very elegantly formulated and solved by Solow (1973), who shows, in addition, how a land-rent surface can be generated as an endogenous element of the model. Under appropriate assumptions about tastes and preferences, the mobility of population, and the fluidity of the built environment, the model can be shown to reproduce experimentally a realistic pattern of urban settlement such that both population densities and land prices decline steadily from the city centre outward. Furthermore, the model can be very considerably enlarged so as to incorporate within its terms of reference such phenomena as residential segregation, traffic congestion, polynuclear cities, and so on. An elementary generalization also permits extension of the model from the case of private individuals to the case of firms. In brief, firms will seek out a location such that profits are maximized, where profits are identified as being equal to total revenue minus total costs (including land rents). The general problem remains, however: does the manifest correspondence of the output of the general neoclassical urban model with the main lineaments of urban space signify the inner scientific prowess of that model? Here it will be argued that the model is, in practice, not only weak in explanatory value, but also positively hostile to penetrating social enquiry, in that it ejects issues of fundamental significance from the realm of debate. This argument will consist of five main lines of attack. First, on the basis of a critique of neoclassical consumer psychology, it will be shown that the model as such is very largely a tautology. Second, it will be shown that the conflation in neoclassical theory of market structure with economic and urban structure generally results in a serious misrepresentation of the nature of contemporary society. Third, it will be shown that the market is in any case susceptible to persistent failure in the urban context. Fourth, it will be shown that, contrary to the neoclassical point of view, land is not simply a neutral 'factor', but also the focus of specific human and political interests. Fifth, it will be shown how neoclassical theory leads to an inadequate problematization of State activity (and hence of urban planning) in capitalist society.

Right at the outset, then, though without going so far as certain Marxian theorists who refuse to accord any significance whatever to consumer choice behaviour and associated demand functions (cf Lipietz, 1977), it may be affirmed that consumers' 'tastes and preferences' represent pure epiphenomena within the total structure of social and economic reality. On the basis of what has already been said in chapter 2, it is evident that economic consciousness ('tastes and preferences') makes its historical appearance in a way that is dependent upon and secondary to a wider sociohistorical process, namely the evolutionary development of a mode of production and, as a corollary, of a constellation of social, political, and legal relationships governing human interactions in the processes of production and exchange. It is *in the context of* a specific mode of production and some derivative social formation that human beings acquire their tastes and preferences, or, more accurately, their historically determinate needs. These needs emerge, not out of a free-floating subjectivity, but out of given life situations whose broad configurations are predetermined within the context of some specific social formation. In contrast to the world of the neoclassical theory of consumer choice, economic reality does not simply grow out of an autonomous system of wants and predilections; economic reality as an aggregate, evolving macrostructure already has an existence prior to consumer preferences as such, and, in relation to this aggregate, consumer choice behaviour represents a definite (indeed crucial) but contained and subjacent moment. In a word, the social relations of production precede both in the order of discourse and in the order of reality, the system of consumption, just as (in line with the argument proposed in the conclusion to chapter 3), the set of real housing choices in urban space is not unilaterally created in the mind but is *given* by the immanent dynamic of urbanization within a system of capitalist social and property relations. For example, the neoclassical assumption that bidders for urban land will desire to substitute accessibility for space at high-rent sites close to the city centre but will desire to substitute space for accessibility at low-rent sites towards the urban periphery corresponds to, but as already suggested at an earlier stage does not explain, the structure of urban space; thus, while this assumption seems at first to have a certain *prima facie* validity, it is found on closer examination to be hopelessly inadequate as a starting point for the analysis of urban land-use patterns. By the same token, any attempt to establish the phenomenon of demand as the privileged foundation of any prospective urban theory is simply to beg the question by taking that which is to be explained as the would-be explanation.

Ultimately, the doctrine of consumer sovereignty that is enshrined in neoclassical theory bears a disconcerting resemblance to Hegel's idealist philosophy of history in which the World Spirit (appearing out of nowhere) is supposed to make itself manifest in material reality. In the same way, the doctrine of consumer sovereignty is idealist in the sense that it presumes that objective sociohistorical conditions are simple matters of subjective decidability, whereas human subjectivity (intentionality) in fact acquires a real as opposed to a metaphysical existence only in the context of a given historical situation. For this reason, neoclassical urban models, despite the fact that they are frequently highly elaborated as symbolic and mathematical statements, represent a largely emasculated social logic. Thus, and to dramatize the point: to attempt to conceive of the history of capitalist cities since, say, the year 1800, as the history of changing tastes and preferences, succeeds only in raising the more fundamental and refractory question as to how it came about that *those* tastes and preferences came to find a place in human consciousness in the first place. Neoclassical models in the style of Alonso (1965), Mills (1972), and Muth (1969) fail precisely at this point. They take consumers' tastes and preferences as an exogenously given datum and on this basis they then proceed to derive an urban reality. However, the scientific nullity of this procedure is made finally evident by the fact that neoclassical models fail persistently in practice to establish the alleged dependence of urban space and structure upon consumers' tastes and preferences. For in such models, tastes and preferences are always themselves taken to be revealed in the *realized* pattern of land uses. This is to beg the question with a vengeance. But in addition, all such analyses encourage a profoundly quietistic view of the world; for if current urban patterns are nothing more than the expression of consumers' tastes and preferences, then on what grounds (in a democratic society) can public intervention ever be justified?

The preceding remarks raise a number of questions about the scientific value and social meaning of consumer choice behaviour *as formalized in neoclassical utility theory*. These remarks are *not* intended to signify that choice behaviour is impossible or that market phenomena must be considered as chimera, but rather to suggest that demands (or needs) must themselves be explained within the context of the macrostructure of society. As it is, the neoclassical paradigm turns things upside down by dissolving the social and property relations of capitalism into overhasty assumptions about the ultimate sovereignty of economic psychology. This procedure immediately paves the way for the emergence of a further paralogism, namely, the neoclassical attempt to identify the market as the foundation and cornerstone of modern society, whereas the market is, in practice, only one of its outer and derivative surface forms. To compound the error, neoclassical models seek not only to give an indicative account of capitalist society *qua* 'market society', but also to suggest that this account must be taken seriously as a *normative* representation of some ideal state of social being.

Consider the case of land. Land is a scarce resource which, in neoclassical theory, is supposed to be perfectly and rationally allocatable among competing users via coordinated supply-and-demand mechanisms. Bidding for land secures an agreement between buyers and sellers about mutually satisfactory prices, and this bidding process also ensures that the quantity of land offered for sale will be equal to the quantity actually purchased. The resulting market equilibrium will, in theory at least, be Pareto-optimal in the twofold sense that (a) once firms are assigned to locations then no firm can be reassigned to any other location without a reduction in total resource efficiency, and (b) once individual households are assigned to locations then no household can be reassigned without a reduction in its aggregate level of utility. In the light of these putative qualities of the theoretical model, and given the real internal logical coherence of the neoclassical paradigm, it is scarcely surprising that it has given rise to a widespread if not doctrinaire belief in the finality and universality of the market mechanism. Over a century ago, J S Mill (1848; 1920 edition, page 920) expressed this belief in the following terms:

> "... throw in every circumstance, the burthen of making out a strong case, not on those who resist, but on those who recommend government interference. *Laissez-faire*, in short, should be the general practice: every departure from it, unless required by some great good is a certain evil."

Then, as now, the dominating implicit norm of exchange theory economics is this: let the market work, and if the market should in practice falter then resuscitate it, or remove those hindrances that stand in the way of its effective operation. Belief in the compelling rationality of the market mechanism is so great that neoclassical theorists suggest that, even when the mechanism does not work, planners and policymakers can do no better than to impose a solution that is delineated as if the market *had* worked[1]. The reason for this of course is that in theory the market mechanism promises efficiency (in capitalistic terms, that is) in the allocation of resources.

---

[1] For example, Nowlan (1977, page 20) writes: "... any reasonably efficient pattern [of property development] that might be determined outside the market—by bureaucrats, say, administering publicly-owned land—will exhibit the same basic features as the market-determined pattern". In fairness, it must be added that Nowlan later goes on to acknowledge certain exceptions to this observation.

We shall see that in the urban context this promise (even in those terms) is not and cannot be fulfilled.

Certainly it is the case that a land market is *one* way of allocating land to different uses and, from certain points of view and in certain circumstances, it can be both an economically and an administratively efficient way. It is also the case that if the urban process at large were capable of attaining to the state of harmony projected by theoretical neoclassical models then there might in some sense be some merit in giving free rein to the market in determining the pattern of urban land uses. Urban reality, however, is more complex and considerably less smoothly running than the world of pure market theory. In particular, and as will be shown rigorously and at length in subsequent chapters of this book, the operation of market processes in the urban context consistently triggers off negative and disruptive land-use outcomes that threaten (in the absence of planning intervention) to destroy such balance as may already exist in the urban system. The self-serving proposition that competitive market allocation of urban resources is necessarily Pareto-efficient or 'rational' loses sight entirely of the evident circumstance that in the urban context *all* land-use decisions are characterized by a political or quasi-political component in that land users (firms and households) in urban space, acting in conformity with the broad structural logic of capitalist society, continually confront one another with problems and predicaments that can have no spontaneous integrative resolution via market relations. To be sure, private decisionmakers in urban space may be expected to make individually optimal decisions and, to the degree that this process puts society as a whole closer to rather than further away from the efficiency frontier, it has much to recommend it; unfortunately, in urban space, there can be no guarantee that such a process does indeed put society closer to (or even close to) the efficiency frontier. Two brief observations (to be expanded at length at a later stage) may be adduced in support of this contention. In the first place, any specific land-use decision, however rational it may be from the point of view of the individual decisionmaker, generates overspill effects (via the system of differential locational advantages) throughout the urban land nexus, and this phenomenon (no matter whether positive or negative) produces precisely the sort of market failure described by Bator (1958). In the second place, any attempts on the part of affected land users to cope with these overspill effects by readjusting their investment levels at specific sites are invariably delayed over lengthy periods of time by reason of the intrinsic slow convertibility of the built urban environment. Optimal private decisions in urban space have an inborn propensity to render all prior locators' decisions immediately suboptimal. But in any case, even the most cursory examination of contemporary urban quandaries suggests that the universal equilibrium and rationality promised by market models of the urban process exist more in the realm of abstract thought than in that of empirical reality. Consider only the following commonly observable urban dysfunctionalities which are produced, in one way or another, not because their underlying behavioural structures escape the austere discipline of market exchange relations, but precisely because, in the context of capitalist society, market exchange itself generates one set of negative urban outcomes (together with corresponding human struggles) after another: property booms and busts; land hoarding; urban sprawl; leapfrogging suburban developments; urban blight; the dispersal of firms and households from the inner city, leaving behind a functionally and fiscally crippled municipality; disruptive land-assembly procedures; the persistent overdevelopment of the central business district while alternative and socially efficient subcentres of activity remain undeveloped; the maldistribution of service outlets (such as supermarkets or banks) in response to the pressures of spatial competition; the demolition of urban amenities by private redevelopment; the phenomenon of invasion and succession in residential neighbourhoods; the disruption of tightly organized communities by incursions of business and commercial activity; gentrification (aggravating an already severe shortage of low-income housing); urban poverty and unemployment; racial ghettoes; and so on. To this indictment may be added two further general observations. First, the market falls short in the control of such externality effects as pollution, congestion, visual disamenity, etc. Second, the market fails spontaneously to provide in socially rational quantities such essential urban goods and services as mass transport, low-income housing, utilities, parks, cultural and recreational facilities and all the rest. Need one labour further the point that the theoretical dream of ultimate urban harmony in capitalism via market relations is an impossible dream in practice? *Some* urban activities are, and can be, effectively coordinated by a market. Urban phenomena as a whole, however, are vastly more labyrinthine than the simple and schematic world as posited by neoclassical market theory. What this theory fails, above all, to capture is the predicament-laden process of the dense human occupation of land within commodity-producing society. In spite of these strictures, a recent polemic in favour of the wider encouragement of market rationality in urban affairs claims that

"... the market mechanism, although imperfect, works reasonably well in allocating land between alternative uses. There is little evidence of market failure ..." (Smith and Walker, 1977, page 22).

In the urban context, and as will be further argued in later chapters, the market mechanism is not simply 'imperfect'; it is a smouldering time bomb.

But there remains, in addition to these criticisms, a whole underlying dimension of reality that neoclassical ideology not only fails persistently to confront but, more importantly, that it actively obscures. The neoclassical paradigm abstracts away from the social meaning of the property arrangements of capitalist society so that the various factors of production—capital, labour, and land—lose their concrete specificity as articulations of human and political interests. They are simply reduced in neoclassical urban models to the status of abstract and mutually substitutable *technical inputs* to a neutral process of production that is presumed to reward them according to their marginal productivities. In particular, this cryptic conception of the nature of economic reality conceals the true character of urban land, and hence fails to grasp its twofold and contradictory significance as (a) a human product that is collectively produced yet whose specific use values depend upon the uncontrollable ways in which it is privately utilized, and (b) a human product that is collectively produced yet whose benefits are appropriated as rent by private landowners. Instead, in the neoclassical paradigm, social relations are reduced to the trivial (and depoliticized) case of coequal buyers and sellers confronting one another across a counter. This failure of the neoclassical model to grasp the peculiar nature of land as it is situated within the system of capitalist social and property relations has grave policy implications. Neoclassical urban theory suggests that there are *no* immanent irrationalities (social, economic, or political) in the ways in which urban land is produced, exchanged, and utilized, and that such problems as may crop up from time to time are mere anomalies, simple market imperfections that can be corrected *ad hoc* in a series of fine tuning operations. As a consequence, neoclassical policy recommendations are only a sophisticated means of masking and preserving the *status quo*.

One final point of criticism of neoclassical theory seems well worth mentioning at this stage. In the light of what has already been said about the nature of the capitalist State in chapter 2 above, there is little reason to accept either as a statement of fact or as a *desideratum* the liberal notion of the State that is implicit in the neoclassical paradigm generally; that is, the notion of the State as a disinterested referee lying above and outside of society as a whole, and intervening in the affairs of society only when called upon to do so by the abstract imperative of some formalistic (usually Pareto-theoretic) criterion of social optimality. On the contrary the logic of State intervention is linked organically to the logic of the civil society within which the State is historically embedded. By overlooking this structured relationship between the civil and the political in capitalism, and by seeking, as a consequence, to construct disembodied and abstract norms of policy intervention, the neoclassical paradigm has in fact thrown itself into something of a crisis of credibility, and nowhere more so than in its prescriptions for urban society. Despite the fact that the neoclassical paradigm constitutes a clearly dominant ideology in North America today, urban planners in practice tend to dispense very largely with the recondite problems of activating and stimulating the market process, and they proceed, as they must, on the basis of what it is necessary *politically* to do in confronting and assuaging the awkward problems generated continually by the urban land nexus as it emerges out of the capitalist mode of production. The current realities of urbanization and urban planning are not to be discovered in textbooks of neoclassical urban economics which *explain away* reality in the interests of smooth abstract theorizing, but in the mass of extant planning documents, government memoranda, and consultants' reports which, in their pretheoretical way, express, without seeking to conceal, the real political dilemmas and discontinuities of modern urban life. It is precisely these dilemmas and discontinuities that give rise to urban planning as a necessary activity of the capitalist State. Notwithstanding the ill-considered normative agendas of neoclassical urban theory, urban planners are indeed engaged in practical work whose purpose is not to achieve full Pareto efficiency via remedial adjustments of the urban land market, but to resolve in political terms the disruptive effects and failures of that market in relation to the functional imperatives of commodity-producing society. As Hason (1977) points out, the fact that urban planners are themselves often among the last individuals to identify correctly this role is no especial evidence against the suggestion that this is what in fact they do.

In the very recent past, much has been made of the rather artificial and unrealistic assumptions that are commonly made as a prelude to neoclassical urban analysis: perfect competition and perfect knowledge, the absence of social and legal restraints, ubiquitous transport facilities and monocentric cities, instantaneous and costless residential relocation, and all the rest. In fact to criticize neoclassical urban models for these purely technical (and entirely rectifiable) drawbacks is to miss the whole point: in short, the fundamental and irredeemable inadequacy of the entire neoclassical theory of the internal structure of capitalist cities conceptualized as simple systems of exchange relationships.

5.3 The manipulated city

In recent years a rather fulsome body of writings has accumulated around the issue of the alleged domination of contemporary urban society by a power elite of businessmen, banks, development companies, conservative municipal politicians, and the like. The main conceptual thrust of these writings is designated here (in terms of its central sophism) *manipulated-city theory* (cf Gale and Moore, 1975). This theory is highly critical of much mainstream urban sociology and economics, and yet because it too (as will be shown) is mystified as to the inner mechanisms of capitalist society, it fails conspicuously to transcend the mainstream and tends simply to gyrate around it, while continually confronting it with disjointed complaints and rhetorical sallies based on the real (but in manipulated-city theory, imperfectly problematized) injustices of society.

Manipulated-city theorists tend to see the city as congeries of neighbourhoods and communities dominated as a whole by an ascendant political faction which fixes, in its own interests, the rules by which the urban game is played. The core of this power group is seen as emerging out of a coalition between finance capital (banks, trust companies, insurance firms, etc) and the real estate interests (developers, real estate companies, landlords, etc) together with a sprinkling of co-opted urban politicians. Thus Lorimer (1976, page 98) writes of the Canadian scene:

"... city governments in Canada are strongly and directly tied to the property investment and land development industry, with the strongest links being the arrangement which puts a hard-core of small-time property industry people like contractors, real estate agents, architects, developers, and real estate lawyers onto city councils. These politicians with property industry connections form the centre of a majority voting bloc which implements policies protecting and promoting the interests of developers, property investors, and other industry members."

This coalition then exerts a sort of class-monopoly effect in the urban land market (cf Barker et al, 1973), and, by virtue of its supposed control over the urban land development process, it manipulates the spatial evolution of the city, and, in the same process, extracts enormous superprofits out of the mass of powerless users of urban land. The instruments with which the coalition sets about these tasks consist, among others, of such diverse means as red-lining, profiteering, land hoarding and speculation, blockbusting, the currying of political favour, and so on. In this manner, old neighbourhoods are destroyed, ethnic groups ghettoized, the citizenry herded into sterile high-rise apartment buildings, urban amenities wrecked, and excessive profits marked up; in brief, city life is rendered intolerable and oppressive, all in the merely pecuniary interests of what amounts to a minor conspiracy.

Now, it must be admitted that many of the complaints put out by manipulated-city theorists are perfectly real and legitimate, and they accurately identify a number of pressing contemporary urban problems. Where these theorists are in error, however, is in their conception of the social logic underlying these problems, and, as a consequence, in the policy pronouncements that they put forward. Having rejected capitalistic rationality as a norm, manipulated-city theorists seem to deny its empirical existence as well. To them, there is no immanent structural logic (to be discovered by rigorous enquiry) that will account for urban land problems as a general social phenomenon. These problems are seen, rather, as the immediate result of the actions of an unprincipled clique of individuals who, it would appear, have chosen out of a purely idiosyncratic ethical lapsus to pursue a set of private interests that are by faith and definition opposed to those of 'the people'. This position, of course, is heavily imbued with precisely the same idealist preconceptions that pervade the general neoclassical urban model. But more importantly, the singling out of a small group of business interests (the property development industry in particular) as the root cause of modern urban problems reveals the fundamental weakness of the manipulated-city hypothesis. Any attempt to discover the ultimate genesis of urban problems cannot stop short at a description of a purely intermediate set of relationships within society; it must rather be resolutely pushed right back to an examination of the very fountainhead of capitalism as a total structure; namely, to the system of commodity production and the web of social and property relations that sustains it. From the observation that the activities of the property development industry generate uniquely problematical outcomes, the manipulated-city theorists have been lured into the belief that the general social logic leading to these outcomes must itself be unique. This is entirely false. For the uniqueness—real as it is—of those outcomes is not due to some unique logic governing the property development industry, but rather to the application of a perfectly general capitalistic logic to a specific object of production and exchange: urban land and property. For this reason, the repeated attempts on the part of the manipulated-city theorists to reform the city via attacks on the property development industry (while neglecting the wider issue of capitalist production relations as a whole) have always fundamentally failed. A scientifically and politically viable analysis of urban land and property development processes must be grounded in a conception of capitalist society as a whole, and tendentious allegations as to the existence of conspiratorial class monopolies scarcely offer a very promising springboard from which to mount such an analysis. Well over a century ago, Engels (1872; 1970 edition) showed in his spirited attack on Proudhonist philosophy that the rhetorical banner of that philosophy—"property is theft"—is both scientifically and politically null; scientifically, because property owners and developers extract their share of total surplus labour not by theft or manipulation but in the perfectly normal course of business as usual; and, politically, because to the degree that property owners and developers are indeed engaged in predatory fiddles, then to the same degree can they be dealt with by existing legal arrangements. The fundamental core and the central question of capitalism is not to be found in the domain of business ethics but in the process of the production and appropriation of surplus labour. This process is hidden within the deep structure of capitalist society, and it is not peculiar, as the manipulated-city theorists seem to suggest, to the land and property development interests, but is all-pervasive within the capitalist mode of production. In spite of these criticisms, the spirit of Proudhon continues to live on, and it seems to reemerge persistently and periodically, especially during urban property booms when land-use conflicts begin to proliferate throughout the urban system. The fact that it then seems to fade away as the specific issues that called it forth also fade away is only further testimony in favour of what has already been suggested above: that manipulated-city theory is incapable of penetrating beneath the superficial appearances of things.

The theory of the urban land nexus that is proposed below is, it is suggested, more far-reaching than any of the current theoretical formulations described and criticized in this chapter. It paints a view of an urban reality that is at once more tractable than the rather desolate metropolis of the classical urban ecologists, more concrete and conflictual than the theoretical wonderland of the neoclassical urban economists, and incomparably more complex and deeply structured than the manipulated world of the New Proudhonists.

Urban patterns 1: production space

6.1 Introduction

The roots of the contemporary city in North America and Western Europe are to be found in the Industrial Revolution that accompanied and underpinned the emergence of modern capitalism in the eighteenth and nineteenth centuries. Embedded as it is, historically, in the capitalist mode of production, the contemporary city acquires a predominant and prototypical function: it becomes a vast machine for the production, circulation, and consumption of commodities. This machine is held together as a unitary geographical aggregate by its own basic centripetal effects. To begin with, the capitalistic logic of commodity production and exchange encourages the emergence of a land-use system that tends to minimize the transport costs incurred by the massive circulation of goods and labour set in motion by the production system. This tendency leads to the development of physically compact cities. In addition, the desirable (profit-enhancing) effects of this compactness are reinforced by the appearance of powerful positive external economies as commodity producers and households come together in close proximity to one another in the urban land nexus. Thus, in commodity-producing society, the physical costs of overcoming geographical space encourage the dense agglomeration of firms and households, and agglomeration (up to a certain point at least) tends to beget yet more agglomeration.

At the same time, this tendency to concentration and compactness in the urban land nexus is complemented by an equally strong tendency to geographical separation and divarication. In particular, the prodigious bipartite split within capitalist society between the production system and the reproduction system is directly recorded in what is certainly the most salient feature of the geography of the contemporary city: its dichotomization into a production space and a reproduction space, each with its own characteristic qualities and functional relationships, and each linked to the other (thus forming a composite urban totality) via a subjacent space reserved for the purposes of circulation. So lacerating and apparently aberrant an event was the massive geographical manifestation of this dichotomy between production and reproduction in the early industrial town, that a great many nineteenth-century utopian reformers, like Fourier, Owen, and Morris, spent much of their energy and ingenuity attempting to devise programmes for the retrieval of some sort of unity of work and life within the human community. This dichotomy, however, has, if anything, tended to become more and more pronounced with the passage of time, and it has been compounded by a subsidiary process involving the yet further internal differentiation and segregation of land uses within each major type of space.

Production space, reproduction space, and circulation space represent the basic building blocks of the contemporary city. They are the essential functional elements of a complex geographical system whose forward evolution is largely dependent on their inner workings and mutual interaction. But this evolution is far from being smoothly self-regulating; on the contrary, it continually encounters internally generated breakdowns that call at once for collective urban intervention in the form of planning. In order to lay the foundations for an effective understanding of the dynamics of the city as a whole (including the dynamics of urban breakdowns and the planning responses that they provoke) it is of some importance now to elucidate the structural details of these different kinds of spaces. In the present chapter, the developmental logic of production space is discussed at some length. In the succeeding chapter, reproduction space and circulation space are described both as composite entities and as they relate to the urban production system as a whole.

6.2 Production space in general

Production space in the urban land nexus is the geographical expression of the utilization of land by three main types of economic activities, namely, (1) industries, (2) offices, and (3) retail and service activities. Although urban analysts (geographers in particular) tend to treat these three kinds of activities as being somehow intrinsically different from one another, they in fact represent only special cases of the general process of commodity production. In other words they are all human activities whose essential character is that they consist in a process that produces exchange values (whether in the form of physical objects or in the form of intangible services) by the combination of materials and labour so as to realize at least a normal profit on capital advanced. This implies directly that the locational geography of industrial, office, and retail and service firms in the modern city must be a function of the dynamics of the rate of profit. From this remark, it follows, in turn, that any really rigorous analysis of the locational pattern of economic activity in the urban land nexus must build on the basic theory of production as presented in chapter 2, and on the preliminary spatial extension of this theory as outlined in chapter 3. What is also implicit in these remarks is a rejection of all those heterodox behavioural theories of the firm which suggest that locational patterns can only finally be elucidated in terms of the personality characteristics and idiosyncrasies of managers and businessmen.

Despite the fact that differences between industrial, office, and retail and service firms are largely formal and dissolve away in the context of basic capitalistic logic, it is nonetheless convenient to treat these various types of firms separately from one another in a first round of enquiry so as to reveal their individual locational characteristics and urban effects.

As will become apparent, however, there are some remarkable similarities between these types of firms, not only at the level of basic economic rationality, but also specifically at the level of locational process.

6.3 Industrial activities
Some preliminaries
In chapter 3 it was shown how geographical space is fundamentally structured as a response to the production relations and interrelations of capitalist firms. It was further demonstrated how geographical space is then dynamically restructured by changes in the technical organization of production. As firms vary their factor inputs (including land) relative to total revenue so the profits (both normal and excess) that they are able to earn in relation to capital invested rise or fall. Firms belonging to branches of production that can generate at least a normal profit at a given set of locations will seek to establish themselves at those locations. Conversely, firms that are unable to generate at least a normal profit at the same locations will seek elsewhere for their land inputs. Over the long run, in a competitive economic system, the rate of profit will be equalized over all sectors and all productive locations.

It is the purpose of the present discussion to show how the changing geographical pattern of commodity production in the modern metropolis (and hence, in large degree, the changing geographical pattern of the metropolis itself) can be generally described in terms of the sort of economic and geographic processes alluded to above. In particular, an attempt will be made here to demonstrate how the persistent historical phenomenon of the decentralization of manufacturing activity in large cities in this century can be analyzed in terms of a basic dynamic involving the progressive substitution of capital for labour in the internal structure of commodity production.

In the present section it is proposed that large cities in recent decades have been consistently characterized by a peculiar form of the Heckscher–Ohlin theorem. It is suggested that inner city locations in large metropolitan areas have evolved in such a way as to develop a marked comparative advantage for labour-intensive economic activities, while suburban locations have evolved in such a way as to develop a marked comparative advantage for capital-intensive economic activities. Accordingly, as the inexorable process of the substitution of capital for labour in capitalist production units has proceeded, so firms have tended more and more to shun inner city locations and to favour locations in the urban periphery. This phenomenon is not totally one-sided, however, and as *some* firms in some branches of production have adopted comparatively labour-intensive production techniques, so they have actively sought out inner city locations. These locational changes have been intimately associated with processes of (a) extensive land-use development in the case of the outward movement of industrial firms, and (b) intensive land-use development in the case of the inward movement of industrial firms. In contradistinction to the usual point of view put forward in the literature, however, it is suggested in the present account that these land-use relationships are probably largely concomitants rather than prime causes of the locational evolution of manufacturing activity in large metropolitan areas. Above all, it is surmised here that the adoption of extensive horizontal plant layouts in urban fringe areas is essentially secondary to (rather than at the root of) the process of urban industrial decentralization. The development of horizontal plant layouts has undoubtedly given a boost to industrial decentralization, but, as will be seen, is almost certainly contingent upon a prior switching-of-techniques phenomenon in urban space.

A lengthy argument in favour of these various assertions is developed in the pages that follow. Because much of the argument is somewhat novel and cuts across the grain of contemporary thinking about industrial location in the large metropolis it is confronted with empirical data at a number of critical points. These data analyses are concerned particularly with questions involving (a) intraurban variations of industrial wages and salaries, and (b) differences between inner city and suburban areas in industrial capital-labour ratios. In the case of the analysis of capital-labour ratios, the enquiry proceeds in a manner that is not unlike the statistical procedure devised by Moroney and Walker (1966) in their attempt to evaluate the Heckscher-Ohlin hypothesis for the instance of industrial location in the South versus the rest of the United States.

The foundations of commodity production in the modern metropolis
Before we examine the process of intraurban industrial location as such, a few preliminary matters need urgently to be clarified. It is above all essential to attempt to identify the key variables involved in this process. Here a number of the major received notions about this matter will be briefly examined and the discussion will then proceed to an elucidation of some first principles. This discussion will involve an investigation of the intraurban behaviour of basic factor and commodity prices as the essential point of departure for any really useful geography of urban industrial production.

A brief comment on the literature
Much of the existing literature that is addressed to the problem of intra-urban industrial location is quite eclectic in nature. Most especially, the dominant process of the decentralization of urban industry in this century is frequently discussed in terms of a forlornly hopeful but analytically self-defeating 'shotgun' or 'shopping-list' approach. The literature commonly adduces such disparate factors as rising land values in the core of the city, traffic congestion, antiquated physical plant, lack of space for *in situ* expansion of facilities, racial tensions, high taxes, deteriorated central infrastructure, new production technologies requiring horizontal plant

layouts, active trades union organizing in inner city areas, and all the rest, as being variously responsible for the abandonment of central locations by manufacturing firms in favour of the suburbs. Exceptions to the process of decentralization (as in the cases, for example, of clothing, printing, or furniture industries in many Canadian and US cities) are invariably explained away by invoking (but rarely problematizing in rigorously determinate ways) 'external economies of scale' and/or 'incubation' effects (cf Hoover and Vernon, 1959). Now, many of these factors that are alleged in the literature to govern the location of industry in the modern metropolis most certainly contribute something to the overall process; others are mere contingencies; while yet others must be seen as pure chimera. Even in aggregate, however, it is suggested here that these factors still do not provide all the necessary foundations for a definitive identification of the problem of intraurban plant location. As already indicated above, this can only be achieved by mediating the locational process in the first instance out of the theory of capitalist commodity production.

In conformity with this latter comment, an obviously primary task is to attempt to decipher the spatial dynamics of industrial profits within the urban land nexus. However, this task is itself in large part dependent upon a prior analysis of the various forces shaping intraurban differentials in basic factor and commodity prices. In what follows, then, an attempt is made to describe the spatial and temporal variation in these prices in the modern metropolis over the last several decades, and then to integrate this description into an analysis of the locational process proper. Thus, we now consider the changing geography of the prices of basic capital inputs (and commodity outputs), the wages of labour, and the price (or rent) of industrial land. In practice, the latter variable is not especially problematical, for unlike the capital prices and the wages of labour, both of which appear to have undergone some remarkable spatial mutations in large metropolitan areas in recent decades, land prices have tended fairly persistently over time to decline steadily with distance from the urban core. The crucial and highly problematical variables at this stage are the prices of capital and labour, and these are now discussed in detail below. Note that in the present instance we are concerned with capital defined (*à la* Sraffa) as commodity capital, that is, the set of physical inputs to production, and these inputs consist both of fixed or sunk capital and of circulating capital.

Spatial and temporal variations in capital prices in the large metropolis
Throughout much of the nineteenth century and the early part of the twentieth century, a high proportion of the industrial base of large cities was composed of heavy industry. Circulating capital inputs to such industry typically consisted of raw and semifinished materials whose bulk and weight made them very sensitive to transport cost variations.

Accordingly, firms tended to locate close to central rail and water transport terminals through which they could draw their basic inputs at minimal possible cost. Location close to rail and water conduits also facilitated the use of rail cars and barges for local interindustry commodity flows. Firms that located away from these major transport facilities had to rely upon the horse-and-cart for transport of their main capital inputs. This, however, was an extremely expensive mode of transport, costing some ten to thirty times more per ton-mile than either rail or water transport (cf Fales and Moses, 1972). Consequently, in the nineteenth- and early twentieth-century city, the overall cost of capital input items tended to increase very markedly with distance from the central core.

After about the 1920s, however, as road transport technology suddenly and very noticeably began to improve (especially as a result of the widespread introduction of the motor truck) this general situation was drastically modified. The costs of moving physical capital inputs across urban space now began rapidly to fall so that, at the intraurban scale at least, spatial variations in the cost of transporting industrial commodities were progressively annihilated. At the present time, indeed, road transport has become so effective that for many (though by no means all) kinds of commodities, transport costs are largely invariant with respect to location in the city.

The exceptions to this latter assertion were, and are, of considerable importance in the modern metropolis. These exceptions concern above all certain kinds of industrial firms whose inputs (and outputs) are constantly changing as a function of the inordinately wide variety of the demands for their products, the pressures of insistent economic competition, and the vagaries of the market. The clothing industry offers the most typical example of such firms, but jewellery producers, printing firms, furniture makers, and certain sorts of metalworking firms may also be included in this category. These sorts of firms are generally describable as having a high velocity of turnover and short production runs, and they characteristically possess intricate backward and forward input–output linkages with one another so that they can be said to constitute definite complexes of economic activity. Since production runs are short, such firms tend to purchase their material inputs in minimal quantities. Hence, they lose the advantages of economies of scale in the transport process, and transport costs per unit of input are invariably high. In addition, however, it is very frequently the case that inputs must be mediated by means of face-to-face contact between interlinked firms. In other words, because of the particularized and incessantly changing structure of production combined with many small specialized demands, firms must necessarily engage in the costly personal negotiation of their inputs (and outputs). Again, because the quantities moved between firms are small, the unit costs of this operation are extremely high. This adds yet more to the overall input costs that these firms must bear. It follows that as the distance (and hence time costs) separating any output unit from any corresponding input unit increase, so must the transfer costs of the associated flow increase rapidly. These costs can only be effectively reduced by either (a) spatial agglomeration of individual firms, or (b) standardization of production allowing for a larger and more consistent flow-through of materials over many production periods. As will become apparent, both of these strategies help to explain much of the spatial dynamics of industrial production in the modern metropolis.

Spatial and temporal variations in labour prices in the large metropolis
Like the transport costs on physical commodities, the transport costs on the movement of workers through urban space have tended to decline fairly steadily since the end of the nineteenth century, and above all since the widespread utilization of the private car for the purposes of commutation. This decline, however, has probably been overall rather less dramatic in the case of the movement of workers than it has been in the case of the movement of many kinds of physical commodities. This is especially the case if we take into account, as we ought, not only the direct money costs of commutation, but also the time costs (evaluated at the going wage rate) and the high frequency of their recurrence (cf Wingo, 1961). These time costs may attain to the level of five to eight hours per week, which is close to the equivalent of a single work shift.

The view from the secondary sources. In principle it would seem likely that variations in the costs of the journey to work might have some effect on realized industrial wages (as paid at job site). If this were so, then, depending on the spatial distribution of jobs and population, wage rates would be expected to vary (around some socially given 'average' wage) across urban space. Unfortunately, there has been little disciplined discussion in the literature of the issue of intrametropolitan wage-rate variations, and the gap in the literature is all the more astonishing in contrast to the extraordinarily intensive effort that has been devoted to the description and analysis of urban land price surfaces. Given the importance of urban industrial wage rates in the present context, we must proceed with some sort of an attempt to come to terms with the problem, though because existing research is so sparse, the present account must necessarily retain a somewhat speculative flavour. We are fortunate to have available one fairly detailed and painstaking statistical study of urban labour markets (Rees and Shultz, 1970), though even this study pays scant attention to the geographical dimension as such. Notwithstanding this shortcoming, Rees and Shultz have shown that industrial wage rates (in the Chicago labour market) do tend to increase significantly the further workers must travel to work. This would appear to be the equivalent of the more analytical proposition that the higher the demand for labour at any location, then the higher the wage must rise in order to draw in workers from a wider and wider labour shed; conversely, the lower the demand for labour, and the higher the local supply, the lower the realized industrial wage. Further evidence in favour of these ideas is developed econometrically by Moffitt (1977); and some general theoretical conjectures consistent with the same line of thinking are to be found in a brief statement by Moses (1962). At the same time, Hoover and Vernon (1959) have developed some invaluable and revealing data on the changing spatial pattern of the wage rates of manufacturing production workers in the New York Metropolitan Region between 1899 and 1954 (cf table 6.1). These data provide indirect corroborative evidence of the tentative argument that is in the process of being developed here.

Hoover and Vernon show that, at the turn of the century when industry was predominantly clustered at the centre of the city, industrial wage rates, as expected, declined uniformly with distance from Manhattan. By about the time of the Second World War, wage rates were still for the most part inversely correlated with distance from Manhattan, but in conformity with the growing demand for industrial labour in the suburbs as a consequence of early rounds of industrial decentralization, a strong secondary peak in the wages surface was now beginning to appear in the inner suburbs. By 1954, as the process of industrial decentralization was attaining its apex, wage rates were now definitely and steadily *increasing* with distance from Manhattan out to the inner suburbs, beyond which wage rates once more declined as distance increased. Even in the outer ring of the Metropolitan Region, however, wage rates by 1954 were still markedly higher than at the centre. This latter overall configuration of the intrametropolitan wage-rate surface has also recently been observed by Stone (1974) for the case of Boston.

A brief statistical analysis. In view of the lacunae in the literature in this matter of intraurban industrial wage-rate variations, an attempt was made to explore the matter further on the basis of some simple statistical analyses of industrial wage rates in the Toronto Census Metropolitan Area for 1971–1972. It is intended to describe these analyses at length elsewhere, and, given the limitations of space and time in the present circumstances, only the main results will be laid out here.

Two main dependent variables were examined by means of regression analysis. These variables were (a) the average annual wage (w^p) at place of

Table 6.1. Average annual earnings of manufacturing production workers in zones of the New York Metropolitan Region as a percentage of wages in Manhattan, 1899-1954. Source: Hoover and Vernon (1959).

	1899	1919	1929	1939	1947	1954
Manhattan	100·0	100·0	100·0	100·0	100·0	100·0
Core (excluding Manhattan)	93·0	93·2	88·0	96·1	91·7	105·2
Inner ring	88·7	90·4	83·2	96·3	96·8	120·9
Outer ring	83·5	87·0	78·0	89·2	92·4	117·5

work of production workers in industry and (b) the average annual salary (w^a) at place of work of administrative, office, and other nonmanufacturing employees in industry. These variables were defined for each of twenty-six (out of a total of twenty-nine) small administrative subunits or areas within the Toronto Census Metropolitan Area. The data reveal steady increases in both wages and salaries from the centre of Toronto out towards the periphery. In the case of the average wage of production workers, the computed regression equation for the jth area is

$$w_j^p = 10725 \cdot 0 I_j^{-0.176} \left(\frac{L_j^M}{L_j^F}\right)^{0.097}, \qquad R^2 = 0.69, \tag{6.1}$$

and in the case of the average salary of administrative, etc workers, the computed regression equation for the jth area is

$$w_j^a = 16033 \cdot 0 I_j^{-0.169}, \qquad R^2 = 0.40, \tag{6.2}$$

where L_j^M/L_j^F is the ratio of male to female production workers in area j, and I_j is a sort of accessibility index which measures overall labour supply and demand conditions in area j. The variable I_j may be further defined as

$$I_j = \sum_{i=1}^{26} \frac{P_i}{E_{ij}}, \tag{6.3}$$

where P_i is the total population in area i, E_{ij} is the total set of intervening industrial employment opportunities between i and j [1]. Note that the ratio of male to female employees was found to be of negligible significance in explaining administrative salaries, and hence was omitted from equation (6.2). The equations (6.1) and (6.2) (and all of their parameters) are significant at the 1% fiducial level.

The statistical exercise described above effectively relates wages and salaries in the Toronto Census Metropolitan Area to a simple spatially structured model of labour supply and demand. This model is embodied in the composite variable, I_j, which, in association with the computed parameters, signifies that (a) as the proximity of any location to population in the metropolitan area increases, so wages and salaries at that location tend to decline, and (b) as the demand for labour at—and in the proximity of—any location increases, so wages and salaries tend to increase. Certainly, average wages and salaries will also vary as a function of the range of skills and attributes of the labour force employed by firms at any location.

[1] The variable I_j is a very crude measure in the sense that P_j is defined as total undifferentiated population, and E_{ij} is defined simply as total industrial jobs intervening (within a 360° radius of i) between i and j, that is, production jobs plus administrative jobs. In the exploratory phases of this analysis, the ramifications of a wide variety of different measures of I_j were explored (measures based, for example, on such special categories of population as immigrants, nonimmigrants, blue-collar, white-collar, male, female, etc, and with intervening opportunities computed separately for production employment and for administrative, etc employment). It was found, however, that none of these refinements was noticeably more serviceable than the broad simple measure, I_j, as defined above and so the latter measure alone was applied in this exercise.

To some extent, differences in labour quality have already been taken into account in the computation of equations (6.1) and (6.2), and the equations clearly distinguish between production workers and administrative workers, and [in the case of equation (6.1)] between male and female workers. Even so, the modest (though statistically significant) coefficients of determination for these equations would surely be greatly improved if refined data on labour quality variations were available to be built into the analysis.

What is important for present purposes is the strong indication in equations (6.1) and (6.2) that (all other factors aside) spatial variations in the supply of and demand for labour seem to have a determinate impact on industrial wages and salaries. This impact exists in spite of the tendency in many cases for wage rates to be negotiated between management and unions. Furthermore, the equations imply that for any specified increase in the demand for labour at the centre of the city (with its strong transport nodality, its ready access to labour from all over the urban system, and its existing massive and highly liquid labour market) wage rates tend to be extremely stable, whereas for a similar increase in the demand for labour in the suburbs (with their relatively lower overall levels of accessibility and their thinner local labour markets) wage rates are susceptible to dramatic upward shifts. In general, and *in the context of the historically given existing pattern of jobs and population in the modern metropolis*, wage rates as paid at job site will exhibit an augmenting marginal propensity to increase with each unit addition to employment demand as distance from the city centre increases. This effect is quite marked, and (in spite of the small absolute values of the parameters attached to the variable I_j) the equations (6.1) and (6.2) suggest that for even modest increases in employment in the urban periphery, local wage rates may rise by 10%, 20%, and even 30% and upwards. Therefore, whatever the empirically realized form of the wage rate gradient in any particular case (that is, no matter whether it is declining, flat, or increasing on average with distance from the centre of the city outwards) we can be fairly confident that any sudden surge of industry towards the suburbs would tend immediately to push local wage rates up to unprecedentedly high levels.

A short analytical history of manufacturing activity in the modern metropolis
On the basis of what has been transacted above, we are now in a position to develop a succinct analytical account of the recent evolution of the geography of manufacturing in large cities in North America and much of Western Europe. We will structure this account in terms of three main time periods, namely, (a) the period around the turn of the century, (b) the inter-War years, and (c) the post-War years.

Intraurban industrial locational patterns and processes at the turn of the century
We may begin by reaffirming the commonly made observation that manufacturing firms in the typical late nineteenth-century industrial city congregated above all at the core of the city. This phenomenon is describable in terms of two major phases of spatial development.

In the first place, many kinds of materials-intensive manufacturing firms in the nineteenth-century city clustered around major rail and water transport terminals. This dense clustering was essential in order to give firms immediate access to far-flung markets and sources of raw materials and to reduce the costs of transporting bulky and heavy industrial inputs and outputs through the city. Fales and Moses (1972), for example, show how much of the centrally located industry of Chicago in the 1870s consisted of firms whose outputs were characterized by significant reduction in weight and/or volume in comparison to inputs, and these firms huddled close to the transport nodes through which they drew many of their basic inputs. In this way, the emergent industrial core of the modern city appeared, and the working population then established itself in dense residential districts distributed tightly around this central nucleus (cf Moses and Williamson, 1967).

In the second place, a group of firms very different from those that were drawn insistently to the central transport terminals of the city also clustered tightly together in inner city areas in the late nineteenth century. This second group of firms was characterized above as being bound together by intricate and impromptu interfirm linkages incurring very high transport costs. Therefore at the outset these firms were (and are) under strong pressure to assemble together in geographical space so as to reduce to the minimum the onerous transport costs on unit inputs. Accordingly, purely *economic* complexes of such firms have tended to coalesce out in the urban land nexus to form distinctive *geographical* clusters. This bunching phenomenon, nonetheless, leaves open the question as to the precise relative location of individual clusters of interlinked firms in urban space, and there is no immediately obvious reason as to why clustering alone should have invariably caused them to gravitate towards the centre of the city.

Recall that (no matter whether we are concerned with the situation at the turn of the century or with the present-day situation) many of these intricately interlinked firms are uniformly describable as having a high velocity of turnover, short production runs, and frequently changing inputs and outputs. As an immediate corollary of this circumstance, the production processes of such firms have at all times typically resisted routinization and mechanization so that they are invariably highly labour-intensive. This has been an essential variable underlying the persistent development of dense geographical clusters/complexes of these firms *at the centre* of the urban system over both the nineteenth and the twentieth century. The heavy labour demands of these firms (both individually and collectively) made it imperative for them to be maximally accessible to the urban labour force as a whole, and thus to locate in inner city areas. In this way, they were able to minimize their wages bills, and thus to enhance their profits. For, even though (as was suggested earlier) industrial wage rates in the late nineteenth-century city tended to be at their highest at the centre of the city and then to decline steadily with increasing distance outwards, any other geographical configuration of the main labour-intensive industrial cluster(s) in the city would at once undoubtedly have caused local wage rates to escalate uncontrollably upwards. It is to be added that many analysts have proposed that proximity to major final markets in the central business district has also been a definite factor in the centralization of these firms. This would seem to have been especially so in the case of printing, which is as much a sort of retail activity as it is a manufacturing industry in the narrow sense. However, although there is no attempt here to discount entirely this factor of proximity to discount entirely this factor of proximity to the central business district (which would quite definitely reinforce the advantages of a central location for many varieties of small labour-intensive firms) it is surely to be of negligible importance when compared with the powerful centralizing impulse exerted by the dynamics of the urban labour market. As so much else in this area of analysis, matters must remain at this rather impressionistic level until the necessary focussed research has been accomplished.

The inter-War years
The development of truck transport in the 1920s, and the concomitant reduction in transport costs for many kinds of industrial commodities now set the scene for the beginnings of a massive decentralization of economic activities in large metropolitan areas. Once locational constraints on the capital cost side were relaxed, decentralization provided firms with the economic advantages of relatively cheap peripheral land inputs and (to begin with at least) relatively cheap labour. For all the reasons discussed above, however, only those firms that could achieve some significant degree of routinization of their input and output needs (hence, also, bulk packaging and transport, and above all, routine and relatively infrequent ordering) could be considered as effective candidates for decentralization. Such firms, moreover, were precisely capital-intensive firms, or else firms that were now in a position to switch to new capital-intensive techniques of production. Thus a first major generation of decentralized firms in the inter-War years was evidently composed of activities that were able at a very early stage to make use of relatively advanced production technologies. These tended to be firms belonging to such branches of production as heavy engineering, textiles, and chemicals. Their impulse to decentralize at an early stage was further stimulated by the circumstance that capital

intensification usually allowed them to reduce to a significant degree the ratio of circulating capital inputs to total outputs.

In spite of the positive wage differentials that existed between the urban core and the periphery in the inter-War years, firms belonging to the central labour-intensive complexes tended to remain firmly in place. These firms could not escape collectively from the high land and labour costs of the centre by reason of the dynamics of intraurban wage rates in relation to the spatial pattern of labour supply and demand; and they could not escape individually by reason of the complex and costly input–output relations that caused them to agglomerate together at the outset. Even if, by decentralization, these kinds of firms were able to achieve potential trade-offs between increased physical input costs and reduced labour and land costs, it seems evident that capital-intensive firms would almost always have been able to outbid them in competition for suburban sites. This remark is underlined by the observation that, under modern urban conditions, wage rates in peripheral areas appear to be highly susceptible to rapid upward movement contingent upon any increase in the local demand for labour. No doubt many kinds of small and relatively independent labour-intensive firms were able to escape from the high land and labour costs of the urban core in the inter-War years; but, again, for any given complement of labour there remains the strong likelihood (given the dynamics of industrial wage-rate determination in peripheral areas) that capital-intensive firms would always have been able to move that much further away from the core.

In the inter-War years, then, the complex Heckscher–Ohlin relationship described at the beginning of this chapter was apparently firmly established in most large metropolitan areas.

The post-War years
As implied by the Hoover and Vernon data given in table 6.1, the whole phenomenon of industrial decentralization caused a rapid upward ascension of peripheral wage rates and, in the years following the Second World War, industrial wage rates in the suburbs now generally began to exceed those that prevailed at the core of the city. The emergence of a high ratio of suburban to central industrial wage rates has no doubt been in part due to a tendency for firms to employ more highly skilled fractions of labour in the suburbs than in the inner city. However, as made clear by the relationship revealed by equations (6.1) and (6.2), much of this phenomenon must also be seen as being the result of a purely spatial redistribution of generalized labour demand conditions. These post-War changes in the geography of intrametropolitan industrial wage rates have greatly emphasized the comparative advantages of the central city for labour-intensive production activities, and of the suburbs for capital-intensive production activities. In brief (all other things being equal) those few branches of production that continue up until the present time to be highly labour-intensive are now even more

likely to remain at the centre of the city, even when they can otherwise free themselves from the severe constraining effects of the high transport costs on their unit inputs (and outputs). However, this comment needs to be qualified by the additional observation that central cities in Europe and North America have very recently begun persistently to lose their blue-collar residential functions. Such a turn of events is likely in the future to modify once more the spatial distribution of comparative advantages in the city, and to set in motion some new mutation of the intraurban locational process. This is an important point and it will be picked up again more thoroughly at a later stage in the argument. One effect of the appearance of high wage rates in the suburbs relative to the core areas would seem to have been a limited but discernible trickle of small (labour-intensive) firms away from the suburbs and back to the central city (cf Struyk and James, 1975).

As a result of the post-War reinforcement of the typical twofold spatial pattern of comparative advantages in large metropolitan regions, the decentralization of industry has become ever more insistently geared to the fundamental process of capital intensification and reorganization. High rates of capital intensification in industry have of course been very characteristic in the post-War decades, and, indeed, many branches of production that were even until quite recently typified by a stubborn resistance to automation (and vertical integration) have now also begun to substitute capital for labour on a significant scale and to migrate away from central city areas. Such is the case, for example, with firms producing cheap standardized clothing, highly automated printing shops, many kinds of metalworking enterprises, and so on. Concomitantly, decentralization has proceeded apace in the post-War decades.

Systematic development of some conjectures and hypotheses
The analytical bases of the discussion that follows are in part discoverable in the early work of Moses (1958), who with some success, though at a high level of abstraction, attempted to combine the theory of location with the general theory of production. Whatever novelty may accrue to the argument presented here resides substantially in the application of the broad logic of location-cum-production as described by Moses to an analysis of the peculiar spatial pattern of manufacturing in the modern metropolis.

Under conditions of competitive equilibrium, the rate of profit on invested industrial capital will tend to constancy across urban space. In reality, however, such a tendency is continually being upset by the accumulation of capital and by technological innovation, both of which incessantly threaten to disturb previously established economic and locational equilibria, for they tend persistently to open up new opportunities for firms to earn excess profits in urban fringe areas. As shown above, the effects of accumulation and innovation in the modern metropolis are (a) to free firms more and more from spatial dependence on one another, (b) to reduce inputs relative to outputs, (c) to cause a decline in the ratio of labour to capital used in the production process, and concomitantly (d) to encourage the ever widening decentralization of commodity production.

Now, over short- to medium-run periods when there is momentary stabilization of economic and technological conditions, previously created opportunities for firms to earn excess profits in urban fringe areas will be rapidly reduced, if not entirely eliminated. In the first place, as more and more firms decentralize, so wage rates towards the periphery of the urban system escalate rapidly upwards. In the second place, land rents at suburban locations would also rise somewhat in response to the increasing demand for industrial land at those locations. Decentralization would thus begin to be dampened down as total industrial profits in the suburbs are cut back to the normal level by a pincer movement, as it were, due to both rising labour costs and rising land costs. In a *ceteris paribus* world of henceforth unchanging production technology, the economic geography of the city would at this point be largely frozen in stasis. Production technology, however, is never in capitalism permanently fixed, and new rounds of capital intensification and technical innovation will always reappear, thereby fuelling in turn new rounds of urban industrial decentralization. Moreover, the deeper the process of capital intensification, the further outwards from the centre of the city are firms likely to locate. This follows directly from the observation that only highly capital-intensive firms are effectively in a position to trade off the premium wages that must invariably be paid at inaccessible locations against the comparatively low land costs at such locations. In harmony with these various remarks, we would expect to observe a vigorous historical process of centrifugal locational activity on the part of industrial firms in the modern metropolis, complemented by a very sluggish process of centripetal locational activity as a few industrial firms continue to adopt labour-intensive production technologies. The centrifugal effects of capital intensification would be augmented by the circumstance that as firms substitute capital for labour so they tend to require more punctilious production workers and increased inputs of administrative staff, and these are precisely the kinds of labour that are at once mobile (that is, characterized by high rates of car ownership) and most likely in any case to be found in suburban communities. As shown in chapter 3 firms locating towards the centre of the city will tend to make comparatively sparing use of land inputs, while firms locating in the periphery will tend to make comparatively lavish use of land inputs. It must be stressed once again, however, that in view of the reasoning developed here these land-input relationships are unlikely to be the ultimate determinants of the industrial geography of the modern metropolis; rather, they are undoubtedly themselves dependent upon prior changes in the internal structure of the production process in the context of existing spatial variations in urban land prices.

Out of all this there emerges the dominant central idea that industrial land use in large cities in modern capitalist society has been characterized by a powerful Heckscher–Ohlin relationship. Central city areas have had a distinct comparative advantage for labour-intensive activities whereas peripheral areas have had a distinct comparative advantage for capital-intensive activities. This idea translates into the following specific hypothesis: *As urban industrial firms adopt increasingly capital-intensive production technologies so (with branch of production held constant) they tend to locate further and further away from the centre of the city.* It must be observed at once that the requisite data (on capital–labour ratios for individual firms) to test this hypothesis directly are quite elusive. Accordingly, for purposes of statistical testing, the hypothesis is recast into a more convenient and tractable though possibly less powerful form. The derivative hypothesis may be formulated as follows: Let $X_{i\tau}^m$ be the total output in the ith branch of production at time τ in some given metropolitan area; and let $X_{i\tau}^c$ be total output in branch i at time τ in the central city belonging to that metropolitan area. Then, for any given branch of production, and any given metropolitan area it is hypothesized that *the change from time τ to time $\tau+1$ in the proportion of industry located in the central city $(X_{i\tau+1}^c/X_{i\tau+1}^m - X_{i\tau}^c/X_{i\tau}^m)$ is an inverse function of the change over the same time interval in the average metropolitan capital-labour ratio for the given branch of production.* Before proceeding to test this hypothesis directly, it is worth remarking that Massey and Meegan (1978) have demonstrated that much of the current movement of industrial jobs away from the centres of large British conurbations has been consequent upon industrial reconstruction and reorganization in the direction of greater capital intensification. Conversely, Struyk and James (1975) have observed that labour-intensive branches of production (for example, apparel, furniture, and printing) in a restricted sample of US metropolitan areas are highly concentrated at central locations, *and, at the same time, are growing relatively rapidly at central locations.* Let us add that further indirect confirmation of these relationships is to be found in an otherwise rather puzzling statistical regularity that is frequently remarked upon in the literature, namely, the widely observed positive correlation between size of firm and distance from the city centre (cf Cameron, 1973). This regularity conforms to, and in part corroborates the argument set out here by reason of the evident connection between firm sizes and capital–labour ratios: on the one hand, labour-intensive firms in any branch of production at the centre of the city would possess few internal economies of scale; they would therefore tend to be small in size. On the other hand, capital-intensive firms in the urban periphery would possess marked internal economies of scale; therefore, even at the risk of driving local wage rates yet higher, they would tend to be large. Incidentally, this reasoning runs parallel to but also in part rectifies the competing but rather formalistic 'incubation' hypothesis (cf Hoover and Vernon, 1959). The incubation

hypothesis asserts that small new firms are economically fragile, but that
their chances of survival are maximized if they locate near to the centre
of the city where an abundance of external economies (in addition to
simple accessibility effects) are said to be available. In this nurturing
environment, firms prosper and grow, until, having reached a certain size,
they are able to provide internally for themselves many of the positive
benefits that they previously consumed as externalities, and therefore they
now decentralize. In the present account, by contrast, the spatial dynamics
of urban industrial firms are more rigorously and specifically derived as an
outcome of capital–labour ratios in the context of a complex spatially
structured system of labour and land markets.

An empirical test of the Heckscher-Ohlin theorem in large metropolitan areas
With the above remarks in mind let us now set about empirically investigating
the second major hypothesis identified above.

The data
The hypothesis to be tested here was confronted with readily available
published data on industrial locational patterns and processes in the three
major Canadian census metropolitan areas, Montreal, Toronto, and
Vancouver. For each metropolitan area, statistical tests of the hypothesis
were run for each of the three-year time periods 1956–1959, 1961–1964,
and 1971–1974. The choice of these time periods was very much
conditioned by the nature of the data available. The basic data relevant
to the present exercise are described in the appendix along with a discussion
of the main problems and assumptions involved in assembling workable
data sets. The data described in the appendix represent for each of the
three census metropolitan areas and for each of the years 1956, 1959,
1961, 1964, 1971, and 1974, (a) the proportion of total industrial output
in the metropolitan area that is concentrated in the central city for two-
digit major industrial groups (that is, $X_{i\tau}^c/X_{i\tau}^m$ where $X_{i\tau}^c$ and $X_{i\tau}^m$ are
measured in terms of total dollar value of output); and (b) the average
metropolitan capital–labour ratio for two-digit major industrial groups
(that is, $K_{i\tau}/W_{i\tau}$, where $K_{i\tau}$ consists of estimated fixed capital depreciation
plus circulating capital, and $W_{i\tau}$ consists of total wages and salaries). Raw
data were derived from two sources published annually by Statistics Canada,
namely, *Manufacturing Industries of Canada: Geographical Distribution*
and *Fixed Capital Flows and Stocks*. Because of Statistics Canada
disclosure rule and other problems (see appendix) the number of major
industrial groups in the computed data sets varies from metropolitan area
to metropolitan area and from time period to time period.

The test
Taking each metropolitan area individually and in turn correlation
coefficients were then computed between (a) a dependent variable, $Y_{i\tau}$,

defined as the net change in the proportion of industry of group i located in the central city between time τ and time $\tau+1$, that is,

$$Y_{i\tau} = \frac{X^c_{i\,\tau+1}}{X^m_{i\,\tau+1}} - \frac{X^c_{i\tau}}{X^m_{i\tau}}, \tag{6.4}$$

and (b) an independent variable, $Z_{i\tau}$, defined as the proportional change in the capital–labour ratio for industry of group i between time τ and time $\tau+1$, that is,

$$Z_{i\tau} = \left(\frac{K_{i\,\tau+1}}{W_{i\,\tau+1}} - \frac{K_{i\tau}}{W_{i\tau}}\right) \bigg/ \frac{K_{i\tau}}{W_{i\tau}}. \tag{6.5}$$

Notice that correlation coefficients are computed for change data only, and no attempt is made to correlate magnitudes of the original undifferentiated variables ($X^c_{i\tau}/X^m_{i\tau}$ and $K_{i\tau}/W_{i\tau}$) with one another. In this manner, complications due to variations in the ages of different plants in different branches of production are largely abstracted out of the data. In addition, changes alone are examined because the data employed here run over the gamut of two-digit major industrial groups, and it seems evident that different branches of production, characterized as they are by a variety of idiosyncratic locational needs and histories in addition to their basic centrifugal/centripetal tendencies, will be arranged in widely differing spatial distributions at the outset. Thus, for example, two arbitrarily chosen branches of production (say i and j) may well be internally organized in such a way that firms in each are arranged in a pattern of labour-intensive firms at the core and capital-intensive firms at the periphery; however, it is not necessarily the case (given the special locational and technological pressures to which each of these branches may be subject) that if $K_{i\tau}/W_{i\tau} > K_{j\tau}/W_{j\tau}$ then branch i as a whole will be more suburbanized than branch j as a whole. This remark is borne out by scrutiny of the data. Thus, certain branches with high average capital–labour ratios (for example, food and beverage industries) are concentrated in central areas alongside branches with low average capital–labour ratios (for example, clothing industries); while a similar jumbling of high and low capital–labour ratio branches (for example, paper and allied products on the one hand, and electrical products industries on the other hand) is apparent in suburban ring areas. Moreover, in the central city areas of Montreal, Toronto, and Vancouver, there is to be found a wide variety of capital-intensive raw-materials processing industries clustered around the port areas of those cities. What is important for present purposes, however, is to abstract general incremental directions and tendencies from a mass of heterogeneous data. For this reason, in addition, it was felt to be more consistent with the spirit of the hypothesis to be tested to define the independent variable, $Z_{i\tau}$, as a proportional change [cf equation (6.5)] rather than as a simple first difference, because in the form of a proportion the variable $Z_{i\tau}$ roughly measures the *rate* of change in capital-labour ratios, and is, at the same time, independent of the initial magnitude of any given capital-labour ratio.

Results

The interrelationships between $Y_{i\tau}$ and $Z_{i\tau}$ for the three metropolitan areas and the three designated time intervals are shown graphically in figure 6.1. The main results of the statistical computations are shown in table 6.2. By and large, the computed correlation coefficients between $Y_{i\tau}$ and $Z_{i\tau}$ are modest in absolute value, though this circumstance is perhaps only to be expected in view of the disparate and makeshift qualities of the data employed. It might be said, indeed, that the correlation coefficients are

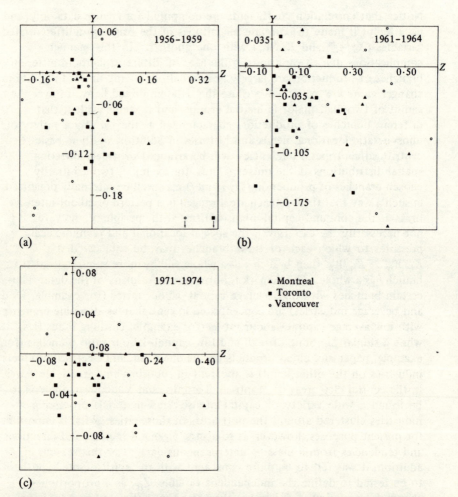

Figure 6.1. Changes in the proportion of total metropolitan industry in central city areas, Y, versus proportional changes in capital-labour ratios, Z, for major industrial groups: (a) 1956-1959; (b) 1961-1964; (c) 1971-1974.

surprisingly high and they would surely be yet higher if branch of production were held constant. What is especially encouraging about the computational results is that there is a scattering of statistically significant coefficients in table 6.2, and, in addition, that all the coefficients have the correct negative sign with the single exception of Toronto in 1971-1974. The overall consistency and coherence of these results conduces to a reasonably high level of confidence in the hypothesis that is being tested. Additionally, regressions of the type $Y_{ir} = \alpha \pm \beta Z_{ir}$ were computed for each of the nine experiments. The results of this exercise were again all remarkably consistent. On average, the computed α values took on a magnitude of -0.04, indicating that in the three metropolitan areas in question there is an autonomous although very restrained process of industrial decentralization of the order of 4·0% drop in the proportion of industry in the central city every three years, or 1·3% *per annum*. In brief, any branch of production whose capital-labour ratio remained unchanged from one year to the next would experience some decentralization, but certainly not enough to account for the dramatic industrial land-use changes that have been evident in large Canadian cities since the Second World War. Further, and again on average, the computed β value was -0.3, indicating that a 100% increase in any capital-labour ratio over a three-year period would induce a drop of the order of 30·0% in the proportion of industry located in the central city.

In general, then, these results seem to confirm, modestly but unambiguously, the initial theoretical analysis. Whenever there is an intensification of labour inputs in any branch of production, new firms in that branch tend to locate in the central city. This relationship no doubt continues to be especially strong in Canadian metropolitan areas where large concentrations of low-skilled immigrant workers (including female workers) are still to be found in core residential areas. Whenever there is an intensification of capital inputs in any branch of production, firms in that branch tend to locate in peripheral areas. It must be affirmed at this stage, however, that although the statistical tests carried out above provide definite testimony in favour of these notions, the tests are nevertheless not finally conclusive. For there still remains the tantalizing possibility that what these tests have captured is nothing more than an accidental

Table 6.2. Correlation coefficients. Figures in brackets show number of cases involved in computing associated correlation coefficients.

	1956-1959	1961-1964	1971-1974
Montreal	−0·56* (14)	−0·62* (17)	−0·27 (16)
Toronto	−0·82* (17)	−0·10 (16)	+0·52* (14)
Vancouver	−0·37 (13)	−0·30 (14)	−0·51 (9)

* Significant at 95% level of confidence.

correlation between two independent and autonomous time series processes, the one involving the progressive suburbanization of industry and the other involving the progressive substitution of capital for labour in the production process, but without any organic functional relationship between the two. In point of fact, this extreme possibility is already to some degree precluded by the circumstance that, in the numerical data employed here, there is observable a small but definite countertendency to the process of suburbanization and increasing capital–labour ratios, namely, a proclivity for *some* firms to take up central city locations while simultaneously reducing, or at least only modestly increasing their capital–labour ratios (cf figure 6.1). Even so, additional evidence and analysis seem to be called for (including, in particular, additional confirmation of the tendency for relatively labour-intensive firms to shift to central locations) before the results established here can be considered to be reasonably definitive.

A back-up test

By way of consummating the above discussion, let us consider, specifically, the case of the recent evolution of the locational pattern of the clothing industry of Montreal and Toronto. As Steed (1976) has shown, there is a clear positive relationship between the degree to which clothing plants in Montreal and Toronto produce standardized outputs (that is, are able to make long production runs of a single item before it goes out of fashion) and the distance from the city centre at which plants locate. Now, as argued earlier, a high degree of standardization of output suggests that capital plays a comparatively important role in the production process, whereas a low degree of standardization of output (as manifested in short

Table 6.3. Clothing industries: degree of centralization of plants, 1949–1973.
Source: derived from data in Steed (1976).

Standardization group	Plants in each group locating downtown (%)			
	1949 (all plants)	1950–1960 (new plants)	1963–1967 (new plants)	1971–1973 (new plants)
Montreal				
A	33·4	21·3	16·3	13·7
B	15·2	12·2	1·9	5·3
C	1·0	2·4	1·3	0·0
total plants	1233	1112	463	205
Toronto				
A	51·2	47·0	43·3	68·6
B	19·2	24·5	19·4	7·1
C	5·9	8·6	2·0	0·0
total plants	601	418	150	64

production schedules with frequently changing inputs and outputs) implies a heavy reliance on direct labour in the production process.

Consider table 6.3, which shows the percentages of clothing producers in specified production groups locating in downtown Montreal and Toronto in the four time periods 1949, 1950–1960, 1963–1967, and 1971–1973. In this table, clothing producers are aggregated into three basic categories according to the degree of general standardization of their output. Following Steed (1976), hats and caps, embroidery, and women's factory clothing and contractors form a first category (group A in table 6.3) representing the *least* standardized types of clothing production; men's factory clothing and contractors and children's factory clothing form an intermediate group (group B); and knitted goods, hosiery, and foundation garments form a third category (group C) representing the *most* standardized types of clothing production. Two tendencies are very clear in the data presented in table 6.3. The first is that over the aggregate period from 1949 to 1973, fewer and fewer new clothing industry plants as a whole have chosen to locate in the downtown area; this tendency is consistent with an overall process of capital intensification in the clothing industry. The second is that in any given time period *new* plants which are unstandardized (and hence, relatively labour-intensive) tend to gravitate towards central locations, while new plants which are standardized (and hence relatively capital-intensive) tend to gravitate to noncentral locations. To repeat the arguments which have already been elaborately dealt with at an earlier stage, this centralization of unstandardized labour-intensive plants is a direct outcome, first, of their need to cluster together, and second, of their composite need to be maximally accessible to their overall sources of labour. Conversely, decentralization of standardized capital-intensive firms is the consequence of their search for cheap land inputs in the context of diminished locational constraints on the capital cost side combined with escalating wage rates in the urban periphery. The finding in the present instance that labour-intensive firms tend to gravitate towards the centre of the city seems sufficiently strong to eradicate any remaining ambiguities in the main statistical test described in the previous section. What is more, because the data in table 6.3 for the three time periods 1950–1960, 1963–1967, and 1971–1973 concern only new plants, we can immediately discount any untoward and complicating effects due to variations in the ages of different plants at central versus noncentral locations.

In contradistinction to this brief but revealing analysis of the recent locational activity of clothing producers in Montreal and Toronto, it has been commonly proposed in the literature that clothing firms (as well as other varieties of typical central city industries) gravitate towards the urban core in order to avail themselves of comprehensive positive agglomeration economies. However, this notion needs to be reproblematized and more rigorously posed. We need first of all to break down agglomeration economies into transport effects on the one side and external economies of scale on the other side. We need second of all to distinguish between the simple spatial clustering of small labour-intensive firms and their tendency (within composite industrial complexes) to gravitate to the centre of the city. Thus, on the one hand insofar as agglomeration economies are identifiable as simple transport cost effects they do indeed largely account for the tendency of these kinds of firms to cluster together in urban space. On the other hand, the centralizing proclivities of these firms are very largely the direct result of their labour-intensiveness. To be sure, it has been suggested in the literature [see, again, the classical statement by Hoover and Vernon (1959)] that there are definite external economies of scale (in the true sense) to be obtained in maximal quantities at the centre of the city and that these are to a large degree capable of accounting for the centralization of small labour-intensive industrial firms. These externalities would involve such phenomena as jointly owned machinery, shared premises, the formation of local high-density markets with efficient dissemination of price signals, and so on. However, it is difficult to see how such externalities would induce the *centralization* of firms, though they would most assuredly encourage the *clustering* effects that are induced in the first instance by the need to minimize overall transport costs.

The general role of industry in the urban land nexus
As the dominant process of industrial decentralization in large metropolitan areas has proceeded over the decades, so the working population has tended resolutely to follow behind. Indeed a pronounced multiplier effect, operating in part via the wages system, seems to have been set in motion as a reflection of the interdependent out-migration of firms and households. Decentralization of industrial firms has encouraged increasing suburbanization of population, and increasing suburbanization of population has encouraged further outward movement of firms. This whole multiplier effect appears to have been magnified by the massive expansion of transport systems in major metropolitan areas in the post-War decades, and in particular by the pervasive tendency for circumferential linkages (connecting different suburban districts along the urban fringe) to spring up within predominantly core-focussed networks. The net consequence of this multiplier effect has been an augmenting series of waves of decentralization of both jobs and population; and given the leads and lags involved, together with the inertia of preexisting industrial and especially residential geographies within the city, it is scarcely surprising that the whole decentralization process has been so slow, staggered as it has been over several decades. Even so, it would seem that the out-migration of industry from the central city has been more rapid than the out-migration of the working population (cf Gripaios, 1977), and, in conformity with this observation, excess demand for industrial labour has tended to shift in the recent past from the urban core to the inner peripheral areas of the city.

This tendency is directly reflected in the wage rate data presented in table 6.1.

At the present time, the mutually reinforcing multiplier effect whereby the decentralization of industry helps to beget the decentralization of population and vice versa has proceeded very far indeed, and nowhere more so, it seems, than in the large British conurbations (cf Foreman-Peck and Gripaios, 1977). Here, the loss of economic activity and population from inner city areas to the suburbs and to the new and expanded towns has advanced particularly far. The loss of population from the inner reaches of the large British conurbations has been so great that even highly labour-intensive kinds of activities have now apparently begun to migrate outwards on a significant scale in search of sources of labour as well as cheap land. As a result of these trends, British inner city problems (unemployment, fiscal austerity, decay of social services, etc) have become so severe, and the economic bases of inner city areas so eroded that there are now concerted moves (as in North America) to reverse the official policy of employment and population dispersal that has hitherto been in existence in various forms since the Second World War. Nonetheless, in Britain, Canada, the United States, and elsewhere, the out-migration of industrial firms from inner city areas seems very likely to continue apace, unless perhaps there were a quite unexpected drop in central city land prices. As things stand, there is now perceptible, in addition to the suburbanization process as such, a pronounced tendency for industrial firms to scatter even far beyond the bounds of existing metropolitan regions as the technical reorganization of industrial production moves forward.

6.4 Office activities

One of the most rapidly expanding spheres of economic production in modern capitalist society is represented by those forms of clerical, bureaucratic, and administrative labour performed in offices by white-collar workers. The significance of this sphere of production is openly proclaimed in the urban landscape by the multistorey office blocks that crowd in on the central business districts of virtually all large metropolitan regions. In addition, there is to be found, to an ever increasing degree, significant but subsidiary scatterings of offices in subcentres of development throughout most urban areas. Like the urban geography of manufacturing, the characteristic locational pattern of office activities is in principle explicable in terms of the functional effectiveness (profitability) of individual office firms in relation to basic capital, labour, and land inputs. Note that, for present purposes, government offices (which are not bound by the strict rationality of capitalistic economic calculation) are excluded from the analysis. In geographical terms, the main question that must be addressed here is why it is that in spite of excessively high land costs at the urban core, the central business district continues to retain a predominant locational hold over office activities. This hold remains powerful notwithstanding the evident decentralization of many office firms in recent years (cf Daniels, 1977).

Before this question is confronted directly, two major general features of office work must be observed. First, the inputs and outputs from office activities consist less of tangible physical commodities than of intangible and often quite ephemeral services, advice, information, and the like. Legal, financial, and business service activities come immediately to mind as producing and consuming these kinds of inputs and outputs. Second (and not unlike the case of commodity flows between certain kinds of labour-intensive industrial firms in inner city areas), such inputs and outputs are rarely standardized; they must in general be treated as flows of one special case after another; and as such they must be mediated by means of direct contact between producer and consumer. Such contact may be by letter or by telephone. Frequently, however, nothing less than personal, face-to-face meeting will be effective in the transmission and receipt (that is, *negotiation*) of the requisite inputs and outputs. It goes without saying that the potential costs of such transactions are high, though they are much reduced where the participants in the transactions have ready access to one another by reason of their location close together in both space and time. This access is crucial where the value of the negotiated inputs and outputs (information) deteriorates as it ages.

As a direct corollary of the above main point, much office work is highly labour-intensive. This follows at once from the unstandardized nature of so many interoffice inputs and outputs. Not only must these inputs and outputs commonly be mediated personally by individual agents, but their unstandardized nature means also that many intraoffice tasks must vary widely from case to case, thus requiring a large direct application of labour. It is true, of course, that in contradistinction to these remarks a very pronounced process of capital intensification has proceeded in the sphere of office activities in recent decades. This has involved the substitution of electronic communications devices for face-to-face contact, and the development of many different kinds of mechanical and electronic laboursaving instruments suitable for application in an office work environment. Thus, for example, whereas the quantity of office floor space in major cities has tended to increase enormously over the last couple of decades, office employment has expanded at a much slower pace. This remark is well illustrated by the specific case of Toronto (see table 6.4). Here, an insistent process of intensification of central office land uses has proceeded over the last couple of decades, while the number of individuals (mainly office workers) travelling in to the core area between 7.00 a.m. and 9.00 a.m. on an average weekday morning has tended to remain fairly constant over the same period. Daniels (1975) provides data for London which more directly corroborate the same point that office floor-space/worker ratios have tended dramatically to increase in central city areas in recent years. In spite of this apparent trend in the direction of increasing capital-labour ratios, office activities remain quite certainly among the more labour-intensive forms of economic production in modern capitalist society.

The various points developed above provide significant clues as to the locational pattern of offices within the urban land nexus. On the one hand, the interoffice transmission of inputs and outputs is frequently extremely expensive; and on the other hand, large (though, in relative terms, diminishing) quantities of labour are required in order to sustain office functions. As already indicated, this situation is not unlike the case of some varieties of labour-intensive manufacturing firms. Thus, in the first instance, office firms tend to *cluster* together in order to minimize the onerous costs of shifting inputs and outputs from one firm to another; and, in the second instance, the resulting spatial aggregation of office firms typically occupies a *central* location so as to be maximally accessible to the totality of white-collar and clerical workers in the city. In response to this same process, white-collar and clerical workers distribute themselves in communities scattered throughout the urban land nexus around the central office nucleus. One effect of this overall geographical pattern is that *office* wage rates at the present time seem to decline systematically with distance from the core of the city outwards, though this pattern is likely to change (as it did in the case of industrial wage rates in the years immediately following the Second World War) as more and more office firms begin to substitute capital for labour, standardize their input-output relationships, and accordingly decentralize. Even so, at the present time, the centripetal attraction of the urban core as a location for office firms is continually being reinforced by public investment in high-speed commuter

Table 6.4. The changing relationship between office floor space and office labour requirements in the core of Toronto, 1963-1973 [a]. Source: City of Toronto Core Area Task Force (1974).

Year	Office floor space in the core area (10^6 ft^2)	Total inbound passengers to the core by all vehicles, 7.00 a.m.-9.00 a.m.	Ratio of floor space to inbound passengers
1963	14·2	103850	136·7
1964	14·1	108499	130·0
1965	14·5	105638	137·3
1966	17·7	104088	170·0
1967	19·6	109219	179·5
1968	20·1	91687	219·2
1969	21·3	106047	200·9
1970	22·1	112096	197·2
1971	24·5	104903	233·5
1972	27·4	110723	247·4
1973	28·2	106988	263·6

[a] The definition of the core area for the case of office floor space counts differs in minor respects from the core area for the case of inbound-passenger counts.

transport links running between the central business district and the outer suburban communities. This increases the ratio of the costs on input–output flows to the costs of moving labour between home and work and underpins the economic advantages of the centre as a location for offices. The accessibility of the core to white-collar labour is yet further enhanced by the incipient appearance in many large cities of an exchange of population between the inner city and the urban periphery in such a way that blue-collar workers migrate outwards so as to be close to industrial employment opportunities in the periphery, while small but increasing numbers of white-collar workers move inwards so as to be close to office employment opportunities in the centre.

The preceding comments suggest that to the degree that office firms can reduce their dependence on shifting inputs and outputs via direct personal meetings and interviews, to the same degree can they free themselves from the high land costs at the core of the city, and move out to more peripheral locations. However, any reduction of dependence on the need for face-to-face contact is in turn contingent upon the degree to which any firm is able to standardize its input–output requirements or, alternatively, to substitute other forms of communication (electronic in particular) for direct physical meeting. It is contingent, that is, upon the ability of any firm to substitute capital for labour in its basic operations. Dramatic exemplification of this point is provided by the observation that among the more persistent types of offices seeking peripheral locations in recent years have been the computer sections of many banks, insurance companies, financial institutions, data-processing firms, and so on. These computer sections are, of course, extremely capital-intensive, and moreover, it is easy to communicate with them from any location in the urban system by means of remote terminals connected to them via telephonic links. On the basis of this same logic, it seems evident, in addition, that the higher the capital–labour ratio that any office firm can achieve (thus reducing upward pressure on local wage rates) the further outward from the city centre it would tend to locate. In these senses, there is little intrinsic difference between the locational logics governing the intraurban distribution of manufacturing and office land use: in both cases, the impulse to outward dispersal seems to be limited above all by the degree of capital intensification that firms can accomplish.

There is much theoretical and empirical evidence to suggest that once any office firm *is* able to substitute capital for labour and/or to reduce its reliance on face-to-face negotiation of inputs and outputs, it is then able to free itself from the necessity of locating within the central business district, and can thus substantially reduce its overall costs. Pye (1977) provides a general theoretical statement of the kinds of economic calculations involved in the office decentralization process. Consider any individual firm that is faced with a decision to relocate away from the centre. Let n be the number of jobs that the firm intends to shift; σ is the weekly saving per employee as a result of decentralization; l is the number of employees who will have to travel to the centre after relocation in order to attend personal meetings; m is the number of such trips per week; t is the fare per trip; v is the value of any communicator's time; and τ is time spent in travelling. Then, if it is found that

$$n\sigma > lm(t+v\tau), \tag{6.6}$$

it is economically rational for the firm to move from the centre to the periphery. Obviously, as the potential applicability of telecommunications technology increases, so the value of the function $lm(t+v\tau)$ will tend to fall, and so by the same token, will decentralization become increasingly attractive to office firms. In addition, much empirical work suggests that office wages and rents are significantly reduced (thus tending to increase the value of the function $n\sigma$) by decentralization. For instance, Daniels (1975) reports for the case of London that average time spent in commuting decreases as a function of the distance that any office moves from central London. Presumably this finding implies that wage rates fall concomitantly. Daniels measures the decrease in time spent in commuting as a result of decentralization by means of the regression equation

$$\bar{\tau} = 39\cdot64 - 6\cdot85d, \quad r = -0\cdot46, \tag{6.7}$$

where $\bar{\tau}$ is mean trip time, and d is distance in kilometers that any office moves from central London. Similarly, Rhodes and Kan (1971) indicate that for a sample of offices dispersing from central London, average staff-cost reduction was $9\cdot4\%$ per employee. Such a reduction is to be expected given the existing heavy concentration of demand for office labour in the centre of London. Overall, Rhodes and Kan report that any office that moves out of central London can expect to benefit by a reduction of the order of 20% of total costs (staff costs, rent, taxes, etc). In broad terms, the degree of feasible decentralization of any office firm is established by the precise form in each specific case of the two functions $lm(t+v\tau)$ and $n\sigma$ in relationship to distance from the core of the city. The propensity of any firm to decentralize is increased (a) the lower the slope of the function $lm(t+v\tau)$ (the higher the potential capital intensity of the firm), and (b) the steeper the slope of the function $n\sigma$ (the greater the potential saving per employee). A hypothetical graphing of these two functions within a spatial system is shown in figure 6.2.

At the present time, the core of the city remains the predominant focus of office employment, though considerable decentralization of offices has been evident over the last couple of decades as the massive substitution of capital for labour in office activities has started to get under way. As more and more offices decentralize, so office wage rates in the urban periphery will rise, thereby reinforcing the emerging comparative advantage of the periphery for capital-intensive firms. Given that accelerated rates of capital intensification in office activities seem likely in the future, the pace of decentralization away from the central business district will probably continue to increase. Goddard (1973) has recently estimated that some 80% of all interoffice contacts in central London are of a type that could be potentially carried on away from the centre by means of newly developed telecommunications technology, and this estimate seems to give a fairly realistic idea of the approximate magnitude of what is likely to be actually attainable in this regard in the very near future. It may well be, of course, that as the division of labour in capitalist society widens, so more and more specialized office firms with more and more emphasis on personal contact and subtly negotiated inputs and outputs will come into being, and will continue to sustain the economic viability of central business district areas. But if the incipient process of office decentralization represents only the early stages of a massive abandonment by office firms of central business district locations (as was at an earlier period the case with manufacturing firms) then some very serious policy questions begin to pose themselves. For if office activities move away *en masse* from the central business district, then the already serious economic crisis of core urban areas in much of North America and Western Europe is likely to take on something approaching disaster proportions.

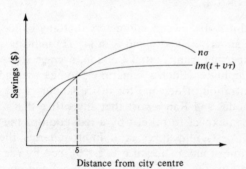

Distance from city centre

Figure 6.2. Savings versus costs of decentralization for an office firm as a function of distance from the city centre. Here, decentralization is economically feasible beyond the distance d_δ from the city centre.

6.5 Retail and service activities
Retail and service activities are typically spread out across urban space in a regular pattern of hierarchically ordered clusters dominated by the massive agglomeration of retail and service firms in the central business district.

These kinds of firms seek out locations with high levels of accessibility to consumers. At such locations they can achieve rapid rates and volumes of turnover and hence maximum profits. This positive relationship between accessibility and turnover in the retail and service sector follows from the circumstance that total demand for retail and service items is not simply a function of prices at point of sale but also of the travel costs that consumers must incur in travelling to shop. The sensitivity of retail and service firms to accessibility, however, varies considerably depending on type of activity. Certain activities, such as car dealers or jewellery stores, are characterized by relatively high prices and a low frequency of demand, so that the marginal effect of consumers' transport costs on final demand is fairly negligible; these kinds of activities are known as high-order functions. Other activities, such as grocery stores or newspaper vendors, are characterized by relatively low prices and a high frequency of demand, so that the marginal effect of consumers' transport costs on final demand is in this case quite significant; these kinds of activities are known as low-order functions. In the vocabulary of central-place theory (see Berry, 1967), high-order functions are said to have a large threshold and range, while low-order functions are said to have a small threshold and range. Here the term *threshold* designates the total population needed to support one unit of any given type of retail and service activity at normal profitability; and the term *range* designates the outer geographical limit of the effective spatial market for that activity. Thus, there are relatively few high-order activities in the urban system, and these tend above all to be concentrated in the central business district. By contrast, there are relatively many low-order activities, and these are very widely scattered throughout the urban land nexus. Economic competition between like kinds of activities ensures that each is more or less regularly distributed through urban space in conformity with its particular threshold and range. Nevertheless, retail and service activities in practice display a higher degree of clustering and centralization than they would if their geographical distribution were accounted for solely by threshold and range variations and pure spatial competition, for the emergence of significant (and genuine)

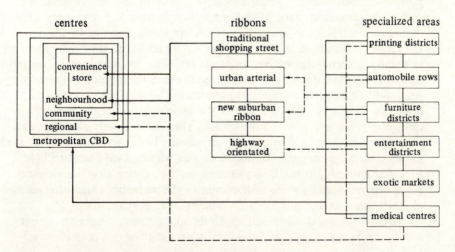

Figure 6.3. Schema of the structure of intraurban retail business. Redrawn with minor modifications from Berry (1963, page 20).

external economies of scale encourages firms to congregate together into groups of varying sizes. This tendency is particularly sustained by the circumstance that an aggregation of retail and service firms at any location invariably attracts more shoppers than would the same set of firms if they were widely and individually scattered throughout urban space. As a consequence of these different relationships, the basic pattern of retail and service distribution in the city takes on the manifest form of a spatial hierarchy of nodes of activity ranging from the central business district at the highest level, through regional, community, and neighbourhood centres, down to the individual street corner store at the lowest level (figure 6.3).

However, in addition to these main processes governing the level and distribution of tertiary activity in the city, there are two further factors that help to modify somewhat the basic pattern of retail and service land use. First, there is a definite tendency, especially in the central business districts of large cities, for highly specialized retail subnuclei to emerge. For example, such activities as automobile showrooms, furniture stores, entertainment, and so on commonly segregate out into specialized land-use areas within more extensive shopping districts; and this is no doubt a response to the behavioural characteristics of consumers who tend to make comparative assessments of prices and available merchandise (goods and services) before actually making a purchase. Second, because of the existence of linear transport paths through the urban system, homologues to the nucleated centre come into being in the guise of ribbons of retail and service firms spread out along major arteries of communication.

The spatial structure of retail and service business is thus intimately intertwined with the geographical pattern of urban population and population movements. Retail and service activities represent the most visible and proximate face of the production system as it encounters the reproduction system in the sphere of exchange. Because of this situation the impact of changes in the retail and service sector on the urban economy as a whole is highly distinctive. In particular, since retail and service outputs do not enter directly as intermediate inputs into the production of other commodities, changes in retail and service price levels have no direct influence on prices elsewhere within the production system. However, any change in retail and service prices would always effectively alter the level of real wages. Increases in such prices would always provoke some upward pressure on wage settlements, and decreases would always tend to hold back (temporarily, at least) wage increases. For this reason, an efficient system of retail and service distribution in the metropolis (and this implies also efficiency in the matter of consumers' transport inputs) is of considerable importance in helping to maintain money wages at current levels, and hence in helping to maintain a rapid pace of accumulation.

Urban patterns 2: reproduction and circulation space

7.1 Urban population distribution

Urban population is typically distributed in a wide circular band whose inner boundary circumscribes the central business district and whose outer boundary coincides with the furthermost limits of the city. Within this band, population density characteristically attains to its maximum value near the centre, declines steadily with distance outwards, and falls to its minimum on the periphery of the urban system. The regularity of this pattern is, with minor and rare exceptions, broken only by the appearance of subsidiary peaks of population at scattered subcentres of development within the urban system. In broad terms, this pattern of population distribution is universally describable by the celebrated negative exponential function first proposed by Clark (1951). This function (which has a strictly descriptive, nonexplanatory value) may be written

$$D = \alpha \exp(-\beta d) , \qquad (7.1)$$

where D is the population density at any point in urban space, d is the distance of that point from the centre, and α and β are parameters to be estimated in any empirical case. Over time, the urban population density curve as described by equation (7.1) has a marked tendency both to rise upwards and to become flatter (thus signifying both increasing population densities and increasing outward movement of population). In addition, with the course of time, the typical urban population density curve tends to develop a cavity towards its point of origin, reflecting the tendency of population at the centre of the city to fall as inner city neighbourhoods are destroyed by the encroachment of central business district activities. These various tendencies are demonstrated in figure 7.1, which shows in comparative format how the spatial distribution of population density evolved in Chicago between 1860 and 1956.

In consumer sovereignty theories of the formation of urban space, the behaviour of urban population densities as described above is largely reduced to a single cause: it is ascribed above all to the structure of consumers' tastes and preferences identifiable in terms of some exogenously given utility function. Much neoclassical urban economic theory, in particular, suggests that relatively high population densities near the centre of the city and relatively low population densities near the periphery are nothing more than the result of the indifference of consumers as between (a) high accessibility to the city centre combined with reduced living space and (b) low accessibility combined with expanded living space. It may very well be that the preferences underlying this state of affairs exist as observable psychic tendencies; it is certainly the case that the urban system as currently constituted *offers* these kinds of basic choices in the matter of residential accommodation. However, the choices are also quite certainly not created subjectively, but are given by the innate logic of the urban system within the capitalist mode of production. To assign a privileged analytical position to these preferences is therefore to translate into psychologistic terms the basic *structural* forces which, as shown earlier in chapter 3, must exist within any centripetal system of accessibilities. These forces manifest themselves in an urban development process that tends to give rise to intensive land use towards the centre of the city, and extensive land use towards the periphery. All that is necessary for this process to work is that differential land rents should emerge in inverse proportion to transport costs throughout urban space, that is, essentially, that the law of exchange of equivalents should prevail. Under such conditions, all locations will possess equivalent prices once location-specific costs (in the present case differential rents and transport costs) are added up at each individual site. Clearly, the operation of this law transcends by far the personal idiosyncracies (tastes and preferences) of the innumerable individuals whose actions mediate it into concrete realization. Then, over the course of time, capitalist housing suppliers, in pursuit of augmented profits, will begin to differentiate their output (relative to prevailing techniques of production at any given moment) over urban space. Housing

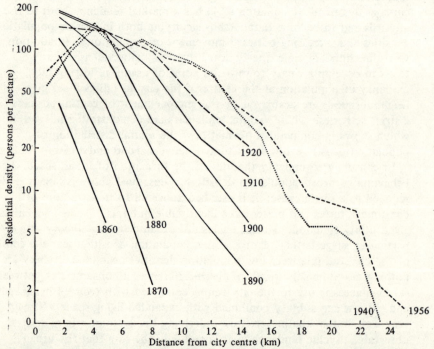

Figure 7.1. Population densities in the Chicago Metropolitan Area. Source: Clark (1968, page 344).

suppliers will tend to produce relatively land-use-intensive housing at high-rent locations, and relatively land-use-extensive housing at low-rent locations. Under current urban conditions, the net result of this will be a system of population densities that diminishes steadily with distance from the city centre outwards. Irrespective of any metaphysical conceptions about the nature of housing preferences 'in abstract', housing demand as a whole will conform to this pattern of production as the rational counterpart to a basic structurally determined set of alternatives: high-density housing and high accessibility at the centre versus low-density housing and low accessibility on the urban periphery. The particular idiosyncratic choice that any individual makes with respect to the alternatives is a pure epiphenomenon: a given degree of freedom within a predetermined structure. This matter will be taken up again towards the close of the present chapter.

7.2 The internal differentiation of urban residential space

These remarks on the broad geographical pattern of population and housing in the city now need to be tempered by consideration of the ways in which reproduction space itself breaks down into a congeries of subspaces, neighbourhoods, and communities. In what follows a brief attempt will be made to analyze the manner in which residential activity in the city as described by equation (7.1) is differentiated along several different lines of social cleavage. In the first instance, the general empirical testimony of urban factorial ecology will be described. At a later stage, an attempt will be made to relate the broad outlines of this testimony to the wider system of commodity production.

Urban residential space observed

Descriptive factorial ecology (cf Schwirian, 1974) has shown time and again that out of the apparent sociocultural chaos of the North American city there emerge three basic dimensions of variation (or factors) representing the dominant pattern of urban society. These three dimensions are commonly designated social rank, ethnicity, and familism. *Social rank* emerges as the preponderant dimension of variation in factorial ecological analysis. This dimension invariably accounts for up to 40% to 50% of all statistical measures of sociocultural variation in the city, and it can fairly be regarded as representing the fundamental core of urban society. Very generally, this factor represents a continuum running from a white-collar social fraction on the one hand to a blue-collar social fraction on the other hand. These fractions tend to be distributed geographically in the city in alternating sectors radiating out from the centre (cf Murdie, 1969). *Ethnicity* typically accounts for some 10% to 20% of sociocultural variation in the North American city. The ethnicity factor identifies social groups such as blacks, Puerto Ricans, recent central and southern European immigrants, and so on, namely working-class groups that are in some fairly overt way imperfectly assimilated into North American society as a whole.

These ethnic groups tend to dwell in distinctive neighbourhoods scattered in discrete clusters around the central business district. *Familism* also generally accounts for some 10% to 20% of urban social variation. It represents a dimension of variation having to do with family structure and life-style, and it characteristically distinguishes the conventional nuclear family on the one hand from single individual families on the other hand. The nuclear family tends above all to be found in suburban areas, while single individual families tend to be concentrated at inner city locations. These three dimensions of variation do not exhaust the entire harvest of urban factorial ecology, but in quantitative terms they do represent by far the greater proportion of that harvest. Furthermore, they constitute a set of statistical regularities that is reproduced consistently in case study after case study throughout North America and much of Western Europe.

Factorial ecology normally goes not much further than recording these empirical observations, commenting upon them in anecdotal fashion, and describing their comparative variations in different cities. It is possible, however, to go far beyond the restricted empiricist interpretations of urban factorial ecology, and on the basis of the theory of modes of production, which problematizes and synthesizes *all* social phenomena, to show that the factors of social rank, ethnicity, and familism as both general social variates *and* spatially determined phenomena, are essentially intermediated expressions of fundamental capitalist social and property relations. It is suggested here that the empirical patterns observed by factorial ecologists are first of all outcomes of the division of labour as established within the system of commodity production, and second of all reflections of the innate logic of reproduction processes that are specific to capitalist society. In line with this comment, it may be observed that precisely the first and most basic line of disjunction within the division of labour in modern capitalism is massively recorded in the structure of urban society: the disjunction, that is, between white-collar intellectual workers on the one side and blue-collar manual workers on the other side, as embodied in the ecological factor of social rank. The ethnicity factor, too, really represents a social fraction whose origins reside within the division of labour, for ethnic groups as identified by urban factorial ecology are primarily composed of unskilled blue-collar and manual workers who happen to be characterized by the added peculiarity, for reasons to be discussed below, that they disaggregate out in urban space so as to form distinctive neighbourhoods. In the same way, the familism factor also bears a definite, if mediated, relationship to the labour process and its needs in capitalism. As will appear more clearly at a later stage, the kinds of social phenomena represented by the familism variable reflect above all the role of urban residential space in the rearing and nurturing of children and in their socialization into the main current of society.

These three main social dimensions as recognized by urban factorial ecology are thus reflections of the global functions and purposes of capitalist society, and, in particular, of capitalist production and reproduction relations. Once determined within the broad structure of society, they are cast out, as it were, into urban space *where they coalesce out into distinctive geographical entities*. In other words, these factors, so far from being chaotically intermingled throughout the urban land nexus, have a marked spatial as well as sociological expression. The hypothesis that now inescapably presents itself for examination is that the neighbourhoods and urban communities that emerge out of this process of spatial disaggregation play some vital role in the further propagation of society as a whole and, more particularly, in the provision of differential reproduction needs. Let us examine this hypothesis, together with its specifically urban implications, by first of all making a brief historical detour. This detour involves a consideration of the role of residential space in the functioning of the nineteenth-century industrial city.

Socialization and reproduction problems in nineteenth-century cities
Without any doubt, the major problem faced by urban society in the early stages of capitalist development was the problem of the socialization and reproduction of the labour force as a whole. In the big manufacturing towns, squalid, crowded, and unhealthful living conditions [as described by scores of observers of the urban scene from Engels (1845; 1969 edition) to Mearns (1883; 1976 edition)] imposed a serious limit on the degree to which large sections of the industrial proletariat could be expected to supply effective labour-power for use within the ever growing and ever more technically evolving production system. So long as the factory system remained at a fairly rudimentary stage of development, the manifest intellectual and moral deficiencies of the labour force were of no great moment, and could in any case be fairly adequately countered by means of close supervision and strong disciplinary measures on the factory floor. In the course of time, however, as economic production processes steadily grew more complex and sophisticated, so the economy as a whole began to call on a much larger scale than hitherto for a labour force with certain minimal standards and skills: the ability to follow written instructions, the ability to work harmoniously in teams, the psychological ability to sustain intense levels of concentration, the ability to assume a certain measure of self-discipline, and so on. All this, however, presupposed a degree of general socialization (including a rudimentary education, together with effective ideological conformity to the exigencies of the labour process) that would certainly have largely been unrealizable within the framework of the decayed social and physical conditions that prevailed in many, if not the majority, of the working-class sections of large industrial towns towards the end of the eighteenth century and the beginning of the nineteenth. These conditions of course were also part and parcel of the problem of the subsistence wages that prevailed in the early stages of capitalist industrial development; but even towards the end of the

nineteenth century, when industrial wages began steadily to rise, there was no *necessary* equilibrium (nor is there even today) between the logic of the wages system as such, and the logic of reproduction. In short, it is essential that a certain number of intervening variables come into play before the wages earned in commodity production can be translated into labour-power that is useful in capitalistic terms. Among these intervening variables, living conditions ranks as being of the first importance.

The real practical importance of workers' living conditions and their effects on the development of capitalist production in the nineteenth century is evident in the early, faltering, and finally abortive experiments carried out by a handful of maverick capitalists who individually—and without being unduly self-conscious of the social logic of their actions— attempted to confront head-on the problems of socialization and reproduction among the industrial proletariat. These experiments consisted for the most part of company towns located well away from existing urban centres and harnessed to a single factory which provided the sole means of local employment. Examples of such experiments are to be found in the well-known cases of New Lanark, Saltaire, Ackroyden, Bourneville, and Port Sunlight, among many others. What these experiments made possible above all was the combination of ordered and healthful living conditions together with some measure of direct supervision and control over the labour force outside as well as inside the factory. Sir Titus Salt, who built Saltaire in the 1850s, not only provided a remarkably high quality of housing for his workers, but also such additional inducements to effective labour as a mechanics' institute, a public park, a hospital, bath houses, and churches galore; needless to say, the consumption of alcohol was resolutely discouraged in Saltaire by a total ban on public houses (cf Stewart, 1952). Even as late as 1914, Henry Ford in Detroit was intervening directly in the living arrangements of his workers in attempts to ensure that his generous five-dollar eight-hour day was being accurately translated into the kinds of mental and physical qualities necessary for a sustained cadence of teamwork on the assembly line. Flink (1975, page 89) writes of this phenomenon:

> "A staff of over thirty investigators ... visited workers' homes gathering information and giving advice on the intimate details of the family budget, diet, living arrangements, recreation, social outlook and morality .... The worker who refused to learn English, rejected the advice of the investigator, gambled, drank excessively, or was found guilty of any malicious practice derogatory to good physical manhood or moral character was disqualified from the five dollar wage and put on probation."

In spite of these experiments, and in spite of the evident success of some of them, it was clear that attempted solutions to the problems of socialization and reproduction among urban industrial workers by means of individual company towns and individual capitalist initiative could work only in very special circumstances. In the first place, the economy as a whole could never operate effectively if it were to be widely dispersed across the landscape; the cost of transporting interindustry inputs and outputs (combined with the positive agglomeration effects that become available when industries cluster together in geographical space) made it imperative for most individual producers to concentrate together in large manufacturing towns. In the second place, so long as production (hence reproduction) was by and large concentrated in existing urban centres, few individual capitalists could be expected to attempt unilaterally to improve the living conditions of their workers, for in the absence of an effective monopoly over the benefits of any such attempt, it would only have provided, via the collective labour pool, an expensive positive spillover effect for other and more cautious capitalists to exploit. For the vast majority of capitalists, then, private solutions to the reproduction problem were neither economically, administratively, nor politically feasible.

What in fact occurred was that a collective solution to urban residential problems was gradually, laboriously, and in large part spontaneously pieced together over the second half of the nineteenth century out of lessons learned from a mass of particular experiments and social explorations. It was a solution that radically transformed the living environment of the city; and it was underpinned and motivated by the piecemeal, but continual and effective intervention of the State, which, in Britain, for example, towards the end of the nineteenth century, began to pass copious amounts of legislation on matters of urban design, public health, building regulations, housing conditions, slum clearance, commuter transport services, and so on. Thus, as Harvey (1976) has so clearly shown, there gradually came into being an ideology of urban living (sustained by steady improvements in the quality of general urban conditions) involving a complex of such sociocultural traits as widespread aspirations to individual homeownership, the quest for healthful and satisfying residential environments, particularly in the newly developing suburbs, and the general promotion of a sense of belonging and community. This is, in part, what Walker (1978) has called "the suburban solution", and, as such, it sustained above all the functional viability of the emerging white-collar fraction of the labour force. But the solution as a whole in fact went far beyond the development of suburban life and culture, for it also involved widespread and dramatic improvements in housing conditions in inner city areas, with concomitant socially desirable impacts upon the quality and character of the urban proletariat that continued predominantly to inhabit those areas.

Unquestionably, the unfolding of these developments was largely a matter of trial and error, or, rather, a matter of a historical logic that was mediated by various social and political practices through a complex sequence of stages. As each potential line of social choice made itself apparent, so it was discovered, in social terms, to be a significant factor (or not) in the satisfaction and concretization of latent historically determinate needs. Thus streetcar suburbs, commuter railways, slum clearances, municipal housing schemes, the City Beautiful Movement, the urban parks movement, land-use zoning, garden cities, landscaped suburbs, and so on, came forward—each in its turn—as a potential contribution to the overall solution, and was then exploited or allowed to fade away as it proved itself in practice to be a meaningful or a merely fanciful response to the perplexing problems of socialization and reproduction in capitalist cities towards the end of the nineteenth century and the beginning of the twentieth. And workers, recognizing their own immediate self-interests, that is, their historically determinate needs, were by and large willing participants in the installation of each viable element of the solution as it made its historical appearance. Hence, around the turn of the century, there gradually came into existence a composite urban environment that made possible the emergence of a new kind of labour force, and that, in particular, reinforced the distillation and internalization of those psychological and ideological habits necessary for the successful prosecution of the more advanced and complex stage of capitalism that was beginning to make its appearance. This environment constitutes (then and now) a significant component part of the general process whereby the individual worker (whether white-collar or blue-collar) acquires 'market capacity', which is to say, that bundle of social and mental attributes (education, skills, personal appearance and conduct, etc) that looms so large in the determination of the exchange value of labour-power in modern capitalist society.

The role of urban neighbourhoods
In the light of this historical digression, let us now return to our main argument and consider more systematically the role of urban neighbourhoods within the reproduction process. The preceding discussion has suggested that there is a direct and powerful connection between the physical qualities of the urban environment and the functional effectiveness of the urban labour force. As important and real as this connection may be, however, it is only finally potentiated after a certain number of secondary events have come into play. Above all, the physical attributes of the urban environment are fully appropriatable as finished use values in the production of labour-power only after they are complemented by the emergence of *distinctive and socially uniform residential neighbourhoods.* The use values are yet further enhanced by the tendency of urban residential neighbourhoods to exhibit (though not without notable exceptions) qualities of social stability and harmony, cultural homogeneity, and intracommunity association. In large degree, then, the slow evolution of the realized historical solution to the problems of socialization and reproduction in the urban environment has been strongly contingent upon

the predominantly spontaneous tendency of distinctive neighbourhoods to disaggregate out in urban space.

Urban neighbourhoods, as such, function as foci of socialization and reproduction in three quite distinctive senses: (1) they help to underpin the rearing and nurturing of children in socially functional ways; (2) they facilitate the development of active networks of social and ideological relationships among groups of individuals with similar life experiences and life expectations; and (3) they signal and in turn partly determine a particular level of social status. I will briefly consider the meaning and urban consequences of each of these three points in turn.

In the first place, then, urban neighbourhoods perform a definite function in the process of socializing children into specific social fractions. The local residential context surrounds children with an everyday environment that sustains the ideological orientations, identity, and behavioural peculiarities of the dominant neighbourhood group. Socialization is further reinforced by children's peer groups (confirming values inculcated in the home) and, particularly in North America, by the local school system. Typically, indeed, neighbourhood schools in North America are characterized by curricula that directly express local socialization imperatives: programmes that are open to such issues as self-awareness, personal effectiveness in small groups, 'creativity', etc, in white-collar neighbourhoods; programmes that are more resolutely focussed on hard-core utilitarian education in working-class neighbourhoods. The general findings of Kohn (1969; 1977 edition) on the interrelations between occupational status and group norms further clarify the social meaning of these observations. Kohn has shown in elaborate detail how the nature of the work tasks performed by individuals translate into specific kinds of value systems which in turn have a powerful impact on child-rearing aims and practices. On the one hand, individuals with high social status (white-collar workers employed in nonroutine jobs that are free from close supervision) tend to put a high premium on those child-rearing procedures and environmental cues that encourage responsibility and self-direction in their children. On the other hand, individuals with low social status (blue-collar workers employed in routine jobs that are generally closely supervised) tend to put a high premium on those child-rearing procedures and environmental cues that encourage conformity to external authority in their children. These various socialization objectives are sustained by neighbourhoods via their definite (though always imperfectly secured) tendency to social uniformity and the concomitant ideological homogenization of local schools, peer groups, friends and neighbours, social networks, and so on. As factorial ecology makes clear, white-collar families (and, to a somewhat lesser extent, blue-collar families) seek to secure their child-rearing objectives by moving out to appropriate suburban neighbourhoods. In such neighbourhoods, effectively removed from the continual land-use conflicts and social breakdowns that occur in the central city, the socialization and nurturing of children proceed under especially favourable environmental conditions.

In the second place, neighbourhoods contain within themselves significant networks of social interaction and information. Such networks help to maintain a pattern of overall cultural homogeneity, just as they help to produce and reinforce socially useful attitudes and points of view. They appear to be of especial importance in working-class and ethnic neighbourhoods where they function as the basis of an informal system of mutual aid and support, in struggling through periods of hardship, in finding jobs, in confronting officialdom, and so on. This role of local neighbourhood networks is of major significance in ethnic neighbourhoods, whose inhabitants are invariably at a particular disadvantage relative to the rest of society by reason of their race, language, or culture.

In the third place, and in part as a corollary of the preceding two points, urban neighbourhoods play an important role as tokens and as sources of social status. Urban residential space acts as a sort of variegated semiological code (cf Krampen, 1979), which, like other similar codes (dress, life-style, habits of speech, behavioural patterns, and the rest) signifies the social position and market capacity of different individuals, depending on their appropriation of various elements of that code. Certain elements of the code also help to legitimate privileged social positions in that they imbue those positions with a ready-made mystique. In the same way, the differentiated semiological quality of urban residential space, as intangible as it may at first appear to be, is of the first importance in a society like that of North America today. Here, in the almost total absence of residues of precapitalist superstructural forms and conventions, overt expression of personal success and accomplishment, here and now, is always taken as the most convincing gauge of any individual's worth and standing. Hence, the permanent, constant, and endemic anxiety in North American society about the acquisition of status symbols as the outward signifiers of personal merit. By the same token, for white-collar middle-class fractions, place and quality of residence (the 'desirability' of local neighbourhoods), are of the utmost importance.

In each of these ways, neighbourhoods ease the process of socialization, enhance the efficiency and effectiveness of reproduction, and help to sustain the exchange value of different categories of labour. In view of these positive uses of urban neighbourhoods, it is scarcely surprising that various social groups tend to form distinctive geographical entities in the urban land nexus in a struggle—that is always more or less imperfect, however—to secure for themselves an exclusive stretch of territory and hence to generate a maximum possible realization of those positive uses. In this way, a somewhat restless hierarchy of urban neighbourhoods—white-collar, working-class, ethnic, etc—comes into being, first as an expression of the social division of labour, and second as an expression of concomitant socialization and reproduction needs. Once established, these neighbourhoods are extremely durable so long as they are left undisturbed by outside forces; but they are also remarkably fragile once any disruptive element makes its appearance. This paradoxical quality of urban neighbourhoods is well illustrated by certain inner city blue-collar neighbourhoods that on the one hand continue to exist long after the industries that provided the basic livelihood of their inhabitants have migrated out to the periphery of the city, and that, on the other hand, are destroyed almost overnight once intrusive land-use redevelopments begin to alter the established pattern of community living. In passing, it is worth remarking that white-collar communities in North America have amply protected themselves from such disruption—including disruption due to encroachments of working-class and ethnic families—through the deployment of powerful exclusionary zoning devices.

7.3 Reproduction space: the problem as a whole

The view developed here of the structure and functions of urban neighbourhoods has little relationship to the neoclassical economic theory of housing choices that simply evades the problem by reducing it directly to a question of exogenously given tastes and preferences. Nor does it accord with the romantic and utopian vision of community living as evoked, for example, by many manipulated-city theorists in their more positive and optimistic moments. On the contrary, the historical process of the formation of residential space is the outcome of a set of structured imperatives reflecting the evolution of commodity-producing society generally. Hence, the historical emergence of the classical pattern of low-density white-collar communities in the suburbs and high-density working-class and ethnic communities in central city areas in North America has not been the result of some presumed *a priori* marginal propensity of managerial and bureaucratic strata to substitute living space for accessibility to the centre, balanced by the assumed countervailing tendency of blue-collar workers to prefer accessibility to living space. The emergence of this pattern has been the result of the confluence of two main structurally determined tendencies: on the one hand, a building and construction process that unfailingly gives rise to extensive low-density land-use developments on the periphery of the urban system and to intensive high-density land-use developments towards the centre; and, on the other hand, (a) the preemption by managerial and bureaucratic strata of that portion of urban living space that has lent itself preeminently to transformation in conformity with the ideology of quasi-natural and secluded urban living that began first to appear towards the end of the nineteenth century as a reflection of the reproduction needs of those strata, combined with (b) the consequent concentration of blue-collar workers in inner city areas close to centres of industrial employment in the core. This basic pattern of social segregation was then boosted to a high level of rigidity and yet further internal differentiation by the gradual institutionalization (in school systems, zoning ordinances, urban design criteria, housing provision, etc) of the differential socialization imperatives proper to each group. In the same way the incipient restructuring of this pattern as a consequence of the recent and evidently accelerating migration of white-collar workers to inner city neighbourhoods, and of blue-collar workers to the suburbs is not the outcome of some self-determinate change in basic preference functions but is, once more, a response to deeply rooted changes in the architectonics of the urban system. Lastly, in continental Europe, a land development process similar to that which prevails in North America, but a rather different urban history (see chapter 10 below), produced a situation that is in many cases precisely the reverse of the situation in North America, for in many continental European cities, the classical pattern of land use is one that is characterized by high-density middle-class communities near the centre and low-density working-class communities in the suburbs. Whatever their specific locational pattern, however, urban residential communities represent functional organic entities, held together by significant positive external effects reflecting concrete reproduction imperatives set in motion by the capitalist mode of production.

7.4 Circulation space

The spaces in which production and reproduction take place in the modern city are tied together as a functional geographic whole—the urban land nexus—by a third kind of space reserved for the purposes of circulation. In contemporary capitalist society, this latter type of space is for the most part (for reasons that will be discussed in the next chapter) controlled by the State, and this means that basic urban transport networks and equipment are supplied largely out of public funds. Then, in reaction to public investments in circulation space, various spontaneous and privatized responses are triggered off among firms, households, and landowners in the rest of urban space. Obviously, the most important function of the urban transport system is to sustain the various spatial connections between and within production space and reproduction space. However, and in view of the opening remarks above, urban transport may also be seen as a major interface in the urban land nexus between a public realm as represented by the actions of the State, and a private realm as represented by the behaviour of innumerable individual firms, households, and landowners. In this sense, analysis of urban transport as a specifically private–public interface provides some significant clues as to the outlines of a putative urban political economy. Urban transport, in short, has powerful differential impacts on various social *interests* in urban space, while it is at the same time deeply rooted in the whole process of the production and reproduction of capitalist society generally. Clarification of the nature of this public–private interface is of considerable significance and interest, not only in its own right, but also for the light that it sheds on the problem of public goods provision generally in capitalist society, for urban transport is in the end only a special case of all politically furnished goods and services (such as schools, parks, postal service, public housing, street lighting, and so on). It is, however, a special case that is of overwhelming importance in the urban context, for it is the essential medium that integrates the urban land nexus (a system of differential locational advantages) into a functioning totality. Thus, no special apology seems to be required for singling out the urban transport sector for special treatment here, although only a very partial analysis will be attempted in what follows. In its functional role as a system of spatial linkages and interactions urban transport is already exhaustively treated in the literature which covers in great detail such problems as modal-split patterns, the journey to work, route layout and alignment, etc; and given, in addition, the rather formalistic qualities of these problems, they need not concern us unduly in this account, important though they may be in strictly practical terms. Instead, the treatment of circulation space that follows is concerned above all with the perplexing problem of the social and urban dynamic that flows from the situation of the transport process at the critical interface between a public realm and a private realm in the urban land nexus.

This public-private interface can be most effectively described in terms of the set of relationships sketched out in figure 7.2. This figure makes immediately clear the position of the urban transport system at the point of interchange between the public appropriations of the State on the one hand, and the private appropriations of firms, workers, and landowners on the other hand. At particular issue here are the interconnected questions as to how the State organizes, runs, and finances urban transport, and how

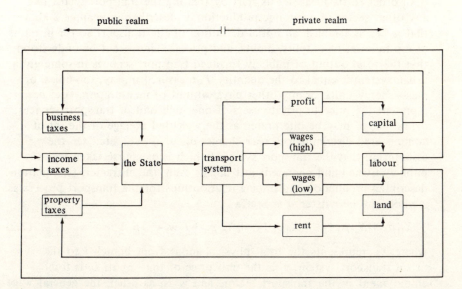

Figure 7.2. Framework for a political economy of urban transport.

private agents in urban space manage to secure for themselves derivative benefits. More generally expressed, the problem is to elucidate the role of urban transport in the determination of both the magnitude and the distribution of net urban income. Remark at the outset that the State imposes taxes on the total net income generated by commodity production; that is, the State imposes differential taxes on profits, wages, and rents, thus diminishing these quantities. These taxes are then spent on the provision and subsidization of urban transport services (among other public goods). Then, as the effects of these transport services are mediated through urban markets in commodities, labour, and land, so they are differentially capitalized in the form of increments (or decrements) to profits, wages, and rents. In this manner, the urban transport system plays a significant and highly complex role in the distribution and redistribution of income shares to firms, workers, and owners of land. As a corollary, the State, as the agency that controls the underlying configuration of the urban transport process, becomes itself a significant secondary circuit of appropriation of net income shares in addition to the primary circuit as represented by the market mechanism in its pristine form. Notwithstanding the ambiguities and complexities of the role of the State in this regard, its inner meaning is expressed in the continuing, if not escalating, urban political conflicts (in the form of clashes with the State apparatus) that break out periodically in large metropolitan regions over various types of transport issues. In order to understand the bases of such conflicts, let us examine in more detail some of the descriptive details of this secondary circuit of appropriation as it manifests itself in the urban transport system.

In order to fix ideas, let us start by treating the transport sector like any other sector of economic production as described in chapter 2 above; that is, let us establish an initial definition of the transport sector in terms of a simple set of outputs, inputs, and prices. Thus, let it be understood that the total output of publicly financed transport services in some given urban system is equal to the quantity T, measured in, say, ton-miles, or mass-energy units, or any other physical unit of mensuration. Let p_t represent the price to private users of one such unit of transport services; or, rather, p_t may be interpreted as the weighted average of the set of administered discriminatory user charges $p'_t, p''_t, p'''_t, ...,$ etc. On the assumption that the transport system (which is of course taken to be publicly owned and operated) just breaks even, the characteristic equation describing production and pricing relationships for the transport process as a whole can be written à la Sraffa

$$X_{1t}p_1 + X_{2t}p_2 + ... + X_{it}p_i + ... + X_{nt}p_n + L_t w = Tp_t , \qquad (7.2)$$

where X_{it} represents the total physical input from branch i to the urban transport system, p_i is the unit price of that input, L_t is total employment in the transport sector, and w is, as usual, the general wage rate. There is of course no rate of profit on the aggregate capital outlay

$X_{1t}p_1 + X_{2t}p_2 + ... + X_{it}p_i + ... + X_{nt}p_n$. Undoubtedly, a more common situation than that represented by equation (7.2) is the case where the State runs the transport system at a loss and makes up the deficit out of a public subsidy. Ultimately, this subsidy must come out of profits, wages, and rents (however indirectly), and it can be expressed as the equation

$$S = \phi_1(\text{profits}) + \phi_2(\text{wages}) + \phi_3(\text{rents}) , \qquad (7.3)$$

where S is the magnitude of the subsidy, and ϕ_1, ϕ_2, and ϕ_3 are rates at which profits, wages, and rents are taxed, respectively, in order to finance the transport system. The characteristic equation describing the economic structure of the transport sector can now be rewritten

$$X_{it}p_1 + X_{2t}p_2 + ... + X_{it}p_i + ... + X_{nt}p_n + L_t w - S = Tp_t , \qquad (7.4)$$

and in this way, the subsidy, S, is translated into a diminished general transport rate p_t. Concomitantly, complex readjustments will begin to take place in production space and reproduction space as the collective decisions of the State are assimilated, via transport prices, into urban commodity markets, labour markets, and land markets. These readjustments will in turn be translated into differential changes in the final levels of profits, wages, and rents. In what follows, a simplified analysis of these differential changes is undertaken by examining the static relationships between profits, wages, and rents on the one hand, and public investment in the transport sector on the other hand; that is, in this analysis, and for simplicity of exposition, all locational variables are held (artificially) constant.

First, then, transport investments and subsidies on the part of the State tend to increase the normal rate of profit by socializing certain basic costs of production. Specifically, improvements in urban transport (a) reduce the final costs of all inputs to the commodity-production process, (b) increase the velocity of circulation of commodities, and (c) reduce the costs of the journey to work thus tending to hold back wage rates. At the same time, because of the dynamics of the equalization of the rate of profit, any transport benefit that tends directly to increase profits in any one branch of production will also tend indirectly to increase profits in all branches of production. Moreover, this effect will not be confined to any one urban centre but will flow over into all cities within the national territory. Mandel (1975, pages 92-93) expresses the mechanism underlying this process in the following terms:

"Capital will relinquish the branches with lower rates of profit and flow into branches with a higher rate. There over-production and over-accumulation will take place, lowering market prices and suppressing surplus-profits, while the branches which have suffered a drain of capital will no longer be able wholly to supply socially effective demand at current output. Market prices in the latter sectors will thus rise again. Equalization of the rate of profit will be the result."

As a consequence of this mechanism, a simple and rather mild policy deduction suggests that to the degree that the rate of profit is indeed increased by some specific transport investment, then to the same degree (at least) should that investment be defrayed out of national business taxes. Even so, in the absence of any sort of adequate urban accounts data, including data that fully report on the rate of profit, such a principle would be exceedingly difficult to operationalize. It is also undoubtedly universally infringed in practice.

Second, public investments in the transport sector tend, in the short run at least, to increase the rate of real wages by reducing personal transport costs, thus leaving workers with an augmented residual money wage. It would seem, however, that this effect is unlikely to be durable over the long run. On the one hand, in a labour market that still retains some degree of competitiveness, decreases in personal transport costs are almost certain to induce a corresponding long-run diminution in wage rates, or, what amounts to the same thing in an inflationary climate, a corresponding diminution in the rate of increase of money wages. On the other hand, reductions in personal transport costs are quite definitely liable to give rise directly to increases in residential land rents. These contentions mean further that public subsidization of commuter transport is in all probability only an indirect means of ultimately subsidizing firms and landowners. If true, these propositions signify that that favourite shibboleth of urban reformers—free public transport—is in fact an infinitely less progressive policy goal than may at first appear to be the case. It is unprogressive, at least, so long as it is advocated in isolation from certain more encompassing and ambitious policy goals that recognize something of the nature of the problem; these goals would include, at the minimum, free transit on a transport system that is maintained strictly out of earmarked business and property taxes.

As Frankena (1973) has shown, the urban transport process also induces very significant intercommunity and interpersonal transfers of income as a consequence of imbalances between taxes and fares paid by various social groups and the burden of use that they lay on urban transport services. These transfers lie in the background of, and in turn contribute to, an ongoing pattern of territorially based conflicts in the modern metropolis. Nowhere are these conflicts more apparent than in the long-standing and smouldering contentions between inner city and suburban communities over the financing (and the environmental consequences) of intraurban expressway systems.

Third, public investments in urban transport almost certainly tend to benefit landowners more than any other social group. Whenever improvements in urban transport infrastructure and services bring about an augmentation of the total set of differential locational advantages in the city, then the general and universal response is an increase in land rents.

The persistence and ubiquity of this response are attested to by the widespread land speculation and redevelopment that are commonly sparked off well in advance of any actual anticipated programme of transport improvement. As a consequence of the tendency of public investments in urban transport eventually to filter out in the form of land rent, the beneficial social effects of public expenditures on the urban transport system are siphoned off time and again into the pockets of landowners, and potentially progressive outlays of public funds (outlays that promise either to increase real wages or to lower prices) are continually deflected from their main aim. In North American cities in particular, the property tax fails notoriously to recapture the unearned increments that persistently accrue to landed property. Thus, in that specific circuit of appropriation which represents the transformation of public funds into privately requisitioned land rent, there appears once more, in one of its most overtly irrational forms, that wider inconsistency in capitalist society generally between the socially interdependent structure of all production, and the privatized but differential nature of appropriation.

In these various ways, among others, the circle between State expenditures on the urban transport system and final profits, wages, and rents, is closed. Nevertheless, an unstable historical dynamic underlies this process; for, as the total surplus produced in urban space is to an ever increasing degree distributed and redistributed by means of political decisions (in matters of transport development as in the supply of public goods generally) so there emerges a concomitant political crisis of urban life. It is a crisis that seems as yet to possess only a diffuse and embryonic form, though the signs of it are clearly apparent in the repoliticization of urban planning at large that has been steadily occurring in North America and Western Europe over the last few decades. As will be shown at a later stage, it is a crisis that is part and parcel of the overall legitimation crisis of the late capitalist State. It is a crisis that follows inevitably upon the historical demystification of social and political relations as the State—the *visible* hand—finds itself ever more deeply involved in the intermediation of the variegated rewards and penalties of individual existence within capitalism. In this process, urban planning, as lived and practical human activity, is rendered transparent, its apologetic camouflage (in the guise of idealist-utopian discourses) dissolved in the daily confrontations between planners and citizens, and its central political meaning revealed.

From both this and the preceding chapter, it is apparent that the urban land nexus represents an extremely complex and multifaceted organism. This organism consists of a hierarchy of activities, locations, spaces, and relationships that extends from individual units of capital and labour at the lowest level, through the aggregate phenomena represented by production space, reproduction space, and circulation space, and forming an integrated urban totality whose ultimate roots are discoverable in the capitalist mode of production at large. In the chapter that follows, the global dynamics of this complex organism will be scrutinized in some detail. It will be shown, in particular, that the urban land nexus, as it makes its historical appearance out of the system of capitalist social and property relations, is inherently unstable, and is permanently vulnerable to its own self-engendered deliquescence. Out of this endemic urban predicament emerges urban planning, that is, a species of collective decisionmaking and action whose function it is to preserve the urban land nexus from the consequences of its own congenital susceptibility to internal decay.

8
The urban land nexus and the State

The composite logic of the urban land nexus flows out of the intersection of three specific spheres of human action and social development. In the first place, the logic of the urban land nexus is in part an expression of the spontaneous decisionmaking calculus of private firms and households in urban space. This decisionmaking calculus is structured by the social and property relations of capitalist society. It leads to uniquely problematical outcomes that call directly for collective intervention. In the second place, then, the logic of the urban land nexus is in part an expression of the rationality of collective political decisionmaking. This rationality reflects the global orientations, biases, and imperatives of the capitalist State as it finds itself inextricably involved in the tasks of managing and attempting to resolve the urban land-use problems set in motion by private decisionmakers. In the third place, the interaction of these two instances—the private and the public—in capitalist urban society gives rise to a field of evolving, but problematical land-use relationships in urban space. Out of this field of relationships grows the specific historical dynamic of the urban land nexus.

The present chapter represents an attempt to reveal the overall historical dynamic of the urban land nexus by describing in systematic terms (a) the crisis-ridden effects of private land-use decisions in relation to the global framework of capitalist society, (b) the consequent character of collective urban intervention, and (c) the ineluctable dilemmas that run through the dynamic reciprocal relations between the private and the public instances in the urban land nexus. This description now opens with an overview of the general process of urbanization within a system of capitalist social and property relations.

8.1 Urbanization in capitalist society
Recall that in the introduction to this book it was affirmed that there is one and only one sense in which an *urban question* can be posed in any other than eclectic and omnibus terms: that is, as a question that is addressed to the dynamics and mutual interrelations of land-contingent phenomena in urban space. From this point of view, poverty, inflation, racism, etc, are *not* urban issues, though they are widely conceived of as such; conversely, the location of industry, the spatial pattern of residential neighbourhoods, the structure of the transport process, and so on, are by their very nature urban issues. They are urban precisely because they play a direct and intrinsic role within the complex of differential locational advantages that is the essence of the city as such. This proposition is in itself based upon a conceptualization of the urban instance (the urban land nexus) as a social artefact that is reducible in the final analysis to a land base consisting of a network of spatial interrelationships. Thus, the urban

land nexus is something quite different from land in its primordial form as a physicochemical entity capable of yielding up agricultural and mineral products. In this sense, the urban land nexus cannot be rigidly delimited in territorial terms but can only be seen as simply fading asymptotically and indefinitely away as distance from its centre of gravity increases. In short, it is less a circumscribable concrete *object* than it is a theoretical construct (but also an arena of political struggle) that poses in dramatic form the urban question in capitalism. This question constitutes a complex of problems that can neither be broken down into a series of more detailed modules, nor made to vanish by osmosis into some wider system of propositions, except at the cost of a vast loss of content and analytical richness. We may at this point begin to identify some of the dynamics of urban phenomena in their specifically land-contingent form by elucidating their distinctive interdependencies within the broad structure of capitalist society.

The production of the urban land nexus

Only in the most primitive and residual sense can the urban land nexus be considered to be composed of raw land. More importantly, as already indicated, it is land that has been built over and used in various ways. It is land on which human beings have expended labour materialized in the form of structural and infrastructural artefacts. It is, in short, a phenomenon that is *socially produced* in a complex dynamic that is in the first instance reducible to two principal phases involving two different modalities of human decisionmaking and action that are different in kind from one another, and, in many ways, incompatible with one another. In one phase of this dynamic, private firms and households develop, exchange, and utilize urban land in conformity with their particular historically determinate motives. In another phase, the State provides elaborate networks of material and immaterial infrastructures that underpin the general processes of production and reproduction with a basic geographical ossature. The combined outcomes of these two phases of the process of land development then give rise to the urban land nexus as a finished use value, that is, as a composite system of *differential locational advantages*, representing, as Topalov (1973) has put it, the "useful effects of urban agglomeration".
In spite of the fact that these useful effects are produced as a result of the aggregate actions of many individual firms and households, together with the political intervention of the State, they are nevertheless finally capitalized for the most part in the form of privately appropriated land rents.

Urban land, then, is *produced* in an intricate communal process. In the one phase of the process, land-use outcomes are the result of the purely private cost-benefit calculations of individual firms and households. This phase is unplanned as a whole, and socially undecidable at the outset. In the other phase, land-use outcomes are the result of the political calculations of the State, which exerts direct control over the quality, location, and timing of urban public works. This second phase is, in principle at least, susceptible to implementation in conformity with general *social* costs and benefits. However, in commodity-producing society (a society in which private decisionmaking is one of the basic conditions of existence of the core structures), it is the first phase that dominates the urban land development process—both as cause and as effect—while the land-use interventions of the State are permanently reduced in practice to rounds of reactive, piecemeal, and palliative 'planning'. From this it follows inevitably that the urban land development process as a whole in capitalism is anarchical, and leads persistently to outcomes that are neither intended nor socially decided. In the light of this manifest urban dynamic we may ask, what social logic structures the mutual interactions of civil society and the State in the production of the general land-use system?

Private and public decisionmaking in the urban land nexus
In previous chapters of this book, an argument has been repeatedly put forward against any attempt to posit the city (the urban land nexus) as a thing-in-itself, or as an 'independent variable'. In fact, of course, urban society is genetically embedded within the structure of capitalist society generally. Urban reality does not derive its various observable characteristics from some autonomous 'urbanism' (in the manner of the Chicago School of urban sociology, for example) but from the global social, economic, and cultural forces and arrangements that make up the totality of capitalist society. It has already been pointed out several times that this notion is not intended to imply that the urban question is an empty question, directly reducible to the question of capitalist social structure generally; nor is it intended to imply that urban phenomena do not generate a degree of restructuring of the very social and property relations that envelop them. What is meant here is that the urban land nexus can only be effectively comprehended to the extent that it can be accurately located within the sociohistorical totality of which it is inextricably a part. Specifically, the internal dynamics of the urban system are in the end direct, but highly distinctive, transformations and intermediations of the social and property relations of the capitalist mode of production generally. As an immediate consequence of this circumstance, one of the prime observable characteristics of the capitalist urbanization process is the salient and two-faceted phenomenon that (a) although individual firms and households exert substantial private control over the development, exchange, and utilization of urban land, nevertheless, (b) none has control over the global outcomes that emerge from this circumstance. This observation immediately raises two major points that are of prime significance in the clarification of the dynamics of the urban land nexus. The first of these points is concerned with the logical structure of the private decisionmaking process that leads to such wayward consequences in the urban land nexus. The second is

concerned with the nature of the collective political response that is concomitantly brought into play.

The domain of private decisionmaking in the urban land nexus
The historic project of capitalism foresaw in private property and freedom of exchange the best basis and guarantee of social equilibrium and concord via the privatized, decentralized decisionmaking of individual holders of resource units. Urban reality, like social reality generally, has turned out somewhat differently. Thus, whereas individual firms and households have always had, and continue to have—in spite of the existence of land-use controls of various sorts—the formal legal right to develop, exchange, and utilize land, they can never be sure that in exercising these rights they will secure, or maximize, their private interests, for the success of any land-use decision is always dependent (via the system of differential locational advantages) upon the uncontrollable outcomes of innumerable other private decisions. This evident discrepancy between the existence of formal legal rights in capitalist society to private land-use control, and the actual absence of real private control over the aggregate outcomes of any specific decision, is so familiar a paradox of the contemporary urban scene that it is frequently taken in mainstream urban theory to be an immutable, universal feature of the urban process, and is reified into various versions of the 'decisionmaking under uncertainty' predicament. This conception only confounds the issue, however. For the discrepancy outlined above, so far from being some transhistorical essence of the urbanization process, is the consequence of historically specific, and hence mutable, social relationships as realized in the urban context. Furthermore, the discrepancy between individual control over particular land-use outcomes and the innately system-wide contingency of those outcomes is not simply a discrepancy between two separate and independent domains of reality. On the contrary, the contingency of land-use outcomes in capitalist cities is the direct result of the existence of private, legal control. In brief, *precisely because urban land development is privately controlled, the final aggregate outcomes of this process are necessarily and paradoxically out of control.*

Now, neoclassical urban theory of course denies or underplays the existence of inherent disequilibria in the urban land nexus. It affirms that the myriad private decisions of landowners and land users are in practice and in principle coordinated by an autoregulating market mechanism which ensures that economic order is preserved in urban society. In this hypothetical world, social equilibrium is seen as emerging directly out of the self-interested decisions and actions of innumerable individual firms and households. Equilibrium is reached where firms have attained to maximally efficient levels of output in the sense that marginal cost is everywhere equated to price, and where individual households have attained to an optimal rate of consumption such that the ratio of the marginal utilities ascribed to any pair of consumption items (including housing) is equal to the ratio of the prices of the same two items. The whole system is assumed to be held together and coordinated by a derivative system of price signals. The consequence of all this, in theory at least, is a tendency to economic stability, high levels of productivity, and efficiency in resource allocation, where the term *efficiency* signifies a situation in which increases in the production of some desired goods and services (housing, transport, parks, etc, in the present instance) are not possible except at the cost of decreases in the production of other desired goods and services. There is only a limited sense, however, in which processes of these kinds can be read off from the structure of contemporary urban reality. On the contrary, the very existence of exchange relations in the urban land nexus produces a concomitant tendency for the urban system to fall into a spiral of self-disorganizing outcomes. That is, and as will be demonstrated in considerable detail below, the market allocation of urban land to competing uses in capitalism must undermine whatever proclivities may otherwise exist in the direction of stability, high levels of productivity, and efficiency. Precisely because urban land is privately appropriated, exchanged, and utilized, and yet can never be produced or consumed in discrete packages like tons of wheat or yards of cloth, but is replete with locational interdependencies that consistently evade the integrative logic of the market, the urban land nexus is endemically susceptible to deviations from even so mild a criterion of efficiency as that defined above. Beneath the apparent short-run order of individual decisionmaking and market outcomes in the urban land nexus, there is discoverable (as will be shown) an omnipresent long-run tendency to decomposition and deterioration. Out of this tendency emerges a series of specific human struggles and conflicts that is superimposed upon and intersects with the wider political dynamic within capitalism as a general structure.

The domain of collective decisionmaking in the urban land nexus
The institutions of private property, freedom of contract and association, and market exchange represent fundamental elements of the system of capitalist social and property relations. As a corollary, individual decisionmaking and action precede—analytically as well as historically—collective forms of behaviour within the capitalist mode of production. However, individual decisionmaking and action are impotent as instruments for dealing with the many necessary tasks of social control that crop up within capitalism generally and within the urban land nexus in particular. Hence a second, and derivative modality of human action is called into being. *Collective action*, that is, makes its necessary historical appearance in capitalist society as a means of occupying and resolving the interstitial decisionmaking imperatives left open by the self-limiting and, indeed, self-negating logic of private action. Collective action, in short, attacks social problems and predicaments that lie well beyond the accessible range of the active potential of private decisionmakers, but whose resolution is crucial for

the continued success and viability of the capitalist system. Concomitantly, collective action seeks to resolve the specific problems created by private decisionmaking and action, and to steer society as a whole into collectively rational options—consistent with existing social and property relations—that are not attainable by private action alone. Above all, and in historically specific terms, collective action is engendered by the peculiar circumstance that the central privatistic kernel of capitalist society—commodity production—with its unique responsiveness to price signals, profitability criteria, and market competition has never in the end been able to provide all the conditions (in the realms of both production and reproduction) necessary for its own existence. Therefore, collective action emerges as a historical and structural necessity, as an instrumentality that is capable of producing in a *noncommodity form* vital goods and services that lie outside of the sphere of operation of the capitalistic logic of private decisionmaking and action.

Collective action, however, is subsequent to the institutional arrangements and habits of civil society. This means, in turn, that *urban planning* must be seen initially as an intermediation of the structure of capitalism generally but, more explicitly, as a response to the specific land-use dilemmas and conflicts created by firms and households as they interact with one another in urban space. It is of some importance to stress, as is done here, this primary genetic dependence of urban planning on the dynamics of the urban land nexus, precisely because so many of the currently influential writers of the French school of urban sociology (for example, Castells and Godard, 1974; Lipietz, 1974; Lojkine, 1977; Preteceille, 1973; and others) persistently describe the city as though it were nothing more than an inert locale, lacking in itself any real specificity or laws of development, and representing simply a *place* in which the grand events of the class struggle are played out in the raw. Important as these events may be in an ultimate sense, they alone can never reveal the origins and peculiar properties of urban planning in capitalism. Before the logic of State intervention in the urban land nexus can be fully disclosed, it is essential to adduce precisely the realm of discourse that Castells and Godard, Lipietz, Lojkine, Preteceille, and the rest have simply conjured away, namely an *urban science* that is unerringly focussed on the dynamics of the urban land nexus *qua* a system of dense differential locational advantages.

Plan of the succeeding discussion
In earlier chapters, an attempt has been made to describe some of the basic elements of just such a science. In what follows now, this discussion will be complemented by a demonstration of the inherently problematical and ill-behaved qualities of the urban land nexus. The argument proceeds along three main fronts. First, it is shown how various general and extra-urban breakdowns in production and reproduction relations (for example, the monopolization of certain branches of production, or the failure of the

wages system to secure adequate levels of housing, health care, and so on) induce the State to provide a basic network of public goods, or noncommodities, in urban space. This level of State intervention constitutes one of the cornerstones of urban planning in practice, though it does not yet constitute urban planning in its final entirety. Second, it is shown how private land-use decisions (themselves partial effects of the State's provision of a basic network of public goods in urban space) lead to diverse urban problems and conflicts. Third, it is shown how urban planning, in its full and definitive sense, emerges as a response to these problems and conflicts, and how it, in turn, leads to yet further problematical outcomes in contemporary urban society.

8.2 Production in the noncommodity form: extraurban imperatives and intraurban consequences

The management of production and reproduction relations

In capitalist society, the necessity for collective action is satisfied for the most part, though not without exception, by the State. For example, in addition to the State, certain types of organizations, such as labour unions, business cartels, trade associations, social clubs, and so on, also accomplish *specific* sorts of collective tasks in capitalist society. Only the State, however, concerns itself with the *general* collective task of ensuring the viability of capitalism as a whole; and, hence, only the State as the agent of general social imperatives represents fully the condensation of all the contradictions of capitalist society. It is necessary to add that only the State possesses the requisite instruments whereby the imperatives of collective action generally can be accomplished, that is, instruments that enable it to carry out its mandate in the form of social intervention that at once breaks and negates, and yet preserves, the social and property relations that call for collective action at the outset. In brief, the State commands, first, a domain of legal and administrative governance, second, the power to enforce collective decisions by what Weber called its monopoly of legitimate violence, and, third, an apparatus of persuasion and public relations in the form of a continuous (ideological) discourse about its own functions and intentions.

These instruments are all in various ways brought to bear upon the problem of the collective supervision of capitalist society. This is not, however, a merely abstract or technical task, lying outside of some given field of historicity; it is, on the contrary, organically linked to the given context of the capitalist system. Thus, the State must on the one side seek to maintain economic order, to underpin the rate of profit, and to ensure the continued expansion of the bases of commodity production; and it must on the other side attempt to guarantee the smooth reproduction of labour and to secure a modicum of social harmony. In brief, the function of collective action as a whole and as a multiplicity of specific projects is to manage the production and reproduction relations of capitalism at large.

In the urban land nexus, this twofold imperative assumes an especially complex character, for it results in two quite separate (but interlocking) domains of collective action. In the first of these domains, the State responds to problems whose sources are in the strict sense extraurban but whose collective resolution results in unequivocally urban consequences. Such problems as the monopolization of public utilities, or the inability of the market to supply many essential infrastructural items, or the perennial shortage of low-income housing in capitalist cities are fairly clearly issues of this sort: they are triggered off by processes that lie outside of the urban land nexus as such, but their ultimate collective consequences contribute markedly to the shaping and reshaping of the overall system of differential locational advantages in the city. In the second of these domains, the State responds to problems that also represent breakdowns in production and reproduction relations, but that are at the same time quite specifically *urban* pathologies. In other words, they emanate directly out of the self-constricting logic of the urban land nexus in the proper sense of the term. In the final analysis, it is of course extremely difficult to disentangle these two classes of problems (together with the political responses that they provoke) from one another. Each merges with the other in some intermediate penumbral zone; and each is inseparably bound up with the other within urban planning as a historically realized administrative arrangement and practice. Despite this difficulty, however, some attempt to maintain a schematic separation between these two classes of problems serves to simplify and clarify the development of the present argument.

In the remainder of the present section, then, attention will be focussed on the former class of problems, while the latter class will be dealt with in detail at a later stage. Here, then, an attempt is made to show how the State sets about the task of mending very general sorts of spontaneous and extraurban breakdowns in production and reproduction relations (thereby socializing to a significant degree the costs of both production and reproduction), and how this same phenomenon produces powerful repercussions on the form and structure of the urban land nexus. At the same time, in order to maintain as clear a focus as possible upon the urban land nexus, this account will be largely confined to two generic cases. One of these cases is the problem of breakdowns in the production of large-scale and indivisible items of urban equipment and services; the other is the problem of breakdowns in the socially necessary consumption of land-contingent goods and services. In treating these two cases it will be necessary to tread a hazardous path between the mainstream theory of public goods and the orthodox Marxian theory of the State. Mainstream public-goods economists, with their predilection for analysis of the technical conditions of market failure, together with their emphasis on Pareto optimality as *the* criterion of political intervention, generally fail fully to comprehend the nature and biases of public policy. By contrast, orthodox Marxian theorists, with their insistence on the analytical preeminence of class struggle generally overlook completely the technical hitches and encumbrances that precede all collective intervention in the urban land nexus.

The case of breakdowns in the production of urban equipment and services

Many of the basic artefacts that are essential to the proper functioning of the urban land nexus participate in a number of common features: they tend to be extremely capital-intensive; and their production invariably incurs heavy fixed costs. The supply of goods and services that possess these sorts of qualities is intrinsically problematical in commodity-producing society for the dynamics of the capital relation lead inexorably either to their monopolization or to their spontaneous disappearance from the commodity form. In either case, the State will often intervene and will regulate or commandeer production. How do these cases come about?

The pervasiveness of monopoly (or oligopoly) in the production of basic urban equipment and services is everywhere detectable in the urban environment. Utilities, bus service, garbage disposal, telephone service, and so on all tend to be characterized by high degrees of monopoly. The monopolistic enterprises that supply these kinds of services are sometimes privately owned (though, more often than not, publicly regulated) and sometimes they are publicly owned outright by the State (or its proxy, the municipality). No matter whether they are privately or publicly owned, however, such enterprises tend to be highly capital-intensive, and this implies that they are likely to be able to achieve significant internal economies of scale by producing at high levels of output. That is, they are likely to be typified by decreasing average and marginal costs across their entire range of feasible output and, under such conditions as these, production is most efficient when it is concentrated within a few large units. In a competitive market situation with rapid accumulation of capital, the force of economic competition among firms in the same branch of production will alone eventually tend to force the concentration of production into a smaller and smaller number of larger and larger enterprises, for larger enterprises, with their definite cost and price advantages, will tend to drive out less efficient smaller production units, and will thus tend to flourish at the expense of the latter. The net result is that the market is highly susceptible over the course of time to domination by a handful of large producers, and, in the extreme case, by a single monopolistic producer.

Once an effective monopoly has appeared in any branch of production, it can begin to charge highly discriminatory prices, and, in the absence of external control, it is often the case that this phenomenon will begin to perturb the efficiency and workability of civil society, especially if the monopolized branch of production occupies some crucial position within the economic system at large. As the output of any monopolized branch of production moves through the input–output structure of the economy, the prices established in that branch are liable to cause a drain of net income (the lifeblood of production) from other nonmonopolized branches of production. Furthermore, monopoly prices are potentially capable of engendering a serious erosion of real wages as the output of monopolized branches enters (directly or indirectly) into final consumption. These problems arising out of monopolization will be exaggerated in the urban context where production units also control *in situ* distributional systems (as in the case of gas or electric utilities) so that to the effects of economic monopoly are added the effects of natural spatial monopoly. Therefore, if—and, it might be added, only if—monopolistic practices threaten seriously to undermine the established arrangements of civil society, the State will interpose its own collective rationality at some juncture in this process, and it will either abolish outright the commodity form by taking into its own hands the management of production in monopolized branches, or, if it permits continued private production, it will do so only under conditions of strict regulation of output and pricing policies. Whether outright public ownership or regulation of private production is selected as a collective solution in any specific instance seems to depend on local factors having to do with the play of political forces within the enveloping social formation. Occasionally, however, the State has little option but to nationalize production in monopolized branches. During times of economic recession, for example, certain types of monopolies are particularly liable to be faced with bankruptcy and extinction. These types of monopolies are above all highly capital-intensive, so that when demand begins to drop off, they are unable to reduce their heavy capital commitments and associated debt at a comparable rate, and they rapidly fall into grave difficulties. In this case, if they are essential links in the overall chain of commodity production, they will be effectively socialized by the State. It seems not unlikely that the acquisition by North American municipalities of many different varieties of urban public services in the period between the two World Wars may owe its origin to this specific logic.

The latter point leads us straight into our second major case of breakdown (and concomitant political intervention) in the production of urban equipment and services. This case involves the not infrequent situation where the fixed capital costs of production are so high in relation to any socially practicable scale of output that private firms could never at the outset be induced to undertake production. In branches of production that are characterized by this problem, there is no attainable combination of production, price, and effective demand that would ensure at least a normal profit on capital advanced, for, at each level of output, average costs exceed the price that would clear the market. In neoclassical terms, these are branches of production in which supply and demand schedules fail to intersect and, as a consequence, production simply cannot be undertaken by private capitalistic firms. Accordingly, where the output of such branches is vital for the continued smooth functioning of capitalism as a whole, the State, fulfilling its historical mandate, will step into the breach and will itself directly organize and underwrite the production process. This, in combination with the tendency to economic monopolization, is undoubtedly one of the principle reasons why the capitalist State persistently finds itself in the business of supplying in the noncommodity form such capital-intensive, indivisible, and high-fixed-cost items of urban equipment as metropolitan subway systems, port facilities, airports, new towns, expressway systems, bridges, and so on. The State then invariably makes these items available for general usufruct at prices far below their actual production costs.

Lastly, certain urban infrastructural services (such as street lighting, urban thoroughfares, or large-scale snow removal) possess a further feature that tends to reinforce their already strong propensity to disappear from the commodity form of production. If any attempt were made to produce these services in the strict commodity form their production costs would immediately escalate in the effort to resolve the problem of collecting user charges. In other words, for these kinds of services, disproportionately large incremental costs would be generated if producers made any attempt to set up effective devices for levying tolls on users. In these cases, then, the problem of initially high capital-labour ratios in relation to total demand is compounded by the problem of the extra investment that would be required in order to generate a cash flow. As a consequence, vital outputs that are susceptible to this kind of market failure are abandoned to the State, which undertakes to produce them out of general tax revenues.

The case of breakdowns in the consumption of land-contingent goods and services
Just as there are cases where certain branches of production are simply abandoned by private capital, so there are certain (land-contingent) goods and services that are crucial to the successful working out of the reproduction (consumption) process, yet that are not consumable in socially rational quantities so long as they remain in the pure commodity form. In order to sustain consumption of these goods and services at levels consonant with basic capitalist reproduction needs, the State must therefore supplement the output performance of private producers. There are two major dimensions to this issue, the first of which is concerned with potential underconsumption in an absolute sense as a consequence of inadequate wage levels, the second of which is concerned with underconsumption in the relative sense as a function of biases in the pattern of consumer spending where the overall structure of selected consumption programmes is inefficient from the point of view of socially determinate reproduction needs.

First, then, in capitalist society, the labour market has a logic that does not, and cannot, automatically register socially necessary consumption imperatives in realized wage levels. This follows immediately from the circumstance that wages in contemporary capitalist society are fixed as the outcome of a series of market processes in the context of an ongoing but fluctuating political confrontation between management and unions, and *not* as the outcome of a calculus of socially imposed needs. More particularly, realized wage levels in capitalist society—and, in particular, the wage levels of the least affluent strata of the working class—can never secure the levels of consumption that are essential for functional reproduction, including the purposes of general socialization and integration. Above and beyond the usual sorts of consumer goods that are produced in the ordinary commodity form (cars, refrigerators, television sets, food products, etc) there exists a vital sphere of consumption that is simply inadequately (in social terms) catered to by private producers. This sphere comprises such goods and services as housing, education, health care, recreation and culture, and so on. In principle there is no technical reason why these items cannot be produced in the conventional commodity form and, indeed, many of them are at least in part just so produced. If they were produced *uniquely* in this form, however, then spontaneous consumer demand for them, at capitalistically determined price and wage levels, would be disastrously low in terms of both the smooth reproduction of social relations and the effectiveness of labour inputs to the process of commodity production. As a result, the work force would quite certainly be inadequately educated, socialized, and physically recuperated by comparison with actually prevailing conditions in capitalist society where the State so assiduously attempts to compensate for the more blatant failures of the normal processes of commodity production and exchange by making available in socially rational quantities and at accessible prices crucial sorts of consumption items. In the urban land nexus, the most palpable sign of this activity of the modern State is the regular appearance across the landscape of such public goods as schools, hospitals, low-cost housing schemes, parks, and all the rest.

Second, even if wage levels were fixed in terms of a calculus of socially imposed needs, there is still no guarantee that they would be unerringly translated by wage earners into such consumption. For wage earners *manage their own consumption* in conformity with mental orientations and habits that give no definite guarantee that they will always be in harmony with the global imperatives of commodity-producing society. Actual patterns of personal expenditure and consumption are in part dependent upon complex psychological activity that lies outside of the domain of commodity production proper and that has little of the rigour and reliability of the laws that govern commodity production itself. Thus, despite the evident fact that the modern capitalist system exerts an immensely powerful influence over those social and cultural forces that encourage the personal assimilation and internalization of an ideology of passive receptiveness with respect to the kinds of consumption patterns that are essential to effective reproduction—as, for example, that complex of psychological, cultural, and urbanistic phenomena known as 'suburban life'—the fact remains that the process of effective consumption remains one of the very weakest elements in the chain of structural logic tying capitalist society together into a workable totality. And this weakness, moreover, becomes increasingly marked with each descending stratum within the overall social hierarchy. The upshot is that collective political interventions—in housing, education, health care, etc—start to appear as a means (in part) of countering the *lacunae* of individual behaviour in the domain of consumption.

It is clear from these two major points that a severe and persistent gap exists in capitalist cities between the production system as such and the reproduction system, over the issue of the smooth integration and functional socialization of labour, and especially of unskilled and manual labour. In view of this gap, the State is called upon to an ever increasing degree to manage the process of reproduction and to ensure a suitable supply at suitable prices of social consumption goods that could never be adequately produced in socially necessary quantities by private commodity producers. So significant and pervasive has this function of the State been throughout the development of capitalist society, that it is precisely in this specific realm of collective action that the main historical origins of modern urban planning are to be found. These origins correspond above all to the activities of the State in the nineteenth century in improving general urban social conditions by means of slum clearances, basic housing legislation, sanitary control and public health measures, and so on. This particular function of the State has grown more or less uninterruptedly ever since, so that it constitutes today a sphere of massive, complex, and all-embracing collective intervention in the urban land nexus.

Towards urban planning
In the diverse ways described above, certain general *extraurban* breakdowns in production and reproduction relations provoke collective responses which profoundly modify the *internal* order and structure of the urban land nexus. In spite of this circumstance, however, and in spite of the further fact that these administrative interventions are intimately bound up with urban planning in practice, *they still do not constitute urban planning in its final totality*. This totality can only be seized in the context of an analysis of that which in the final and coherent sense renders planning *urban*, namely, the fact that it constitutes a land-contingent process of social control called into being by the endemic land-use predicaments that are continually being thrown out by the urban system as such. With this general context in mind, the basic ideas developed here are now reworked by engaging in a systematic examination of the main causes of the land-use predicaments of the urban land nexus, and a first tentative effort is made to derive urban planning out of these predicaments. Thus, the argument at this stage moves from the issue of breakdowns that are essentially extraurban in origin (though they are resolved in terms that are pregnant with

land-contingent consequences) to the core issue of breakdowns that are in both origin and character quintessentially urban. On this foundation, a composite statement about the nature of urban planning is put forward in the ensuing chapter.

Here, then, the crisis-ridden logic of the urban land nexus is elucidated in detail. This logic is described, for simplicity of exposition, as involving two major (but overlapping) sets of land-use problems, the one set static, the other dynamic. These land-use problems are all in different ways outcomes of the peculiar status of the urban land nexus as a system of differential locational advantages situated within the capitalist mode of production. They represent forms of market failure; but, in addition, they are also foci of definite urban struggles. In social formations where political consciousness is highly coordinated by a left-wing party (or parties), as in France or Italy, these struggles tend to merge with the wider social struggles within capitalism at large. In social formations where such coordination is weak or minimal, as in Canada or the United States, they tend to remain isolated as local territorial issues outside of the main thrust of national political debate.

8.3 Static land-use problems
Simple externalities

The urban land nexus constitutes an expanse of territory punctuated by a dense and multifarious variety of locational events. These events interact both positively and negatively with one another. On the one hand, many land users generate extremely beneficial effects that are eagerly sought out by other locators; on the other hand, many land users are also the source of damaging effects that impose severe penalties on other locators in the urban land nexus. Frequently, these effects are involuntarily and gratuitously exchanged between producers and consumers: if positive, they are neither credited to producers nor debited to consumers; if negative they are neither debited to producers nor credited to consumers. In short, their production and consumption are not structured by a market and a concomitant pricing mechanism and, as such, they represent *externalities* (or spillover effects) in the strict sense. Because firms (and households) that propagate externalities across urban space are by definition absolved from taking them into account in their private calculations of costs and benefits, they themselves are liable to function at levels that are quite suboptimal in social terms. If they generate positive externalities (for example, crowds of shoppers that overflow into local retail stores) then they are likely to be less active than they would be if all social benefits were somehow or other accounted for in the decisionmaking process. If they generate negative externalities (for example, smoke or noise) then they are likely to be considerably more active than they would be if all social disbenefits were somehow or other accounted for in the decision-making process. By the same token, consumers of positive or negative

externalities will almost certainly operate at socially suboptimal levels of
activity. In the presence of externalities, then, the net result will be a
pervasive inefficiency in the urban land nexus that is likely to provoke a
concomitant political response once it attains some critical point (in social,
economic, or psychological terms) of functional impairment. In point of
fact, the externalities problem as a whole represents a major dissonance in
the urban land nexus, and it lies in the background of a great many urban
planning interventions. In order now to put some focus on this problem
we will consider here a small set of particularly significant manifestations
of land-use externality effects, namely, (a) the problem of negative spillovers
in the urban land nexus generally, (b) the problem of land development
bottlenecks, and (c) the so-called free-rider problem.

Negative spillovers in the urban land nexus
For ease of exposition, the problem of negative spillovers in the urban
land nexus can be broken down into a series of subproblems depending on
whether the affected parties are firms, households, or governments. These
subproblems will now be treated severally and in turn.

Negative spillovers in production space
The classic example of a negative spillover effect is described by Bator
(1958) where some firm, following its own internal profit-maximizing
logic, establishes a production plan whose marginal *private* costs are far
below the real *social* costs of production. This situation is evident
whenever the production decisions of one firm impose uncompensated
costs on any other group of firms. Thus, a negative spillover effect will
occur if, for example, some firm generates quantities of noise, fumes, or
dirt, that then impinge on other firms in the surrounding neighbourhood,
obliging them to incur incremental expenses in added sound insulation,
or air filtering, or cleaning. A similar problem would emerge in the
circumstance where some noxious activity invaded a shopping district,
driving potential customers away and forcing retail firms to invest extra
capital in attempts to counteract this negative effect. All such situations
involving negative spillover effects can be described analytically in the
following terms.

Suppose that a firm producing, say, heavy chemicals, moves to a location
in the vicinity of a firm manufacturing, say, clothing, and that various
negative spillover effects generated by the chemicals firm (for example,
pollution of stream water used in the manufacturing process of the clothing
firm) begin to cause an increase in the production costs of the clothing firm.
Let us take it that the chemicals firm produces x units of output per
production period at a total cost (in terms of capital and labour) of $f(x)$,
and that the clothing firm produces y units of output per production
period at a total cost (also in terms of capital and labour) of $g(y, x)$, where

$$\frac{\partial g(y, x)}{\partial x} > 0 \,. \tag{8.1}$$

The function g(y, x) thus identifies directly the cost disbenefits that the clothing firm must incur as a consequence of the production decisions of the chemicals firm. Both firms will now seek individually to maximize their profits, and they will accomplish this goal by applying doses of capital and labour to the production process in such quantities and combinations as cause marginal cost to be equated precisely to price (that is, such that the difference between individual revenues and individual costs is a maximum). For the chemicals firm, this condition may be written

$$\frac{\partial f(x)}{\partial x} = p_x \,, \tag{8.2}$$

and for the clothing firm, it may be written

$$\frac{\partial g(y, x)}{\partial y} = p_y \,. \tag{8.3}$$

Evidently, however, the profit-maximizing strategies of these two firms are suboptimal in aggregate social terms, for since the cost of clothing production increases as the output of chemicals increases, the profit-maximizing value of x is in fact higher than is socially desirable, and the profit-maximizing value of y is lower than is socially desirable. In a word, the same aggregate quantities of capital and labour that produce x and y under the conditions given by equations (8.2) and (8.3) could actually produce a higher overall value of output. In fact, a fully (that is, socially) optimal allocation of resources is obtainable only where true marginal costs are equal to price, that is where

$$\frac{\partial f(x)}{\partial x} + \frac{\partial g(y, x)}{\partial x} = p_x \,, \tag{8.4}$$

and

$$\frac{\partial g(y, x)}{\partial y} = p_y \,. \tag{8.5}$$

The socially optimal values of x and y can now be derived by solving the simultaneous equation system (8.4) and (8.5). So long as all relevant decisionmaking is private and decentralized, however, a socially suboptimal outcome will prevail.

To illustrate this general problem further, let us consider a concrete numerical example. Suppose that the chemicals firm produces at a marginal cost—equal to price—of $15 per unit of output. Suppose, in the same way, that the clothing firm produces at a marginal cost of $28. Let us take it that of this latter $28 a total of $22 represents normal production costs, and a total of $6 represents costs that are incurred as a result of the externalities imposed on the clothing firm by the chemicals firm. This means, of course, that the true social cost of the marginal unit of output of the chemicals firm is not $15 but $15+ $6 = $21. From this it follows that the combined production plans of the chemicals firm and the clothing firm are suboptimal in social terms. If the chemicals firm were to reduce its total production by one unit of output, then, in a competitive equilibrium, the factors so released would create goods to the value of $15 elsewhere in the economy. The aggregate result is that society as a whole would be better off to the extent of $6, where this latter quantity represents the difference between the true cost ($21) of the suppressed marginal unit of output of the chemicals firm, and the social gain of $15 resulting from the redeployment of the released factors.

This example illustrates clearly how the urban land nexus as a whole can begin to sink into disorderliness via the system of differential locational advantages. It also illustrates the point made previously in chapter 5 that even in purely neoclassical terms the urban land-use system can never fulfill the promise of market efficiency as held out by mainstream theory. However, as will be made increasingly apparent during the further development of the present argument, the problems raised by the anarchical tendencies of the urban land nexus transcend by far the simple technical question as to whether and to what degree the urban system deviates from the efficiency frontier.

Negative spillovers in reproduction space
Individual households, like individual firms, are also frequently obliged against their will to consume multiple negative spillover effects generated by other locators in urban space. At the very least, these negative effects cause households to incur unwelcome psychic or monetary costs, and, in their more extreme forms, they may seriously undermine the very logic of reproduction in urban space. Among the more familiar examples of negative spillovers imposed on urban households are such nuisances as air pollution, noise, traffic moving through residential neighbourhoods, congested pedestrian thoroughfares, deteriorated local property, socially incompatible neighbours, urban sprawl destroying countryside amenities, incursions of business and commercial activity into the local neighbourhood, and so on. These sorts of externalities all reduce in one way or another the satisfactions and efficaciousness of urban life, just as they tend to raise the costs of urban life. Furthermore, the negative spillover effects that impinge on households are liable seriously to subvert the workability of urban society by compromising the potentially positive contribution of urban neighbourhoods to the process of the reproduction of labour. Some additional comment on this latter point seems to be in order, given its general importance.

As was argued at an earlier stage in the proceedings, urban neighbourhoods that function most successfully as centres of the process of capitalist reproduction are marked to a high degree by qualities of social stability and cultural homogeneity. These qualities enhance the role of neighbourhoods as effective centres of living, socialization, leisure, and social quiescence, as centres, that is, of domestication within the system of capitalist social and property relations. But these same qualities are also of the utmost fragility, and they are liable to be shattered in short order once disruptive spillovers begin to make themselves felt. Residential neighbourhoods are highly susceptible to deterioration as arenas of social reproduction once they are invaded by socioeconomic groups that differ significantly in status from the preexisting dominant group. And they are also severely deranged once conversions to nonresidential land uses begin to occur on an important scale. For example, in many Canadian cities towards the end of the 1960s, the combined effects of the expansion of central business district activities and the concomitant phenomenon of gentrification started to project serious negative spillovers onto inner city blue-collar neighbourhoods. Many of these neighbourhoods were subjected to a veritable onslaught of devastation. Much of the existing housing stock was destroyed and commercial properties put up in its place; white-collar workers, seeking accommodation close to their places of work in the central business district began to buy out and to renovate whole sections of these neighbourhoods; and, in response to rocketing land prices, real estate and construction companies set about assembling tracts of land and converting them to high-rise developments. This combination of events provoked a considerable reaction on the part of the long-established blue-collar residents of these inner city neighbourhoods. Responding to the near-annihilation of their customary patterns of community living, they formed into irate citizens' groups which then engaged in frequent and costly confrontations with urban politicians, planners, and property developers. These citizens' groups pushed actively for legislation and land-use controls that would effectively protect their living arrangements, and their political activity in this regard was all the more intense given their correct assessment of the difficulties of finding suitable low-cost substitute housing elsewhere in the city. In varying degrees this political activity met with a modicum of success, and in Toronto, for example, a concerted effort was made in the early 1970s to preserve inner city neighbourhoods from further catastrophe. At the same time, many of the conflicts and problems generated by the disruption of the blue-collar neighbourhoods in Canadian inner city areas have tended simply to subside as the property boom that initially triggered them off has itself faded away in the mid-1970s. If these conflicts and problems seem to be at a currently low ebb, however, they are almost certainly only in temporary abeyance, for the developmental logic of the urban land nexus remains just as capable of reproducing them in the future—given the right conjunctural circumstances—as it has been in the past. Needless to say, the types of negative spillovers described here are potentially even more devastating in white-collar neighbourhoods than they are in blue-collar neighbourhoods. However, they are warded off with reasonably consistent success in white-collar neighbourhoods by means of the exclusionary zoning devices with which the residents of those neighbourhoods have sought to protect their own amenities and advantages.

Negative spillovers and urban government
Urban governmental units too must frequently bear heavy fiscal and political penalties generated by negative spillover effects from within the urban land nexus.

Spontaneous peripheral expansion, for example, consistently tends to impose heavy external costs on municipal budgets. As the city grows outwards, so the State is drawn into more and more costly rounds of investment in the urban fringe in order to maintain minimal standards of residential amenity. The same growth induces serious overloads on existing service facilities such as sewers, telephone lines, gas and electric distribution systems, necessitating costly investments in additional capacity. Furthermore, low-density suburban development encourages preferential use of the private car for personal transport, and this gives rise to an increasingly pressing need for intraurban expressways to carry commuters between the periphery and the centre; it also gives rise to serious transport congestion in the core of the city requiring additional public expenditure on such relief measures as street widening, traffic control, provision of parking facilities around the edge of the central business district, and so on.

These various events are also implicated in a further significant series of governmental quandaries as a result of negative spillover effects in the urban land nexus. The urban fiscal crisis that has affected so many central city administrations in North America in recent years is directly related to the externality effects sparked off by spontaneous urban growth and development. The crisis, in fact, has its ultimate roots in a number of historical occurrences that date from the turn of the century. Some time toward the end of the nineteenth century, metropolitan areas in North America disaggregated out into two clearly defined spatial-cum-political domains, comprising in the first case, the central city, and in the other case, a zone of independent suburban municipalities surrounding the central city. In this manner, the suburban middle classes sought to emancipate themselves in urban space from the social and political influences and the fiscal burdens of the working-class populations that tended to predominate in central city areas. The problem is that the process of administrative separation of suburban communities from the central city has been only too successful. At the present time, the independent suburban municipalities impose severe and unrecompensed fiscal burdens on the central city, and the weight of these burdens is magnified by the erosion of the central city tax base as a result of the massive and continuing out-migration of jobs and people to the urban periphery. In particular, suburban residents make extensive use of the central city for a variety of purposes (work, shopping, pleasure, etc) and the central city government underwrites the concomitant infrastructural and administrative expenses. The fiscal arrangements of the

central city are yet further burdened by the need for expensive social
assistance programmes to help assuage some of the more pressing social
problems that characteristically make their appearance in central city areas
as local neighbourhoods fall into decay and abandonment. Nevertheless,
that part of the cost of public services that is directly attributable to the
existence of a ring of independent municipalities in the urban periphery
cannot be imputed back to its source, for the central city administration
lacks effective taxing powers beyond its own boundaries. Hence, and in
the climate of general stagflation and fiscal demise that has characterized
economic conditions in the mid-1970s, the financial resources of many
central city areas in North America have been squeezed to the breaking
point forcing many of them to adopt a policy of austerity in which
ostensibly deteriorated urban services are allowed to fall into a condition
of yet greater dereliction and disrepair.

The planning response
Even the relatively restricted class of problems discussed above provokes a
remarkable variety of collective responses as urban planners are called
upon to counter the negative spillover effects generated in various ways at
various locations in the urban land nexus. For example, the urban general
plan is widely used as an instrument in the attempt to control and rationalize
the overall pattern of urban development so as to minimize many of the
negative spillover effects that would appear under conditions of unregulated
growth and expansion. The urban general plan is frequently complemented
by land-use zoning provisions which seek in a more particularized and
specific way to contain such negative externalities as might seriously
compromise the detailed functioning of production space and reproduction
space in the city. As a matter of fact, so imperfect did a free land market
prove to be as a rational sorter and arranger of land uses in North American
cities towards the end of the nineteenth century that a corresponding
major urban crisis was only avoided by the widespread introduction of
land-use zoning procedures. More recently, there have been innumerable
experiments throughout North America with the legal and fiscal control of
urban nuisance effects of many different kinds (air pollution, noise,
littering, visual disamenities, waste disposal, and so on). There have also
been concerted attempts to manage typical sorts of overloading problems
in the urban environment such as traffic congestion, rush-hour peaks in
public transport demand, overdevelopment of office buildings in the central
business district, etc. These attempts have consisted of administrative
measures as well as fiscal devices designed to internalize some (at least) of
the negative externalities generated by these problems. Additionally, a
number of schemes for the rationalization of urban administration by
bringing the central city and the suburbs together within one governmental
unit have been proposed and implemented (as in the case of Metropolitan
Toronto). Such schemes promise to help control the negative outcomes

that spill over existing municipal boundaries, and they also offer the
possibility of significant economies of scale being achieved in the production
of certain urban public goods such as police, fire protection, traffic control
water supply, sewage disposal, etc.

Like all collective interventions in capitalist society, however, these
planning responses represent eclectic, partial, and stopgap measures that
temper but do not abolish the self-constricting logic of the urban land nexus.

Land development bottlenecks

In capitalist cities, the typically fragmented and dispersed pattern of landownership (together with the fact of private landownership itself) interposes formidable barriers in the way of the development and redevelopment of urban land. In the face of this pattern of landownership, the assembly of large tracts of land as a preliminary to efficient redevelopment is frequently rendered time-consuming and costly, and this problem is exacerbated where there are existing fixed capital investments in the land that mature at different points in time. The problem is yet more complicated where individual private owners refuse to part with their land at any price, or withhold sale of their land in the expectation of a concomitant better offer. This barrier effect of private landownership is nowhere more pronounced that in the peripheral zones of large metropolitan regions. As the city expands laterally, massive land-use conversions tend to take place in these zones in order to accommodate ever growing needs for new towns, airports, industrial estates, new suburban subdivisions, and so on. And yet, time and again, development is hindered by complications arising out of the acquisition of the necessary composite land assemblies at uninflated prices. In this way, the atomized pattern of private landownership in capitalism tends to limit the pace of urban expansion, and as a consequence to restrict the smooth accumulation of capital. In this sense, as in so many others, the capitalistic logic of urbanization comes into collision with itself, for the very crux of the problem of land development bottlenecks is that upon which contemporary forms of urbanization generally are predicated, namely, the private and individual ownership of land. Since private land-development companies lack the power and the instruments to overcome the barriers set in their path by the institution of private landownership, the collectivity is inexorably drawn into the issue. Applying its prerogative of eminent domain, the State then sets about the task of breaking the power of private landownership wherever this is essential to ensure the achievement of the overriding capitalistic goal of unhindered expansion of the bases of commodity production. The State accomplishes this task by a wide variety of means depending on local circumstances and political tradition; but among the more commonly used means in North America and Western Europe are local expropriation, enforced redevelopment, compulsory purchase, and land banking. As Topalov (1974) has justly suggested, these sorts of collective activity are typically resolutely sporadic, discrete, and intermittent so that the State in no way begins to pose itself as a threat to the institution of private property as a whole.

A particularly clear example of collective political intervention directed towards the resolution of land development bottlenecks is the recent French experience with two planning devices designated ZAC (*zone d'aménagement concerté* or joint development zone) and ZAD (*zone d'aménagement différé* or deferred development zone). These are both instruments designed to ease the process of urban expansion while ensuring minimal disruption of prevailing social and property relations. The ZAC instrument represents an administrative means of organizing the land planning and development process, while the ZAD is essentially a land banking mechanism. When the French government declares a tract of land subject to ZAC regulations, it takes upon itself the overall task of land assembly and, in various forms of association with private capital, it oversees the actual development of the tract in conformity with some general plan. These procedures are instituted for the purposes of achieving smooth and massive land-use conversions over stretches of land that have become ripe for redevelopment. Significantly, once any specific ZAC operation has been completed, the land is then released back into private ownership and control. In contrast

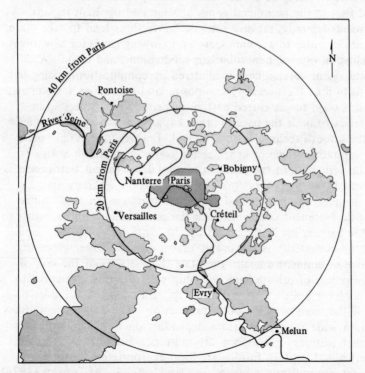

Figure 8.1. Deferred development zones (ZADs) in the Paris region as of 1st January 1975. Based on information in AFTRP (undated).

to the ZAC device (which facilitates the process of immediate land development), ZAD regulations are designed to enable the State to acquire extensive land reserves for development at some indeterminate future date. The State acquires these land reserves within the framework of two main legal dispositions that are immediately enforceable once any specific tract of land has been officially designated a ZAD. On the one hand, the State is able to make compulsory purchases of land in any ZAD. On the other hand, the State may intervene in any private sale of land in any ZAD, and preemptively declare itself the purchaser; at the same time, the State may block any price manipulation (including the effects of land speculation) by purchasing the land at what it takes to be a fair price based on recent land market transactions in the immediate vicinity of the ZAD. Something of the broad social meaning of this process of land banking on the part of the French government may be gleaned from figure 8.1, which shows the geographical distribution of land held in the form of ZADs in the Paris region in 1975. As figure 8.1 demonstrates, land that is subject to ZAD regulations in the Paris region lies well beyond the existing built-up area, and it thus lies strategically well in advance of the path of outward growth of the city. As such, it constitutes a sort of safety valve ensuring the instant availability of new land for development as the city expands. The ZAD process thus eases the whole dynamic of urban growth, eliminating disruptive blockages in land assembly and conversion, thereby helping to ensure the onward march of accumulation and commodity production.

It is evident that the intervention of the State in the elimination of crucial land development bottlenecks is a collectively rational and necessary response within capitalism to the prevailing pattern of fragmented, dispersed and privatized landownership. However, as already indicated, the State tends to attack these problems in ways that concede maximum continuity to the existing arrangements of civil society. That is, the land development activities of the State are in practice governed by local and pragmatic circumstances, internal to and imposed by the social formation. While the diverse policies that the major capitalist States have created in order to deal with these bottleneck problems have largely left existing social relationships intact, they do seem to have been remarkably efficacious from a technical point of view, particularly in much of Western Europe. Here, strong centralized planning bureaucracies have managed successfully to contend with the political opposition of landowners, and especially of those landowners in urban fringe areas where the bottleneck problem has tended to be most acute. Given this efficacy and the consequent alleviation of potentially severe blockages in the forward evolution of the urban land nexus, the nationalization (or municipalization) of urban land as called for by urban reformers of all kinds since the second half of the nineteenth century is no doubt likely to be postponed yet further, if not indefinitely, in capitalist society. Nevertheless, the direct intervention of the State in land-development problems has not been entirely lacking in progressive elements where (as in the case of recent legislation in Britain and France) it has also sought to recover at least some of the incremental land value created by local community activity.

The free-rider problem
The free-rider problem is a yet further case of the failure of private and social decisionmaking to coincide with one another in a common optimal solution. The problem can be described generically in the following terms. Suppose that some specific urban development scheme is proposed, say, a scheme to build a neighbourhood park or community centre. Suppose further that successful advancement of the scheme depends on the purely voluntary contributions and assistance of private individuals and that, once it is completed, it is destined to be freely accessible to all comers. Any potential contributor to and user of the scheme is then caught in a dilemma. On the one hand, if the individual predicts that others will support the scheme then he definitely gains by refraining from making a contribution while nonetheless enjoying the final results of others' efforts. On the other hand, if the individual predicts that others will not support the scheme, then he will perceive any contribution that he might make as being simply wasted. In either case, the individual's economically rational choice (like every other individual's rational choice) is to do precisely nothing, or, in other words, to be a free rider. As a consequence, however, many socially beneficial projects and activities in the urban land nexus that are susceptible to this curious logic remain pure chimera unless accomplished by some decisionmaking unit (for example, the State) whose relationship to society as a whole enables it to transcend the free-rider dilemma. This brief analytical statement may be made more coherent and precise by a discussion of two particularly outstanding examples of the free-rider problem in the urban land nexus. The first example concerns the restricted locational logic of capitalist firms in the city; the second concerns the genesis of certain forms of urban decay and blight.

First, then, the geographical distribution of capitalist firms in the urban land nexus is constricted by a developmental process that no individual firm can overcome. Because of the profit-enhancing qualities of positive agglomeration effects, firms tend to seek out locations within nuclei of economic activity where such effects have already emerged in definite and irreversible form. By the same token, firms tend to shun those areas of the city where agglomeration effects are negligible. This, however, leads to a self-perpetuating vicious circle. Where positive agglomeration effects already exist owing to historical circumstances, they flourish; where they do not exist, they have little chance of appearing spontaneously. This suggests that the privatistic and capitalistic logic of urban land-use development must be self-limiting, for it discourages the appearance of those very social outcomes—the emergence of new poles of activity generating significant positive agglomeration effects—that might further the ends of capitalism as such. In certain cases, then, the State, as the agent of general collective imperatives, will seek to break this vicious circle, and will set about the task of creating new poles of attraction in geographical space as and when these promise to enlarge the sphere of commodity production and exchange.

Second, the origin and perpetuation of much urban decay and blight can be ascribed to the free-rider problem, for once any urban neighbourhood has started to run downhill, individual property owners will frequently and rationally choose to be inactive in the face of the deterioration of their property. For one thing, any new investment in any individual property will always be vitiated to some degree so long as the surrounding neighbourhood remains in a state of blight. For another thing, any new investment will provide highly beneficial but free externalities for adjacent property owners, many of whom may well be business competitors of the original investor. Under conditions such as these, any particular owner, applying a calculus of purely private costs and benefits to the problem, will find it most advantageous to remain a free rider, and simply to reap whatever positive spillover effects may accrue from the improvements that others might make in their property. As a result, however, private renewal becomes indefinitely postponed as property owners await windfall gains that in practice have little likelihood of appearing spontaneously. In North America and Western Europe, many different kinds of government programmes exist in order to combat urban decay and blight produced by this particular manifestation of the free-rider problem. These range from subsidies on housing repairs to full-blown urban renewal projects. Variations of these kinds of programmes are periodically put into effect in North American cities in attempts to ameliorate slum conditions, especially at times when the deterioration of urban slums reaches a point such that the multiple negative spillover effects (violence, racial tension, etc) that flow outwards from those slums into other areas of the city begin to threaten the livability and workability of the urban environment as a whole.

As will be shown at a later stage in chapter 10, the mechanism of the free-rider problem may also be seen as underlying, at least in part, the failure of a purely privatistic solution to appear to the severe and long-standing problem of reproduction in capitalist cities (particularly in nineteenth-century industrial towns), that is, a solution in which each individual firm oversees the reproduction of its own workers. Concomitantly, the State has been persistently obliged to play the role of collective proxy in the management of functionally efficient reproduction spaces.

8.4 Dynamic land-use problems

In addition to the *static* land-use problems described above, the urban land nexus is further endemically typified by various *dynamic* land-use problems. These problems can be reduced to a small number of very broad types, namely (a) the problem of the slow convertibility of the urban land nexus, (b) the problem of the timing of development decisions, and (c) the problem of the temporal myopia of private locational activity in the urban land nexus. Each of these types of problems is again a reflection of a situation in which private control and individual behaviour, structured by capitalist production relationships, give rise to an urban dynamic that is quite perceptibly out of control, and, in aggregate, beyond all real social decidability.

The slow convertibility of the urban land nexus
Harvey (1978, page 124) has captured something of the essence of the problem of the slow convertibility of the urban land nexus in a passage that echoes what has been said previously about the innate discrepancy in capitalist society between the imperatives of private and collective action:

> "Capital represents itself in the form of a physical landscape created in its own image, created as use values to enhance the progressive accumulation of capital. The geographical landscape which results ... expresses the power of dead labour over living labour, and as such it imprisons and inhibits the accumulation process within a set of specified physical constraints. And these can be removed only slowly unless there is a substantial devaluation of the exchange value locked up in the creation of these physical assets."

Remark, at the outset, that if it had been possible to accommodate urban activities within instantly convertible nondurable structures, there would in all probability have been many fewer urban problems in capitalist cities than is currently the case, and the collective undecidability of urban land uses would have posed quite negligible difficulties. In such circumstances, any change in the demand for urban land would always have called forth and been met by an immediate response on the part of private developers in the form of appropriate land-use conversions. Had this been the case, there would undoubtedly have been a vastly more dense development of urban land-use activities than is currently prevalent in capitalist cities. Similarly, had urban infrastructural facilities been sufficiently easily implantable and removable, the fluidity of private land uses would have been vastly increased. Under hypothetical conditions such as these, any analysis of the urban land nexus might well stop short at a description of the simple theoretical landscape *à la* von Thünen as described in chapter 3— a landscape whose use characteristics and geographical articulation are in principle instantly adjustable to meet every possible new contingency. As a corollary, all social conflict in urban areas would no doubt be reducible forthwith into unmediated struggles over the differential distribution of the net product into profits, wages, and rents. Hence, had urban structure and infrastructure been swiftly convertible, collective irrationalities and negative spillover effects in the urban land nexus would have been largely ephemeral. Every perturbation in the existing spatial configuration of differential locational advantages would have instantly produced a counter-response in the guise of an overall conversion of preexisting structures to correspond to this perturbation, and, accordingly, many though by no means all urban land-use problems would have remained only temporary and self-correcting inconveniences. In reality, however, land-use conversions are always delayed in time as a function of the fixed capital invested in buildings and structures. This means in addition that spatial inefficiencies and irrationalities have a strong tendency to become locked into the urban landscape, and the problem is compounded by the multiple ripple effects that run through the urban land nexus so that any single disequilibrating situation may take years, if not decades, to work its way out via a delayed concatenation of private land-use conversions.

It is clear that this state of affairs imposes severe penalties on urban society as a whole. But land users are also liable to find themselves penalized as private individuals by the slow convertibility of the urban land nexus. Thus, a firm may make what initially appears to be a perfectly optimal locational decision. Then, in the course of time, it may find itself faced with unforeseen changes in the configuration of differential locational advantages, such that its production possibilities are now either greatly truncated or greatly augmented. In either case, the firm's original decision, in terms of location and level of activity, is now revealed to be quite suboptimal in its own private terms. At the same time, the firm's fixed capital commitments will prevent it from readjusting to a fully optimal standard of performance over some definite period of time, though it will still, of course, seek to optimize whatever choice variables remain within its command in the interim. The more dramatic the changes in the configuration of differential locational advantages the more pervasive such functional impairments are likely to be. For similar reasons, urban workers and households have often incurred heavy costs as a consequence of urban land-use changes, and most especially as a consequence of the rapidly shifting location of work places relative to the geographical distribution of residential neighbourhoods. This phenomenon has led to many cases of social disharmony and unrest, and to periodic outbreaks of political conflict and demands for higher wages.

Development decisions: timing and choice of land use
In reality, the slow convertibility problem is only a special case, singled out for its particular importance and visibility, of the more general problem of the timing of development decisions in the urban land nexus. This problem consists in a persistent discrepancy between privately optimal and socially optimal land-use conversion times in the twofold sense that private conversions may be premature or they may be long overdue relative to social criteria of evaluation. It is a problem that exists precisely because private landowners make decisions about the timing of land-use conversions in terms of their individual interests and fail entirely, by the nature of the

case, to take account of the externalities generated by their land development activities. In both private and social terms, this problem is immensely complicated for it involves not just a question as to the timing of conversion from one given type of land use to another, but also a question as to timing in the context of multiple alternative land-use choices. In what follows, a treatment of the simple one-variable timing problem will first of all be undertaken and on this basis, the multiple-variable timing problem will then be discussed.

The timing of simple development decisions

Suppose that a given urban site is currently occupied by one kind of land use, say land use of type a, but that conversion of the site, now or in the future, to some other specified kind of land use, say to land use of type b, is an open possibility. Let us designate the stream of potential future revenues generated by the existing land use as $r_0(a)$, $r_1(a)$, $r_2(a)$, ..., etc, where the index 0 denotes present time. Similarly, let us designate the stream of potential future revenues generated by the alternative land use as $r_\theta(b)$, $r_{\theta+1}(b)$, $r_{\theta+2}(b)$, ..., etc, where the index θ denotes time of conversion from use a to use b. We may suppose that the total cost of conversion from use a to use b is equal to the quantity K, which, for simplicity, may also be considered to take into account any scrap value recoverable from the existing use. The owner of the given site will now seek to identify an optimal moment for conversion from use a to use b. Such a moment will be one that maximizes *net present value* of the total property or, in other words, that maximizes the market valuation of the property in terms of present prices. This net present value is equal to the stream of discounted earnings generated by the existing use up to

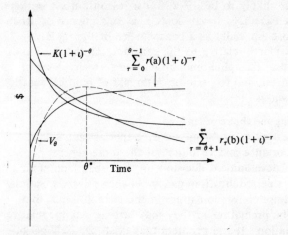

Figure 8.2. Optimal time of conversion (θ^*) from land use of type a to land use of type b.

the moment of conversion at time θ, minus the discounted cost of conversion, plus the stream of discounted earnings generated by the new use subsequently to time θ. In symbolic terms, this problem can be expressed as a programme whose objective is to define a numerical value of the variable θ that maximizes the net present value function V_θ, that is,

$$\text{maximize } V_\theta = \sum_{\tau=0}^{\theta-1} \frac{r_\tau(a)}{(1+\iota)^\tau} - \frac{K}{(1+\iota)^\theta} + \sum_{\tau=\theta}^{\infty} \frac{r_\tau(b)}{(1+\iota)^\tau}, \qquad (8.6)$$

where ι is the prevailing rate of discount. The maximand (8.6) is subject to two general feasibility conditions, one of which requires that V_θ be greater than the sum of all future discounted earnings generated by the present use up to infinity, the other of which requires that V_θ be such that at least a normal profit is earned on the quantity of capital K. These conditions ensure that conversion is rational in capitalistic (profit-maximizing) terms. Figure 8.2 demonstrates graphically how V_θ varies as the value of θ is varied and how the optimal conversion time, θ^*, is derived. It is to be observed that, in a competitive land market, land prices at all urban sites will fully reflect and anticipate, and hence force into existence, all future privately optimal conversion possibilities. To this degree, as Nowlan (1977) suggests, the land market can be considered rational.

However, an immediate qualification of this latter remark is required. The quantities $r_\tau(a)$ and $r_\tau(b)$ constitute revenues that are entirely privately appropriated. As such, they can in no way reflect whatever positive and negative externalities may be generated by the land uses of type a or type b. As a consequence, the privately calculated optimal conversion time, θ^*, is liable to be markedly suboptimal from the perspective of society's costs and benefits. On the one side, private land-use conversion will be *delayed* beyond the time that is socially optimal if either (1) the existing land use generates negative externalities (as in the case of the chemicals firm discussed above) so that $r_\tau(a)$ is an overestimate of the real economic returns to that use, or (2) the alternative use generates positive externalities so that $r_\tau(b)$ is an underestimate of real economic returns. On the other side, private land-use conversion will be *premature* in social terms if either (1) the existing land use generates positive external effects (as in the case of a large department store that attracts shoppers into the downtown area) so that $r_\tau(a)$ is an underestimate of the real economic returns to that use, or (2) the alternative use generates negative externalities, so that $r_\tau(b)$ is an overestimate of real economic returns. As a consequence of these potential discrepancies between private costs and benefits and social costs and benefits in the urban land nexus, there is little guarantee that the process of market exchange in land will in fact be quite so rational as advocates of *laissez-faire* norms assert. Indeed, the social irrationality of the market with respect to the timing of land-use conversions is revealed by the frequency with which the State in practice imposes its own political logic on the process. Thus there arise those familiar situations in which the

State seeks sometimes to accelerate the process of land-use conversion, while at other times it puts impediments in the way of conversions, for example by subsidizing activities whose private costs and benefits are such that they would otherwise have long ago been forced out of existence but whose positive impact on the local economy is so great that it is justifiable in social terms to maintain them in business via collective intervention.

The timing of complex development decisions
The potentially wide discrepancy as described above between privately and socially optimal outcomes in the timing of land-development decisions is fraught with added potential dissonances where there is a multiplicity of choices as to types of new development. This point may be illustrated by briefly considering the logic of private land-use conversion decisions under circumstances where several alternative choices as to type of replacement are available, and by then showing how this logic is liable to produce solutions that deviate from socially optimal solutions.

Table 8.1. The timing of alternative development decisions: development costs, net revenues, and present values (in $)[a]. Source: Nowlan (1977).

Time period	Development alternatives		
	a	b	c
0	−800[b]	0	−200
1	60	0	30
2	60	0	30
3	60	0	30
4	60	0	30
5	60	0	30
6	60	−1600	30
7	60	110	30
8	60	110	30
9	60	110	30
10	60	110	−2400
11	60	110	150
12	60	110	150
⋮	⋮	⋮	⋮
Present value of the property			
$\iota = 0 \cdot 04$	700	909	931[c]
$\iota = 0 \cdot 05$	400	448[c]	382
$\iota = 0 \cdot 06$	200[c]	162	116

[a] Present values represent the sums of positive and negative income streams discounted to the beginning of the first time period. Appropriate formulae for calculating present values are: $V_a = -800 + 60\iota^{-1}$; $V_b = (-1600 + 110\iota^{-1})(1+\iota)^{-6}$; $V_c = -200 + 30\iota^{-1}[1 - (1+\iota)^{-9}] + (-2400 + 150\iota^{-1})(1+\iota)^{-10}$.
[b] Negative entry indicates cost of development; other entries show net revenue per time period.
[c] Preferred alternative for a given value of ι.

Specifically, let us examine the case where three alternative land-use conversion possibilities (designated here a, b, and c) are available at some particular site. A hypothetical economic evaluation of each of these three possibilities is presented in table 8.1. This table shows all revenue streams, capital costs, and net present values (defined with respect to a privately optimal conversion time in each case) for the three different redevelopment alternatives. Alternative a involves immediate conversion of the site at a cost of $800, and thereafter revenue is generated at a rate of $60 per time period. Alternative b represents a situation where the site produces no revenue whatever up to time period 6, at which point conversion occurs at a cost of $1600, and this produces a revenue of $110 in all subsequent time periods. Alternative c consists of two different redevelopment manoeuvres: in the immediate present, a small investment of $200 is made, generating a revenue of $30 per time period up to time period 10 when a further conversion at a cost of $2400 is made, generating an income of $150 in all ensuing time periods. When maximum present value is used as a criterion of evaluation, alternative c will be preferred by private landowners where $\iota = 0.04$; alternative b will be preferred where $\iota = 0.05$; and alternative a will be preferred where $\iota = 0.06$. However, as in the case of the simple timing problem considered earlier, the revenue streams associated with these three alternative land-use projects fail to take into account external costs and benefits. In the case of the problem of the timing of complex development decisions, this means that there is a strong likelihood both that the timing decision itself will be suboptimal *and* that the very choice of land-use alternative will diverge from the socially optimal solution. Once again, then, when this potential maladjustment begins to threaten the bases of a workable urban process, remedial political action may be expected to materialize (in the form of diverse land-use controls and incentives) so as to counteract the more socially deleterious effects of this mismatch between private and collective optimality in the urban land nexus.

The temporal myopia of private locational activity

A sort of location-theoretic counterpart to the timing problems discussed in the previous section appears in certain dynamic spatial processes where, at any time period, new firms face multiple alternative choices of location. When such processes are governed by an individual profit-maximizing decisional calculus they frequently result in locational outcomes that engender extremely high social costs, and, in particular, high overall transport costs. Several decades ago, Hotelling (1929) suggested that even in a purely static environment, private locational decisions in geographical space may well be attended by collectively undesirable results, a proposition later corroborated in part by Koopmans and Beckmann (1957) among others. Once private locational decisions in urban space are analyzed as part of a general dynamic process, however, this tendency to social and spatial inefficiency takes on an especially heightened form. In pursuing their own private and mutually competitive interests, individual land users typically make 'myopic' locational decisions in the twofold sense that (1) they tend to block out the achievement of socially rational land-use patterns at some future point in time, and (2) their own decisions tend (from their own purely private standpoint) to become increasingly inefficient as further private locators enter into urban space. Since the urban land nexus is everywhere characterized by the problem of slow convertibility, these myopic and inefficient decisions become sealed into the landscape, and are accordingly reproduced and cumulated through time.

This propensity to inefficiency in any competitive dynamic locational system may be demonstrated by means of a simple hypothetical example that on the one hand illustrates the self-constricting character of private locational decisions, and that on the other hand illustrates (once more) the clear superiority, from the point of view of social costs, of coordinated decisionmaking and control. The example is based on the work of Teitz (1968), and it can most simply and effectively (though somewhat artificially) be elucidated in terms of a problem in which some fixed number of economic activities, say service centres of some sort, enter one by one into a regular circular region. It will be assumed that a total of four service centres is to be established, one centre being constructed in each time period over a series of four stages. Once any centre is established it is then taken to be fixed in location for all ensuing time periods, up to and beyond time period 4. Let it be assumed that customers for the service in question are evenly distributed over the given circular region. Any customer will then patronize the nearest service centre, and if a new centre is built nearer to that customer than some other centre that he had previously patronized, then he will shift his allegiance from the older to the newer (and closer) centre. This general locational structure will now be briefly analyzed for the two contrasting cases where (1) all centres constitute individual private and competitive firms, and (2) where all centres are publicly owned and operated by a single planning agency.

In the competitive system, each firm, as it comes into the system, is assumed to attempt to maximize its profits by selecting a location which in some way guarantees that the firm is the closest and most accessible

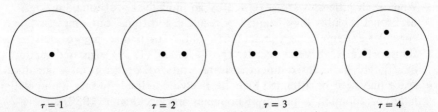

Figure 8.3. A myopic locational process.

centre for the largest possible number of customers. Thus, in time period 1, the first centre locates at the point of maximum aggregate travel for the entire region (see figure 8.3). Where only one centre exists, this location is also socially optimal. However, where other locators are likely to enter the system in the future, there is now only a truncated and constricted space left open to them. In time periods 2, 3, and 4, then, each new centre that comes into the system attempts to find for itself an individually optimal location, but in each case because of the failure of prior locators to take account of social costs, the system only becomes more and more locationally irrational from society's point of view. Indeed, the locational dynamic is such that individual locators themselves are increasingly penalized as new firms enter the system (a phenomenon that is evident from a scrutiny of figure 8.3). The final highly inefficient state of the system as established in time period 4 is now simply reproduced through succeeding time periods. In this hypothetical example, it is assumed that private locators' information about the future is nil, but as has been demonstrated elsewhere (Scott, 1975), even if all information about the future were perfect, the impossibility of socially coordinating all locational decisions would still produce a state of marked spatial inefficiency.

In the case of the planned dynamic locational system, a single decision-making body organizes the overall spatial process in conformity with some general criterion of social optimality. This criterion will be taken here to involve the minimization of cumulated total transport costs. In the first time period, then, a service centre is established at an acentral and apparently inefficient location (cf figure 8.4). Its inefficiency is indeed only apparent, however, for the planned location of this first element of the system leaves open the possibility of correspondingly more efficient locations being established for incoming centres in the future. The first centre, in short, is located within a final spatial structure that is planned and designated from the outset. Similarly, in time periods 2, 3, and 4, succeeding centres enter the system and take up locations in conformity with this overall plan. The final state of the system as established in the fourth time period is highly efficient and in social terms is far superior to the competitively (and myopically) determined pattern. The superiority of the planned system is enhanced by the fact that it now recurs without change through all ensuing time periods.

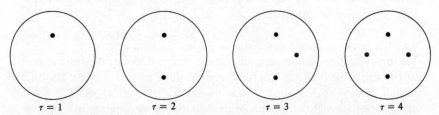

Figure 8.4. A planned locational process.

The two hypothetical problems discussed above represent, of course, extreme and vastly oversimplified cases. In fact, no pretence is made here that real locational systems (whether competitive or planned) conform in any but the most crudely approximate ways to the types of historical sequences and processes discussed above. These two examples are intended only to suggest tendencies and trends in either case, and to demonstrate by means of a deliberately overdrawn contrast between a starkly myopic locational process, and a thoroughly planned system, how the composite and superimposed consequences of private locational decisions can, over time, take the city progressively away from the efficiency frontier. By the same token, then, the peculiar logic of private locational activity contributes *its* share to the tendency for significant breakdowns to occur at various points within the urban system.

In conclusion, it is worth adding that even when private locators attempt to escape from some of the more individually nefarious consequences of their own myopic decisionmaking procedures and to assess the course of future events, the results may prove to be just as disastrous as they are when decisions are made wholly with respect to the immediate present. The simple example of leapfrogging in urban development is a case in point. Locators who engage in leapfrogging seek to take speculative advantage of anticipated continued outward urban expansion; and they locate well beyond the existing built-up area of the city so as to avail themselves of cheap land (though in the same process incurring high operating costs) in the expectation of increased land prices (and lower operating costs) as the built-up area of the city flows outwards. This locational phenomenon imposes heavy costs on the community. It tends to involve the community in high expenditures on basic infrastructure in the urban fringe; moreover each round of such expenditure is geometrically more burdensome on the public purse than the last. But when the looked-for outward urban expansion does not occur, and when associated infrastructural services fail to materialize, then the problem is liable to become even more acute. Hence, at the present time, when an endemic fiscal crisis has resulted in a definite faltering of the previously established pattern of rapid peripheral expansion, so locators who had speculated on a continuation of that pattern are now forced to bear the heavy private costs of their misinformation, while the community as a whole bears the cost of the resulting inefficient pattern of land use in the urban fringe and of the resulting destruction of local countryside amenities.

8.5 The private-public interface in the urban land nexus
The preceding analytical demonstration of the inherent dysfunctionalities of the urban land nexus has fundamental implications for any historically rooted theory of urbanization and planning. It provides us with a series of important insights into the general spatial consequences of private action—as structured by capitalist social and property relations—in the

urban land nexus, and, as a corollary, into the nature, evolution, and limits of planning. In addition, it clearly signifies that there is a realm of potential and actual social conflict in cities that cannot be directly read off from class relationships determined in the domain of production. In the urban land nexus there are *land-contingent* political issues and questions which are admittedly intermediations of fundamental social dynamics emanating out of class relationships, but which are, at the same time, strictly urban, spatial, and territorial in expression, and, as such, often far removed in empirical reality from pure class practices and alignments. Thus, there exists in contemporary capitalist cities the pervasive and refractory tendency to land-use failure and conflict as outlined in detail above, and there exists the derivative and predictable imperative of dealing collectively with this same failure and conflict. Concomitantly, private action and collective action become enmeshed with one another in a dynamic interrelationship of response and counterresponse that carries the urban land nexus forward through a succession of historical mutations. We may begin to discover something of the detailed character of this dynamic by considering three elemental components (or moments) that represent its essential movement, namely, first a private component, second a public component, and third the private-public interface that emerges out of the mutual confrontation between these two components.

The private component in the urban land nexus
As a structured element of the social formation, the urban land nexus is in large degree the spatial effect of capital's insistent search for profits, and, in relation to this, of the search by labour for residential environments that enhance the process of reproduction and that sustain the exchange value of labour-power. However, as a structured element of the social formation, the urban land nexus is also highly susceptible to various pathological states of being as capital and labour seek to satisfy their historically determinate needs in spatial context. In the urban land nexus, that is, a succession of individually optimal land-use decisions leads in the long run not towards but away from social and spatial optimality. Capitalist cities are only prevented from falling into massive disarray by the incessant intervention of the State. Even so, given the nature of the capitalist State, this intervention is always extenuated, and there have been recurrent moments, not only in earlier Dickensian periods of capitalist urbanization, but also in the very recent past when it has seemed as if the city and city life were doomed to be swallowed up in their own self-engendered chaos and irrationality. Thus, in capitalism, the urban land nexus confronts society with difficult and often potentially explosive administrative tasks, and these tasks take on two principal determinate forms. First, the logic of commodity production and the private appropriation of profit call for efficient, fluid, and fully serviced production spaces. Second, the logic of the reproduction of labour calls for the development of secure, secluded,

and socially homogeneous residential neighbourhoods. Since the private appropriation, exchange, and utilization of urban land lead to outcomes that undermine these essential foundations of a viable capitalism, remedial urban planning makes its appearance as a necessary and indissoluble element of the general imperative of social control.

Now, despite the manifest urban land problems that have been lengthily exposed and analyzed in the present chapter, many approaches to urban theory continue to suppose as a basic point of departure that urban society constitutes a naturally self-equilibrating system that is only prevented from attaining to a final state of harmony by the clumsy and gratuitous interventions of planners. Mainstream urban theory, then, produces with astonishing frequency comforting fictions about the supposedly intrinsic rationality of the spontaneous process of urban growth and development together with mystified policy prescriptions built around the notion of market norms as universal panacea (cf Smith and Walker, 1977). Hence, the urban land market is seen as an autoregulating mechanism, as an efficient allocator of scarce land units among competing users, as a maximizer of collective benefits, as a rational sorter and arranger of land uses, as the operationalization of consumers' tastes and preferences, and so on. Quite apart from the criticisms that have been addressed to these points in earlier chapters of this book, the land-use predicaments elucidated in the present chapter pose a central dilemma for mainstream theory. This is not, it should be noted, a dilemma that can be solved simply by rewriting the Walrasian equations of economic equilibrium in such a way as to take account of certain minor technical aberrations in the urban context. It is rather a case of a fundamental, perennial, and intrinsic dissonance in capitalist cities as manifested in the permanent mismatch between urban form as the unintended and unplanned outcome of a private decisional calculus (rooted, in the last analysis, in the logic of commodity production) and the historical imperative of continued social cohesion, stability, and functional effectiveness.

The public component in the urban land nexus
State intervention in the urban land nexus is therefore a social imperative imposed by the self-destructive logic of capitalist society as it is mediated through urban space. The observable material manifestations of urban planning in practice—land-use zoning, building regulations, public health laws, new towns, urban renewal, municipal housing schemes, public transport, and so on—constitute the multifarious and stopgap measures that the capitalist collectivity brings forward as a way of dealing with its own fundamental breakdowns in the urban land nexus. In a word, urban planning constitutes a decisionmaking calculus that seeks to mitigate the deleterious social effects and failures contingent upon the behavioural peculiarities of firms and households in urban space, and to steer urban

society forward into collectively rational choices consistent with capitalist social and property relations.

However, while urban planning is certainly *produced* by capitalist society, it is by the same token *contained* by capitalist society. The State in general is structurally internal to capitalism as a whole, and it does not have, nor can ever have, a mandate to reform fundamental social and property relations. On the contrary, the rationality of the State is itself an element of the rationality of the social system within which the State is historically embedded. As a corollary, urban planning emerges as an active instrumentality of urban change and reform precisely and uniquely to the degree that it serves the very purposes of capitalism and is able to break the inner contradictions of capitalist urbanization (without, however, reconstituting the social logic that produces those contradictions) and thus to open up the way for commodity production and the accumulation of capital to proceed in a more or less workable fashion. In the light of these remarks, it is clear that the conventional theories of collective action and public goods provision (cf Baumol, 1952; or Olson, 1965) are doomed to failure. Such theories get off to a good start by rooting political action in various manifestations of social and economic disintegration, but they fail signally when they cap this insight with an ahistorical and idealist view of the State as *deus ex machina* motivated only by the imperatives of Pareto optimality, and an abstract 'public interest'. The conventional theory of public goods provides few real clues as to why the State will or will not act in specific cases of market failure, and none whatever as to the definite political biases, predilections, and miscarriages of collective action in practice. Nevertheless, in line with the argument developed thus far in the present account it now seems possible to assert that *whereas all collective intervention in the urban land nexus is preceded by some specific dissonance, breakdown, or market failure, not all dissonance, breakdown, or market failure is invariably succeeded by collective intervention; the State will intervene only when the irrationalities and dislocations of the urban land nexus begin to undermine the viability of capitalist society as a whole, and, in particular, the functional effectiveness of commodity production and the reproduction of labour in urban space.* To illustrate the point: it might be felt in some quarters that the worth of human life is so great that the State ought once and for all to resolve the problem of fatal traffic accidents, whatever the cost in economic terms. In principle, this problem is undoubtedly capable of resolution. In practice, however, the capitalist State cannot undertake such a project, for the State is not susceptible to a decisional calculus that enables it to evaluate the costs of fatal traffic accidents above the costs of a severely curtailed system of road transport. Given its historically specific tasks, and given that urban problems tend to emerge slowly and hesitantly rather than cataclysmically, the State understandably tends to search for policies and solutions that promise maximal effectiveness but that disrupt to the minimal extent possible the existing arrangements of civil society. However, in this very process of seeking to remedy symptoms, while neglecting their underlying basic causes, the State inexorably finds itself participating in the creation of new urban predicaments. *Precisely because the State has no mandate to change prevailing social and property relations, and hence is constrained to plan reactively and palliatively it becomes itself an integral element of the urban problem at large.*

In contradistinction to the abstract-idealist formulations of current planning theory, urban planning is not reducible to some *a priori* conception (like systems analysis, or mathematical programming, or organization theory) that appears, literally, out of nowhere[1]. As lived and practical human activity, urban planning is comprehensible only as a definite concrete social phenomenon, that is, as a historical event that grows organically out of the basic contradiction in capitalism between the purposes and objectives of commodity production on the one hand, and the functionally defective behavioural devices that constitute the privileged active core of commodity-producing society on the other hand.

The private-public interface

Urban planning spans and in part resolves this latter contradiction, and in this very process a second broad contradiction is brought into existence, namely, the observable contradiction in urban society between the opposed but mutually interdependent imperatives of private versus collective action. We might call the social dynamic that emerges out of these superimposed and intertwined contradictions—between individual rationality and social irrationality, and between the imperatives of private versus collective action—the double dialectic of the urban land nexus. The opposed imperatives of the private and the public in the production of urban space lie at the root of a powerful evolutionary tendency in the urban land nexus. By way of a preliminary attempt to comprehend this tendency, it may be seized at the outset in terms of a familiar prototypical case:

In their unceasing quest for profits, capitalist firms actively seek out ever more technically efficient production processes. One of the ways in which this phenomenon manifests itself in a land-contingent form is in the continual intensification of land uses at central (that is, accessible, polarized, and economically efficient) urban locations. As the process of land-use intensification proceeds, however, so these central locations become more and more overloaded, and the general level of congestion in the central business district becomes increasingly intolerable, especially where there is, in addition, heavy usage of the private car in the journey to work. These circumstances then provoke a counteractive response on the part of the State, which intervenes by investing large quantities of public money in

---

[1] See, in this regard, the recent exchange of views between Harris (1978) and Scott and Roweis (1978).

basic infrastructure in and around the central business district. This then immediately increases the differential locational advantages (and hence the land rents) of central city locations, and directly triggers off new rounds of land-use intensification. The State then intervenes once more, provoking yet more private land-use intensification, and so on, until this particular chain of actions and counteractions in itself builds up into a composite problem whose ill-behaviour begins to exceed the very problem that set it in motion in the first instance. In large Canadian cities, for example, these continual rounds of land-use intensification began, in the late 1960s and early 1970s, to threaten inner city neighbourhoods as commercial and business activities spread outwards from the central business district, and various forms of local protest and political agitation on the part of inner city residents appeared as a consequence. At the same time, municipal financial resources were severely strained by the burden imposed by the continual need to upgrade central city infrastructure. Thus, many Canadian municipalities now found themselves in the position of having to find new strategic methods for confronting the everlastingly elusive problem of the escalating intensification of central city land uses. That is to say, they found themselves obliged to discover some new apparent form of the same basic logic linking civil society and the State through the urban land nexus into a dynamic system of action and counteraction. In the case of Toronto, to take a very specific example, this reorchestration of that customary theme is now taking definite shape in the form of a burgeoning urban policy that seeks to accelerate the decentralization of central business district firms by encouraging the formation of new nuclei of commercial activity at locations well removed from the core. In this fashion some of the pent-up pressure producing continual land-use problems and conflicts in the core of the city is likely to be released. It need hardly be pointed out, however, that beyond the accomplishment of this new phase of the private–public dialectic in the urban land nexus there unquestionably lie yet further, and only dimly apprehended, rounds of this same powerful overarching logic, and hence yet further rounds of urban problems and conflicts.

The urban land nexus is thus reproduced through time in a complex process involving successions of mutually dependent, but eternally problematical, private and public decisions. Private action gives rise to a persistent tendency to dislocation and conflict in the urban land nexus. The State unceasingly attempts to rectify this situation while itself producing further turbulence in the urban land nexus by shifting around the whole system of differential locational advantages (and concomitantly altering the expectations and rewards that different classes, strata, and social fractions seek to procure from urban life). This then sparks off further spontaneous readjustments in the configuration of urban space. However, these two moments of urban development (the private and the public) do not simply represent two independent and mutually exclusive domains of social action. Rather, they are intrinsically and mutually interrelated in the dialectical sense that they are at once antagonistic to one another and yet intimately contingent on one another. The sphere of private action in capitalism rebuffs collective action as that which is socially antithetical to its own existence and interests; and yet collective action grows out of the sphere of private action for the very reason that it secures and guarantees the continued viability of civil society. Out of this tense force field of relationships there emerges a peculiar historical logic that is universally decipherable beneath the apparent disparateness of the manifold events of the urban land nexus. It is a logic that involves an open-ended sequence of privately induced dislocations in the urban land nexus calling forth corrective measures on the part of the State, which in turn give rise to new privately induced dislocations, requiring new corrective measures, and so on *ad infinitum*. As the capitalist city evolves through history, this dialectical process is constantly recreated at ever and ever higher levels of complexity.

Urban planning, then, is less an autonomous control mechanism than it is itself merely a historical response to prior events in the urban land nexus. Urban planning is *embedded* in the urban land nexus, just as the urban land nexus is embedded in the social formation. This means in practice that the social and property relations of capitalism are taken as a fixed and specific point of reference so that State intervention in city systems is permanently reduced to piecemeal and reactive measures. In these circumstances, it follows that the whole process underlying the growth and development of the urban land nexus is inevitably anarchical, governed as it is, in the final instance, by the anarchical process of private decisionmaking and action. Therefore, under current social and property relations the urban land nexus as a whole is *not* an object of collective decisions and voluntaristic social intentions. Nor can it ever be rationally planned in conformity with socially decided purposes in the context of existing social and property relations.

The origins and character of urban planning

In the present chapter an attempt is made to articulate a coherent general theory of urban planning. To all intents and purposes, this theory has already been laid down in earlier sections of this book, and all that needs to be accomplished here is to recapitulate and synthesize the main elements of the preceding argument. In that argument, planning has been consistently identified as a concrete social phenomenon, hence as a phenomenon that is to be explained and accounted for in terms of its observable material manifestations. These material manifestations appear at the precise interface where the State, as the general agent of collective action in capitalist society, confronts and seeks to counteract the self-disorganizing tendencies of the urban land nexus.

In contradistinction to the general perspective on urban planning developed here, much of the existing literature proposes a conception of the planning process as an essentially abstract, procedural, and voluntaristic calculus. It tends to see planning decisions and actions as being independent of any wider structuring process, and imposed from the outside, as it were, upon existing social and urban patterns. It thus tends to conceive of urban planning as a substantively empty ensemble of technical and operational procedures motivated by some disembodied criterion of rationality. Observe that this latter remark is quite definitely not intended to throw doubt on the importance and usefulness of the various technical methodologies currently in use in planning research and practice (on the contrary, their everyday importance and usefulness are surely entirely self-evident); it implicitly questions only the possibility of constructing an adequate theory that is pitched at the level of the internal operational logic of planning as opposed to the more encompassing level (which includes the former) of planning conceived as a socially and historically determinate practice whose inner workings are established by its external relationships to the rest of society. Much of the planning literature, nonetheless, sees methodology as *the* essential point of departure for any theory of urban planning. In its failure effectively to problematize the phenomenon of planning, however, this same literature condemns itself to a truncated and ahistorical view of the planning process as a collection of decisionmaking schemata similar in epistemological status to mathematical theories in the sense that they are in essence devoid of empirical content. But planning is only in the end comprehensible as a structured outgrowth of the social and property relations of commodity-producing society, and its admittedly ready assimilation of routinized procedural methodologies is entirely secondary to its main purposes and functions as it operates within the urban land nexus. Given the extraordinarily restricted horizons of much of the existing literature, some prefatory comment would seem to be in order here by way of clarifying the meaning, properties, and main objectives of any enquiry into contemporary urban planning. This is equivalent to an attempt to elucidate the tasks and qualities of a viable theory of planning.

9.1 The tasks and qualities of a viable theory of planning

Mainstream theoretical analyses of the planning process invariably proceed out of such disparate, but idealist, points of departure as discussions of planning as a general systems process, or efforts to assimilate planning into mathematical optimization theory, or programmatic statements as to what planners ought rationally to do under specified decisionmaking conditions, and so on. In view of this disparateness, it is of some importance to begin the present discussion by explicitly, though sketchily, outlining some criteria by which any prospective theory of urban planning may be judged. This undertaking is initiated, right at the start, by rejecting any attempt to derive planning theory out of abstract normative principles as to what planning *ought* to be in any and all hypothetical ideal circumstances, and by insisting, on the contrary, that a viable theory of urban planning poses itself the sole task of explaining in strictly indicative terms what planning *is*. That is, in contrast to the purely nonscientific and utopian normative theorizing so commonly pursued in the mainstream literature, the theory of planning that is sought after in this account is derived uniquely out of a logical-cum-empirical effort to discover the roots of planning as a concrete social phenomenon. This line of attack, it might be added, so far from requiring any special apology, is surely the usual, normal and sensible procedure for initiating social enquiry generally. In accordance with this observation, let us establish a few ground rules as to how we might go about identifying a viable planning theory, how we might evaluate it, and what expectations we might reasonably make of it.

Much of the existing literature on urban planning theory proceeds on the assumption that the foundations of any conceptualization of the planning process are discoverable in the universe of abstract analytical categories rather than in the universe of lived and practical human activity. Accordingly, conventional planning theory tends to move forward on the basis of formal and linguistic definitions of planning that have a strictly *a priori* or nominalistic character. For example, one repeatedly encounters in the literature such global descriptions of planning as these: planning is "a process for determining appropriate future action through a sequence of choices" (Davidoff and Reiner, 1962, page 103); or, "planning is that process of making rational decisions about future goals and future courses of action which ... requires explicit evaluation and choice among alternative matching goal sets" (Webber, 1963, page 320); or, planning is "a rational process of thought and action which ultimately aims ... at promoting human growth" (Faludi, 1973, page 25). Now, statements of these sorts, that is, formal linguistic definitions of the planning process at the highest possible level of abstraction are in one sense unexceptionable. Yet the very fact that they are largely beyond reproach is gained at the cost of any real clarification of the genesis and historical evolution of planning in practice. They may well (in certain senses at least) be unassailable statements; they may possibly even be susceptible to certain forms of empirical documentation (as opposed to empirical testing); and yet they remain essentially vacuous and indeterminate statements. If we scrutinize them by confronting them with questions such as: according to what social logic are appropriate future actions determined? what social processes set the goals? what might be some of the typical goals? why would these be typical goals? what in sociohistorical reality establishes the specific nature and content of rationality? what is the precise practical meaning of the notion of human growth? etc, then we can readily begin to see how empty and myopic these statements are. As a result, they can really tell us very little that is worthwhile about the substantive domain of urban planning. This remark is reinforced by the further observation that while the three statements about the nature of urban planning given above are all different from one another, it is nevertheless difficult to think of any empirical test that might *in principle* contradict any one of them.

By contrast consider a statement such as this (even if it is already undoubtedly known to be false): Urban planning in contemporary North American society is an outcome of the attempts of municipal politicians to gain reelection; in pursuit of this goal, politicians pass legislation that (a) maximizes urban net income, (b) stabilizes all processes of urban change, and (c) rearranges zoning ordinances in favour of private voters at the expense of business firms. Or this: Urban planning is a function of the personality types and values of planners; where rigid authoritarian personality types dominate the planning process we find programmes geared to efficiency, growth, and economic productivity; where other-directed nonauthoritarian personality types dominate the planning process we find programmes geared to equity, social justice, and the protection of residential amenities. Or even this, laconic as it may be: Planning is an attempt to restructure the city such that aggregate land rents are maximized. These statements are quite obviously not empty and shortsighted. They are at once highly general, that is, they lay claim to validity over a specified universe of cases, and yet they are scientifically rich in that they are open to immediate and dramatic confrontation with empirical data. Even if they are eventually found to be substantively false, they retain their robustness as theoretical propositions. This is precisely because these statements, so far from being immune to the possibility of empirical refutation, are in fact deliberately structured for maximum refutability. This is one of the hallmarks of any powerful theory. So long as such a theory resists empirical refutation, it provides us with definite and structured expectations about the world of substantive phenomena. And if eventually such a theory should indeed be shown to be false, then we have at least gained the certain knowledge that *this* theory need not be taken seriously in the future.

On the basis of this reasoning, it may be adduced that among the principal initial conditions as to what constitutes a viable theory of urban planning, the following must figure with some prominence. First, any such theory must identify universalized *but concrete* expectations about the phenomenon of urban planning. Second, it must allow the possibility of testing the reliability of these expectations against empirical evidence. Third, it must predict future trends before they actually happen. These criteria are, in part, what distinguishes scientifically viable theory from ideology, folklore, myth, and metaphysics. These points have been discussed here at some length, even though they are after all fairly obvious, only because they are so frequently and persistently ignored in mainstream theories of urban planning. The mainstream literature consistently proposes theoretical analyses of the planning process that are by and large indeterminate with respect to substance and social logic, and utopian with respect to the alleged purposes and functions of planning. The theory that is sought after here, however, is above all a theory that attempts to elucidate the material data of planning, just as, say, neoclassical land-use theory seeks to explain and not to engender *ex nihilo* the material data of land use.

In contradistinction to this essentially *indicative* intent, there is a definite position, widely adopted in the literature, that suggests that planning is by its nature essentially *normative*. In this view, planning theory is not so much a discourse about a specific concrete social phenomenon; it is, rather, seen as a self-constitutive *project* involving a process of the suppression of the irrationalities of the past and the ushering in of a new order of things. Now, it is true, of course, that planning is indeed a vehicle for human intentions, and, as such, it is a mainspring of change in contemporary urban systems. However, it is essential to append to this remark the further point that planning performs this function in the context of an enveloping system of social and historical circumstances that is *given*, and that structures its content and trajectory. To treat planning as lying somehow or other outside of a given social formation and constituting a sphere of pure voluntaristic action would be entirely one-sided. Such abstraction away from real and historically determinate parameters of human activity implicitly assumes that transcendent and ahistorical norms (such as the public interest, Pareto optimality, conservationist ethics, Fourierism, and all the rest) have practical operational meaning and relevance irrespective of existing social conditions. To be sure, there is always the sheer logical possibility of setting up abstract normative theories of one sort or another. However, any attempt to relate such theories to the world of material human reality brings us immediately back to the domain of the indicative; for any such attempt only raises the inevitable questions: under what specific social and historical circumstances will any given imperative be meaningful and applicable in practice? and again: what concrete circumstances *give rise* to this imperative rather than that imperative? These questions are rendered all the more acute in the light of the political tensions and conflicts that are so endemic a feature of contemporary social and urban life. In fact, in capitalist society, urban planning can never be reduced down to a system of socially indeterminate norms. On the contrary, planning as a concrete social phenomenon is a product of and an immediate reflection of the historically determinate social and property relations of capitalist society as mediated through the urban land nexus. We may safely leave to visionaries and utopians the bold but sterile task of constructing abstractly normative blueprints for the future of human history. In the discussion that follows, attention is resolutely focussed on the goal of explaining planning as an observable historical event; and the achievement of this goal is sought without benefit of any aprioristic programme of social reform or utopian reconstruction. This having been said, it must be added, however, that the theory of urban planning that is to be developed below is definitely expected to provide guidelines as to policy formation, political action, and the possibilities of progressive urban change. Such guidelines are expected to emerge, and are actively pursued, precisely because any historically embedded (and hence viable) theory must in part reveal real human interests for what they are, and not for what they are asserted to be in the politically anodyne mainstream theories of planning.

A viable theory of planning should therefore not only tell us what planning is, but also what planners can realistically expect to accomplish in any given set of social circumstances. It should be finally capable of confronting and answering all questions that seek to discover the nature of planning as a concretely realized sphere of social action. Such questions as, for example: what social functions does planning perform? what does planning accomplish? what can we expect planners to do under given specific conditions? in what ways does capitalist society circumscribe the activities of planners? why is planning so pervasive today? why was planning relatively insignificant in the last century? why do planners zone land uses (or undertake urban renewal projects, or develop new towns, or intervene in urban transport processes)? why did the citizens' participation movement emerge as an influence on planning? what can planners do next? and so on. The argument that follows seeks to lay the essential foundations of a theory that goes at least part of the way in providing answers to all questions such as these.

9.2 Urban planning and the State

It follows from the preceding argument that any attempt to construct a credible theory of urban planning must begin by rejecting all preconceptions of this activity as an autonomous 'essence'. In contradistinction to the prevalent idealist interpretation, any historically self-conscious theory of urban planning will always insist on treating urban planning like any other concrete social datum: problematical in itself, and, in principle, explicable in strictly indicative terms that reveal its relational social logic. Accordingly, a viable theory must be somehow or other derivable in terms of some wider conception of society as an evolving total entity. In practice, this proposition is equivalent to an assertion that the origins and character of urban planning are finally discoverable within the structure of capitalist social formations. And this in turn implies that a necessary preliminary step in any attempt to understand the form and content of contemporary urban planning is an analysis of the role of the capitalist State.

The capitalist State: a brief recapitulation
The capitalist State occupies a sphere of collective governance whose function is to secure socially necessary functions that are inaccessible to the privatistic decisionmaking modes of civil society. The State safeguards social and property relations as a whole, and it engages in cautious crisis management and steering tactics as and when these become imperative at any particular conjuncture. In line with these tasks, the actions of the State fall into two major categories of intervention, reflecting the structure and dynamics of commodity-producing society as a totality. On the one hand, the State takes such initiatives as secure continued capital accumulation and economic growth, that is, it seeks to ensure the success and vitality of the material foundations of capitalist society. On the other hand, the State establishes conditions that secure continued assent to the legitimacy of the capitalist social order, and, in particular, that help to keep the struggle between capital and labour over the meaning, purposes, and rewards of existence in capitalist society within manageable bounds. State policies reflect these two broad imperatives with varying emphasis and bias depending on any conjuncture of events. For example, in North America in recent decades an observable pattern of public policy shifts has tended to emerge such that when economic growth is at a high level then programmes geared to equalization (increases in social overhead capital, investment in backward regions, amelioration of environmental quality, etc) are fairly strongly in evidence, whereas when recessionary conditions appear, then programmes geared to growth (tax cuts, reductions of all but the most economically efficient public investments, industrial productivity incentives, etc) are clearly dominant. Given the environment of social and political conflict in which it necessarily exists, the State finds itself in a permanently critical situation as it carries out these complex and often incompatible functions. As Habermas (1976) has pointed out, if the State fails to secure continued capital accumulation and economic growth then productive efficiency and capitalist rationality are severely compromised; if it fails to secure continued assent to the legitimacy of the prevailing social order, then breakdowns in the continuity of social and ideological relations will ensue. In either case, there will be grave consequences for capitalism as a working and ongoing entity.

The capitalist State, then, represents the condensation of collective imperatives within the field of historical action defined by the social and property relations of capitalism. In capitalist society, the State can neither be external to that field of historical action, nor be simply the fief of some powerful and politically privileged clique. The *capitalist* State is, rather, the general expression of collective imperatives in a society whose basic rule is determined by the deeply rooted law of the exchange of equivalents and all that this signifies in terms of democratic order and individual rights. Further, this view of the State runs counter to two alternative views with some considerable currency among social scientists at the present time. It is a view that rebuts on the one hand the liberal consumer-sovereignty theory of the State (together with various accretions from welfare economics), and it rebuts on the other hand that blunt Marxist theory of the State as the executive committee of the bourgeoisie.

The former view is captured precisely by Thompson (1965, page 263) when he describes the political fragmentation of metropolitan areas in North America as a device that is designed to secure the more perfect satisfaction of consumers' tastes and preferences. He writes that such fragmentation serves

> "... to bring together in a given municipality a group who would minimize the public sector in their everyday life, with a volunteer fire department, self-provision of garbage disposal and outdoor lighting of their property, and dependence on personal libraries. Alternatively, another like-minded group of residents may prefer to substitute 'free' municipal swimming pools and golf courses for the more common 'free' paved streets (by retaining dirt roads). A third group may be less distinctive in matters of the quantity or mix of public services than in their desire to exercise close control over the local government that produces these services. This latter group may feel that 'bureaucracy' (diseconomies of scale in administration) more than offsets various economies of scale in production and finance, and so this might be an economy-in-government group."

At the other extreme, the contemporary orthodox Marxian view (as reflected in the doctrine of State monopoly capitalism) is concisely summed up by Leclercq (1977, page 222), who describes the political logic of modern capitalist society as the result of the more or less direct control of the State apparatus by the big monopolies in the context of the so-called overaccumulation–devalorization process:

> "The State now intervenes as the organizer of the capitalist mode of production. In this totality, the determining role resides in the last instance with the monopolies, as a result both of their increasing weight and importance in economic life, and of the influence that they exercise over the State and its policy. This is decipherable in the contradictory growth of capital and the particular expression of this growth in the

falling rate of profit. From this there flows a propensity to an overaccumulation of capital in relation to possibilities for its valorization: excess capital is devalorized and rendered dormant: it does not, or cannot, claim its share of average profit.

Besides the classic form of devalorization—bankruptcy—there now appears a modern form: nationalization. Here, a portion of social capital is permanently assigned to devalorization: it yields zero or negative profit and it contributes to the raising of the rate of profit in other branches. It delays the crisis without suppressing it. The intervention of the State secures also a part of the financing of private monopolistic production (subsidies, consumption by the State, expenses contributing to the development of the social forces of production ...). The State aims also at the reorganization of production. In these conditions, the grand bourgeoisie cannot give up its control over the State."

Given all that has gone before, it is evident that neither of these two views of the State, nor the urban planning theories that they beget (planning as a consumer option versus planning as an expression of the desperate search by the monopolies to shore up the supposedly falling rate of profit) can be even mildly accurate descriptions of the processes of public policy formation in a capitalist society. The former view is simply blind to the fact that modern society is structured from top to bottom by capitalist production and reproduction relations, and it falls by default into an absurdly idealist position that sees the State as being continuously created and recreated in the minds of the general citizenry. By contrast, the latter view is founded on a contrived and dogmatic theory of the dynamics of the rate of profit, and this theory in turn is based upon a mechanical interpretation of the labour theory of value that rigidly insists on accounting for all economic quantities in terms of simple labour hours. This interpretation has recently been discredited yet again—and with immense clarity—by Steedman (1977), and the reader is referred to his work for a rigorous demonstration of the essential superfluity of the standard labour theory of value. In addition to this difficulty, however, and even granting for the sake of argument that the rate of profit does tend to fall over time, the theory of State-monopoly capitalism simply assimilates political action into a sort of conspiracy on the part of the grand bourgeoisie. Without further intermediation, then, such activities on the part of the State as the provision of transport services, land-use zoning, mortgage financing and insuring, urban renewal, and all the rest are seen as being the outcome of monopoly capital's direct or indirect manipulation of the organs of government in order to counteract the nefarious effects of the falling rate of profit. Even setting aside the arguments that have been advanced in the present book purporting to show that the intervention of the political collectivity (in society at large as well as in the urban land nexus in particular) is more subtly embedded in capitalist social relationships than this, the theory of State-monopoly capitalism poses, in its own terms, a number of refractory questions. Thus, if the theory is correct, then at what stage in the process of the falling rate of profit are we to suppose that the grand bourgeoisie, working through the State, will begin to press for the "devalorization of excess capital"? When the rate of profit falls to forty, twenty, ten, ..., percent? Would a rising rate of profit imply a withdrawal of capital from the realm of politics? How do we explain such activities of the State as land-use zoning, the administration of building codes, traffic control, neighbourhood preservation, and so on, which have clearly little or nothing to do with the supposed process of devalorization? The recent study by Lojkine (1977) of urban planning in modern society reveals the mortal weaknesses of the concept of State-monopoly capitalism. Beneath all the complex but overdrawn analysis—itself founded on the doubtful macroeconomic machinery of the labour theory—there is discoverable nothing much more than a reconstructed theory of the power elite. What is more, Lojkine's statement is almost entirely devoid of any real *urban* specificity or meaning in the senses insisted upon at earlier stages in the present argument. Clearly, when the State acts to preserve the capitalist social order, it upholds, by that very process, the prevailing relations of authority and subordination in society. To distort this phenomenon into the recurrent fallacy of the theory of the power elite is to miss all the analytical niceties, and hence also the derivative political tasks, that surround the question of collective action in contemporary capitalist society. The same points are made with some force by Touraine (1973, page 274), who writes:

"The extreme visibility of the State apparatus and of political parties suggests that the State is the central operating principle of society, that society is the product of the State, and that the conquest of the State signifies the creation of a new society .... The State is not placed above society; no more is it a pure instrument of unification of social practices in the service of the dominant class. As the location and agent of communication between levels of social reality, it is always contained within a mode of social domination, but it is not the same thing as this domination."

Like the State at large, urban planning is a social relation that is contained within, but is not the same thing as prevailing forms of social domination in contemporary society. It partakes of the capital–labour relation, but in peculiar, mediated, and occasionally remote ways. Moreover, planning plays a historical role that distinguishes it from the State as a whole, even while it remains an intrinsic element of the apparatus of the State. Given its particular role and functions, urban planning is not, and can never be a simple microcosm of the totality of the State.

The situation of urban planning within the State apparatus
At an earlier stage, it was shown how political intervention in capitalism is engendered in a contradictory way by the various concrete failures and insufficiencies of civil society. This suggests at once that urban planning itself cannot be derived in a simple *a priori* manner out of a globalized description of the functions of the State. Before urban planning can be seized in theoretical terms, and situated in relation to the State as a whole, the intervening variable of the urban land nexus must be adduced. In other words, before urban planning can be adequately conceptualized, it is essential to unravel the complex logic that governs the spatiotemporal development of the urban land nexus, and that causes the urban system to throw endless problems into the lap of society, thus provoking collective remedial action. Urban planning is neither an attempt to operationalize some utopian vision of the ideal city, nor the outcome of conscious political manipulation on the part of the grand bourgeoisie. It is a socially structured public response to the problems and predicaments of the urban land nexus. Urban planning, in sum, is society's way of dealing with the historical imperative of controlling the crisis-ridden land-contingent logic that constitutes the urbanization process in capitalism. As such, planning also has a territorial and geographical expression, so that it is imbued with spatially determinate social conflicts that cut across strictly class lines of demarcation. However, as an element of the apparatus of the capitalist State, urban planning is inescapably marked in various ways by the overall capital–labour relation that runs through commodity-producing society.
In brief, the politics of urban planning can be simply reduced neither to the issue of intercommunity and interneighbourhood rivalry, nor to the issue of pure class relations. It partakes of both of these issues simultaneously, but in unequal and variable degree, and the overall political controversies and pressures that surround the realized actions of urban planners are very much a function of established social practices and political configurations; they are also very much a function of the presence or absence of one or more political parties capable of meaningfully coordinating and integrating urban issues into a general reformist agenda. As it happens, the somewhat peripheral location of urban planning within the capitalist mode of production generally, obscures its essential and ultimate connection to basic class issues. This is perhaps particularly the case in North America where a strong tradition of local government (and the consequent geographical fractionation of political issues) makes it yet more difficult to perceive the organic structural link between politics at the municipal level and politics at the broad national level. Strong municipal government tends to depoliticize urban planning.

At the same time, this ambiguity as to the political functions and biases of urban planning grows in part out of an intrinsic ambiguity in the global structure of the State itself. Given the multifarious character of the different organs of State control and administration, the specific balance of tensions and conflicts that is evident at the level of the State as a whole is far from being replicated in perfect one-to-one correspondence throughout its many component parts. Hirsch (1976) has shown how each particular formation within the State bureaucracy exists within its own specialized environment, with its own specific tasks and projects, and with its own acquired perceptions of things. As a corollary, collective action in capitalist social formations is always to some extent cloaked by the appearance of a lack of coordination, as though the State *really were* involved in a process of muddling through in an entirely aimless and apolitical way. This appearance is magnified by the overt inconsistencies that occur time and time again as different departments of government fulfill their own specific mandates. The net result is a distortion of the perceived meaning of collective action generally, and a concomitant depoliticization of the interventionist tactics of the State. Similarly, the highly specialized functions of urban planners, and their apparent isolation from the realm of national politics contribute still further to the difficulties of discovering the wider significance of planning as an element within the total collective machinery that permits capitalist society to reproduce itself through time. While the isolation of urban planners from the realm of national politics is clearly in the process of being rapidly dissolved away in all the major capitalist societies, planning and urban policy nevertheless still tend to appear as a domain of decentralized, localized, and semicoordinated decisionmaking within a total State apparatus that is considerably less than monolithic.

If the State bureaucracy of capitalism is complex and multidimensional, however, this is only in the end an outcome of the circumstance that it faces a complex and multidimensional task within the context of a single overriding imperative, that is, the historically imposed necessity of sustaining the social and property relations of capitalism. Urban planning, then, takes on specific meaning and content in the twofold sense that (a) it represents collective action in capitalist class society and (b) this action deals with

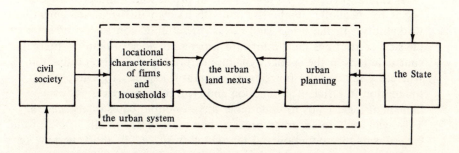

Figure 9.1. Schematic representation of the urban land nexus as a subset of geographical relationships embedded in capitalist society.

the idiosyncratic quandaries and managerial tasks thrown out by the urban land nexus. This notion is identified schematically in figure 9.1, which shows how the urban land nexus grows out of the locational dynamics of firms and households together with the apparatus of urban planning as these in turn are organically rooted in the wider set of relationships linking together civil society and the State.

9.3 The dynamics of urban planning
Urban land problems and the genesis of urban planning
The fundamental structural core of capitalist civil society consists of the institution of commodity production and exchange together with a constellation of derivative social forms: the division of labour, the rate of profit, land markets, the family, residential neighbourhoods, and so on. This structural core functions in conformity with a rationality that is based essentially on price signals, market competition, decentralized production decisions, and such bourgeois legal arrangements as private property, individual rights, and the contractual equality of persons. These legal arrangements are the formal expression of a social system whose basic behavioural logic is codified within a system of individual decisionmaking and action. Civil society, then, can be seen as an ensemble of historically determinate social relationships actualized by a human behavioural process comprising a purely *privatized* system of calculations. By contrast, urban planning constitutes a sphere of *collective* political calculations, and it fills a vital decisionmaking gap within the totality of capitalist society. Furthermore, whereas private action can always be deciphered in terms of the historically determinate interests of individual actors, the rationality of urban planning can never be comprehended in terms of the personal interests of the individual agents (planners) who carry it through. Urban planning is comprehensible only in terms of its functional connection to the various self-negating elements of civil society as they are mediated through the urban land nexus.

As capitalist society expresses itself in urban forms and processes, so it begins to encounter numberless limits to its own further development and workability. In the urban land nexus, these limits consist less of external physical restrictions on the forward progress of society than of internal contradictions in the spatial dynamics of production and reproduction. Whereas a successfully functioning capitalism requires a geographical foundation in efficient production and reproduction spaces, its own immanent logic tends to undermine these essential bases of its success. This logic leads to an urban process that consistently results in multiform breakdowns in production and reproduction space. In short, because of the necessary primacy of individual decisionmaking and action in capitalism, a constant stream of pathological outcomes erupts through the urban land nexus. While these pathologies threaten to impair the functional efficiency of society at large, they are nonetheless immune to curative action via the

normal rationality of commodity-producing society. Consequently, when
the dislocations, irrationalities, and conflicts of the urban land nexus begin
to subvert the smooth perpetuation of prevailing social relationships, urban
planning makes its historical appearance as a means of socially readjusting
the spatial and temporal development of the urban land nexus—a necessity
that cannot be neglected and yet that is constantly in conflict with the
basic conformation of civil society. Urban planning acquires and changes
its specific targets and emphases as well as its supportive ideologies
(planning theory, planning education, professional codes of practice, etc) in
relation to definite urban manifestations of that same necessity. In view of
this remark, urban planning is not, and never can be, a simple homeostatic
phenomenon, such as, say, an invariant and logical system of decisionmaking
rules and procedures. It is, on the contrary, an ever changing historical
process that is continually being shaped and reshaped by reference to a broad
system of urban tensions, of which it eventually itself becomes an integral
element. Thus, North American society, for example, has not engaged in
frequently bitter urban controversies and disputes over urban property
rights, institutionalized zoning, urban renewal, highway construction,
suburbanization, and all the rest, simply because urban realities did not
measure up to certain abstract standards of performance. It was only
when urban growth and development began to produce *real* problems that
society started to act consciously and collectively to counteract them.
Urban planning is thus a historically specific and socially unavoidable
response to the autodestructive social and property relations of capitalism
as they make their way through land-contingent processes into the realized
form of the urban land nexus.

The limits of urban planning
At any given moment in time the limits of urban planning are fixed in
relation to the politically feasible negation of the arrangements of civil
society that is necessary in order to enable planners to make remedial
attacks upon the functional breakdowns of the urban system. Urban
planning is an active social force only to the degree that it acquiesces in
its own containment within the primary structures of commodity-producing
society. More specifically, the history and development of urban planning
is the history and development of an instrumentality that is at once
crucial for the well-being of society, but that is constantly resisted by society.
In contrast to conditions in, say, some hypothetical socialist society
where the collectivity by definition assumes preeminent control over the
production and reproduction of social relationships (hence also generating
a corresponding set of historically specific problems and predicaments),
collective control on the part of the capitalist State is always acquired
in a pragmatic and piecemeal fashion and always in the face of the
grudging assent of civil society. Capital, in particular, is perennially
unwilling to consent to the extension of State intervention and regulation,

and yet, recognizing that its own survival is intimately dependent on some form of collective decisionmaking, it finally accepts—though always fractiously and only after internal struggle—that curtailment of its own sphere of operation that must come about before planning can begin to function as an effective instrument of public policy. Capital as a whole has always fundamentally opposed and sought to abridge the institution of planning while at the same time disconsolately conceding its social inevitability. In other words, planning is hemmed in by the prior structures and imperatives of capitalist society, and its power to resolve the problems of the urban land nexus is permanently and of necessity shackled. This means that the reactive and palliative nature of urban planning in capitalism is not simply the result of some technical, analytical, or human failure; it is the inevitable concomitant of a social logic that sets definite barriers around the range and effectiveness of all political action. Urban planning is a response to the imperative of collective action in the urban land nexus, and yet it cannot transgress the very social relationships from which it springs. It is, in short, a mode of intervention that is put into effect only when it serves the limited purpose of being necessary and useful in strictly capitalistic terms.

The terms that establish the conditions under which urban planning is put into effect or left in abeyance take on varying substance as capitalist society evolves through time, and as it encounters new conjunctures and new political imperatives. In the early industrial towns, for example, the various problems of discordant land uses were for the most part ignored by the State with the exception of very basic but perfunctory controls geared largely to matters of public hygiene and the maintenance of social order. At the turn of the century, nothing less than virtually universal zoning could contain urban land-use problems within socially necessary limits. By the 1930s, the State was deeply committed as a significant partner of capital in the production of urban land by means of massive investments in infrastructure and public housing. At the present time, State control over the entire process of development of the urban land nexus is so great that it is now virtually everywhere systematized within such broad administrative arrangements as national ministries of planning and/or urban affairs, planning enabling acts, a codified body of planning law, the urban general plan, and so on. At each stage in the unfolding of this historical pattern, planning enters onto the scene in the form of an indispensable but always restrained instrumentality for bridging and defusing the specific predicaments of the urban land nexus. However, because it is so highly limited in its range of operation, planning also emerges as a social phenomenon that finally only compounds the overall problem of urbanization in capitalist society by itself sparking off yet further rounds of urban predicaments. Thus, housing clearances for urban hygiene purposes in the nineteenth century led directly to the unresolved problem of lodging displaced families; zoning contributed to the overdevelopment of some urban areas at the expense of others, just as it also encouraged urban social segregation; the participation of the State in the physical production of urban land via the implantation of extremely complex infrastructural artefacts gave rise to the problem of insistent land-use intensification in central business districts while it also encouraged uncontrolled outward expansion of cities; and the generalization and institutionalization of planning practices within a complex bureaucracy has contributed markedly to the repoliticization of urban planning and the incipient but increasing polarization of urban life. Urban problems, then, are not just the by-product of private decisionmaking and action in the urban land nexus; they are also the outcome of foregoing planning interventions which have helped to steer the urban land nexus into configurations that are pregnant with those very problems. In addition to the problems mentioned immediately above we might also note in this context such problems as the contemporary crisis of municipal finance, the massive and dysfunctional use of the private car for urban transport, the ghettoization of racial minorities, and so on. The social and property relations of capitalism give rise to a form of urban planning which, in resolving one set of problems, triggers off yet more. For this very reason, and to repeat, it is evident that the omnipresent failures and shortcomings of urban planning in practice are *not* the result of a failure of planning research, or of the imperfections of planning education, or of the professional inadequacies of planners, etc, etc. One might say, rather, that in the matters of research, education, and professional work, established levels of performance are more than equal to the structurally limited tasks that planners are required to perform. For the failures of planning in practice are less failures of *savoir faire* than they are the inevitable concomitants of collective intervention in a society that at once clamours for and yet rebuffs such intervention.

The opposed imperatives of private versus collective action in the urban land nexus
Since the political collectivity can never transcend the immanent structures of civil society (except, of course, by a forced appropriation of the administrative apparatus of the State) it can never secure final and decisive control over the development of the urban land nexus. Urban planning interventions are, by their very nature, stopgap measures generated as reactive responses to urban land pathologies. In addition, and as a consequence of the inherently restricted scope of collective action in capitalist society, each specific round of planning intervention sparks off new sorts of pathologies in the urban land nexus. Planners are able to control in many cases the outer symptoms of these pathologies, but they can never abolish the fundamental capitalistic logic that produces them. Thus, each time that planners intervene to correct a given predicament in the urban land nexus, so the whole urban system is carried forward to a

new stage of development and structural complexity in which new predicaments begin to manifest themselves, calling for yet further rounds of collective intervention, carrying the urban system forward to a yet more complex stage of development, and so on, in repetitive sequence.

In the urban land nexus, this dynamic relationship between civil society and the State assumes the form of an observable organic private-public partnership in the production of urban land. This partnership is precisely the open appearance in urban society of the fundamental contradiction, outlined above, between the antithetical imperatives of private action— as imposed by the norms and logic of commodity production—and the imperative of collective action—as imposed by the failures and self-negating properties of the institutions of civil society. Furthermore, this partnership between civil society and the State, and, as a corollary, between the market allocation and the political allocation of urban land to different uses, is not simply a *mechanical* relation between two autonomous sets of variables; it is a *dialectical* relation in the definite sense that the institutions of civil society give rise, through successive mediations, to the historical emergence of collective action and, indeed, can only continue to reproduce themselves in the presence of collective action, whereas these same institutions also impede and resist the emergence of collective action. In other words, the social and property relations of capitalism create an urban process which repels that on which its continued existence is ultimately posited: collective action in the form of planning. In this way (and notwithstanding the pervasiveness of planning in contemporary cities) the urban land nexus moves forward through time in a pattern of historical development that is ungoverned, and, effectively, ungovernable. Beneath the appearance of social control over the evolution of the urban land nexus by means of technical fixes, there emerges, upon closer scrutiny, the inexorable dynamic of a complex of land-contingent events that is, to all intents and purposes, quite out of control and, in human terms, irrational.

The capitalist State is thus caught up in a constantly escalating spiral of urban interventions that are essentially preempted by an overarching historical logic. The more it acts, the more it must continue to act, and there can be no practical possibility of withdrawing from or reversing this process except at the cost of a dramatic resurgence of those very problems and predicaments that made any particular interventionist tactic necessary in the first instance. It therefore seems safe to assume that urban planning in general, whatever its realized concrete content, will continue to penetrate increasingly deeply into all layers of urban life. This process, however, carries with it severe political penalties. As the State finds itself in the situation of mediating ever more insistently and intimately the whole process of the production of urban land, so does it visibly modify the distribution of material benefits and disbenefits accruing to various individuals and groups in urban space. As a consequence, urban planning begins to lose its utopian and depoliticizing patina as that which 'seeks to promote human growth', and its true political nature begins to emerge with ever greater clarity. The more the State intervenes in the urban land nexus, the more various social groups and fractions are encouraged to contest the legitimacy of its decisions, and the more urban life as a whole is gradually invaded by political controversies and dilemmas. In this process, the role of urban planning as an instrument for regulating the institutions of commodity-producing society (as mediated through the urban land nexus) becomes ever more apparent; the ideological confusions and distractions (such as mainstream planning theory) that surround the activity of planning start to drop away as they are confronted with empirical circumstances that are increasingly inexplicable in terms of the received wisdom; urban planning experiences the same incipient crisis of legitimation that haunts the State as a whole in late capitalist society; and planning begins to emerge in its true colours as only one more administrative formation within a State that is, in its totality, rooted in the central capital-labour relation of commodity-producing society.

9.4 A concluding comment on planning theory

The theory of urban planning that has been synthesized in this chapter is resolutely nonnormative and antiidealist. It is concerned to discover the material sources of planning as a modality of collective action in capitalism, and it rejects by implication all those views of the planning process which simply assert that planning *ought* to conform in practice to this or that *a priori* methodology. In spite of this reservation it is to be remarked that the theory described above definitely provides a framework for situating in a concrete and nonmystified way the role of different methods and procedures *within* contemporary planning practice. The argument in the present chapter has proceeded, not by inventing abstract analytical definitions of planning [which, as Roweis (1975) has pointed out, may well be valid as definitions of planning in other yet to be realized societies, though most certainly not in contemporary capitalist society], but by the progressive conceptualization of urban planning as it emerges obscurely but resolutely out of the capitalist mode of production. In view of this argument, it is by now abundantly clear that there cannot be a scientifically viable planning theory in the form of a self-contained discourse about the pure logic of decisionmaking and collective behaviour. On the contrary, any really viable theory of urban planning must grow out of some wider theory of the urbanization process, and it must further elucidate this process in terms of its connections to a single field of historical action, the capitalist mode of production. It is to be concluded, then, that the concrete goals and actions of practising planners in matters of urban public health, new towns development, inner city revitalization programmes, environmental protection and control, etc represent the outer manifestation and conditions of continued existence of the deep structures of commodity-producing society as these structures obtrude into the peculiar historical entity that is designated here the urban land nexus.

In the few remaining chapters of this book, an attempt is made, first, to inject some empirical substance into the theory of planning proposed above, second, to use this theory as a point of reference to reveal for what they are the main ideological effusions that currently pass for a reigning theory of planning, and, third and finally, to discuss in a broad way, some of the political implications of the analysis developed here.

Urban development and planning intervention: five illustrative sketches

10.1 Introduction

The argument as developed hitherto has proceeded in a largely theoretical manner. It has been shown in principle and in a broad way how the urban system may be supposed to work, how planning makes its historical appearance, and how both urbanization and planning combine to yield a single dynamic process within the overarching process of capitalist development. It now seems important to flesh out this bare structure with some reasonably solid empirical content.

Thus, the discussion that follows turns to an exposition of five simple empirical vignettes as a means of illustrating the theoretical discussion developed above. These vignettes all show, for a wide variety of different capitalist social formations, how the evolution of the urban land nexus may be consistently described in terms of a dialectic of private versus public decisionmaking and action as structured by the imperatives of the capitalist system. The five examples selected here comprise brief analytical sketches of (a) the relationship between reproduction and urbanization in Britain in the second half of the nineteenth century; (b) the case of Baron Haussmann and the reconstruction of central Paris from 1851 to 1873; (c) the origins and consequences of land-use zoning in North American municipalities; (d) the US urban renewal programme from 1949 to 1961; and (e) transport problems and policies in Metropolitan Toronto from 1953 to the mid-1970s. The example of reproduction and urbanization processes in Britain in the second half of the nineteenth century is chosen to illustrate the defective logic of spontaneous reproduction processes in capitalist cities, and the concomitant need for some form of social control over housing and neighbourhood development in order to enhance the functional success of urban residential activity. The case of Baron Haussmann and the reconstruction of central Paris represents a situation in which the intervention of the State constituted the only practicable means of transcending the inherited physical barriers that in the mid-nineteenth century imposed severe limits on the growth and expansion of the city of Paris. Land-use zoning in North American municipalities exemplifies a widely employed collective method of attempting to contain and to neutralize many different kinds of negative spillover effects in the urban land nexus. The US urban renewal programme from 1949 to 1961 is a case study in one collective attempt to overcome a highly resistant free-rider problem, and it demonstrates how the American government justified its attack on that problem by means of a proclaimed preoccupation with housing while covertly serving the interests of capital. Finally, the analysis of recent transport problems and policies in Metropolitan Toronto provides significant insights into the behaviour and urban impacts of the State as supplier and manager of a system of capital-intensive public goods.

These five brief case studies are intended to serve no more ambitious purpose than one of simple exemplification. Given their inductive and partial nature, they can never function as finally clinching testimony in favour of the theoretical ideas developed in earlier chapters, though they do most certainly dramatically illustrate various facets of those ideas. Despite their selection so as to provide a fairly wide range of historical and geographical cases, they are also, of course, somewhat arbitrary. Equally valid and forceful empirical examples might well have been synthesized out of many other cases of urban development and planning intervention in capitalism, for example, urban public health legislation and planning, new towns programmes, public housing, industrial incentive schemes, the geographical organization of municipal government, and so on. No matter what specific exemplary topics may be chosen, however, a similar broad historical pattern is in one way or another discernible in all; that is, a privatistic process of urban development leading to breakdowns in production and reproduction space, calling in turn for collective intervention whose net effect is a modified urban structure in which the recurrent capitalistic logic of private decisionmaking and action leads on to yet more historically determinate urban breakdowns. Finally, the five empirical examples chosen for particular analysis here all demonstrate the particular point that different capitalist social formations may contain within themselves radically different urban structures and interventionist procedures. In the terminology of Hindess and Hirst (1977), the urbanistic "conditions of existence" of the core relationships of capitalism take on widely varying shapes and forms depending on historical circumstances, local conjunctures, and the overall structure of political alliances and consciousness.

10.2 Reproduction and urbanization in Britain in the second half of the nineteenth century

The rapid and uncontrolled growth of industrial towns in Britain in the early decades of the nineteenth century produced a notoriously squalid and insalubrious urban environment. Caught up in the grip of a relentlessly competitive labour market, the new industrial proletariat lived close to the subsistence level in dense and disease-ridden residential quarters which tended persistently to degenerate into ominous slums. In a celebrated passage from his description of Manchester in the 1840s, Engels (1845; 1969 edition, pages 82–83) dramatically captures something of the dismal character of those slums:

> "Right and left a multitude of covered passages lead from the main street into numerous courts, and he who turns in thither gets into a filth and disgusting grime the equal of which is not to be found—

especially in the courts which lead down to the Irk, and which contain unqualifiedly the most horrible dwellings I have yet beheld. In one of these courts there stands directly at the entrance a privy without a door, so dirty that the inhabitants can pass into and out of that court only by passing through foul pools of urine and excrement. This is the first court of the Irk above Ducie Bridge ... . Below it on the river there are several tanneries which fill the whole neighbourhood with the stench of animal putrefaction. Below Ducie Bridge the only entrance to most of the houses is by means of narrow, dirty stairs and over heaps of refuse and filth. The first Court below Ducie Bridge, known as Allen's Court, was in such a state at the time of the cholera that the sanitary police ordered it evacuated, swept and disinfected with chloride of lime."

An analogous description of social and urban conditions in the low quarters of Glasgow in 1842 is quoted by Ashworth (1954, page 49) from a report of the superintendent of police at that time:

"The houses ... are unfit even for sties, and every apartment is filled with a promiscuous crowd of men, women, and children, all in the most revolting state of filth and squalor. In many houses, there is scarcely any ventilation; dunghills lie in the vicinity of the dwellings; and from the extremely defective sewerage, filth of every kind constantly accumulates. In these horrid dens the most abandoned characters of the city are collected, and from thence they nightly issue to disseminate disease, and to pour upon the town every species of crime and abomination."

Similar descriptions from across the length and breadth of Britain during the nineteenth century might be multiplied *ad infinitum*. For present purposes the significance of these accounts resides in the problem so clearly implied in the final sentence of the second passage quoted above, which is to say that the severely deteriorated living conditions of the urban proletariat gave rise to persistent and long-term breakdowns of public health, and social order. In spite of the valiant efforts of a long line of individual reformers and philanthropists throughout the nineteenth century, these critical breakdowns were most emphatically irresolvable by means of individual initiative alone. Some more potent social force than this was essential in order to counter the global problem of residential disintegration in nineteenth-century cities, and of thus releasing more fully the potential energies and capacities of the urban proletariat. Hence, gradually over the nineteenth century, and always in the context of restless political conflicts, the British State began to bring a series of complex collective responses to bear upon this problem. Let us here consider the particularly subtle and intriguing question of the role of the State in its attempts to enhance the qualities of residential environments as foci of socialization and social reproduction of the urban proletariat in the nineteenth century. It goes without saying that the effectiveness of this role was intimately dependent on the prior success of the State's ongoing programme of public health legislation and physical environmental control throughout the nineteenth century. This programme is forcefully described in Benevolo (1967) and the reader is referred to this latter work for further information on this matter.

The sort of urban conditions described by Engels in 1845 were the inevitable expression in the living place of a labouring class that was for the most part brutalized, indisciplined, and illiterate. At the same time, these same urban conditions sustained and intensified these negative qualities of the proletariat by interposing real obstacles in the way of all but the most imperfect domestication of the human labourer. These negative qualities made themselves manifest in an inefficient work force, street riots, worker rebellions, sabotage of factory equipment, and so on. Indeed, by the middle of the nineteenth century, the defective socialization of the working classes was beginning to constitute a brake on the forward momentum of the accumulation process. British capitalism was now on the threshold of a new phase of expansion and development that called increasingly for a new kind of main labour force: one that had unerringly (if possible) internalized the needs and imperatives of the production system and that was accordingly capable of self-discipline and moral restraint, of taking modest initiatives in the performance of labour tasks, and of enduring the psychological costs of an intensified rhythm of factory work. In practice, the inculcation of these extremely positive attributes into the urban proletariat was dependent in significant ways upon workers' living arrangements, and upon various attempts collectively to upgrade the functional qualities of those arrangements. As Pollard (1965, page 197) has written:

"The conclusion cannot be avoided that ... the drive to raise the level of respectability and morality among the working classes was not undertaken for their own sakes, but primarily, or even exclusively, as an aspect of building up a new factory discipline."

And in pursuit of this surpassing end, it was necessary for society to find some means of attacking the very roots of the problem, namely, family structures, the domestic environment, and the social relations of reproduction.

Already, by the beginning of the nineteenth century, the manifest problems of working-class reproduction in the industrial towns had given rise to a series of manifestos proclaiming alternative ideal models of urban life and society. Many of these manifestos were, in addition, translated into practical experiments in new forms of living and working. For the most part, these experiments were little more than utopian fantasies that failed in short order as the effective impossibility of transforming capitalist society by simple fiat and moral exhortation became readily apparent in practice. Owen's ideal community at New Harmony, founded in the 1820s, or the various social experiments modelled upon Fourier's prescriptions were immediate outcomes of the utopian fervour that swept much of nineteenth-century social thought, though they disappeared, by and large, within only a few years of their initiation. By contrast, a scattering of new factory villages and workers' settlements, in England and elsewhere, achieved a more enduring and practical success. These new communities were founded by individual capitalists concerned only with the comparatively modest task of improving and overseeing the living conditions of their workers without in any sense calling into question the fundamental social and property relations of capitalism. In spite of the circumstance that these communities are persistently confounded in the literature with more purely utopian experiments, they were, in fact, resolutely antiutopian in character and they sought precisely to insert themselves into the *existing* fabric of industrial capitalism. Among the better known of these more down-to-earth experiments are New Lanark (which was established by Owen himself in 1799 in the early stages of his career as social reformer), Saltaire (built by Sir Titus Salt in the 1850s), Bourneville (founded by George Cadbury in 1879), and Port Sunlight (founded by W H Lever in 1888). A plan of Saltaire is given in figure 10.1, which illustrates the clear interdependence between the workers' residential community and Salt's factory. Pollard (1965, page 197) remarks of all such experiments:

"In their attempts to prevent Idleness, Extravagance, Waste, and Immorality, employers were necessarily dealing with the workers both inside the factory and outside it. The efforts to reform the whole man were, therefore, particularly marked in factory towns and villages in which the total environment was under the control of a single employer .... These settlements were founded by the industrialist, their whole *raison d'être* his quest for profit ...."

However, if many of these experiments were highly successful, both in the proximate sense that they vastly improved the living standards of the labour force, and in the ultimate sense that they also brought about a marked increase in industrial productivity, this was essentially a function of a very special and in practice nongeneralizable state of affairs, namely, the peculiar circumstance that the population of these model workers' communities constituted a captive labour force. In the big industrial towns, by contrast, anarchy in living conditions was the inevitable order of the day. There, the law of a competitive, many-sided, and integrated labour market prevailed, and wages (that is, standards of living) were fixed in an entirely impersonal and implacable manner. And, as already pointed out in chapter 7, the curious logic of the free-rider problem effectively prevented capitalists in the major manufacturing centres from taking any significant initiatives in the direction of improving the living conditions of their workers. Every capitalist would of course have drawn considerable benefit from any general enhancement of the reproduction process.

However, any unilateral attempt on the part of individual capitalists to achieve this goal would only in the end have succeeded in bestowing a number of powerful positive externalities on those shrewder and more cautious competitors who logically preferred to reap rather than to sow. In addition, as the experience of Pullman in the United States made plain, it was extraordinarily difficult even for those capitalists who enjoyed a captive labour force to maintain expenditures on workers' welfare in times of economic recession when factory profits were rapidly dwindling. The collective hand of the State was thus not long in making itself felt within this system of predicaments.

Accordingly, over the second half of the nineteenth century, the British State put together—at first hesitantly and tentatively, and then more

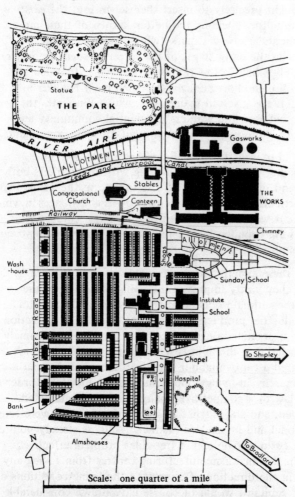

Figure 10.1. Plan of Saltaire. Source: Stewart (1952, page 159).

confidently—a package of legislative arrangements that sought to counteract the manifest problems of reproduction and socialization in the large industrial towns. These arrangements were pieced together bit by bit; they were not planned from the beginning as a totality, nor were they even particularly forseeable from the perspective of the kind of society that prevailed towards the middle of the century. Each iteration of State intervention was shaped and reshaped by some specific urban situation, and by specific political alliances and struggles. As the effects of each such iteration made themselves felt, so new configurations of the urban system emerged, producing yet further measured doses of public intervention. Something of the unplanned and piecemeal nature of the State's attempts to rationalize the reproduction process by means of collective action in the urban sphere can be gleaned from table 10.1, which provides a summary of the more important housing acts and related legislation in Britain between 1851 and 1919. These various collective interventions consisted largely of a two-pronged attack on the functionally defective living patterns of the British urban proletariat. One wing of this attack consisted of an attempt to upgrade the quality of the residential environment in inner city areas; the other wing consisted of an attempt to foster and accelerate the emerging process of suburban residential development.

In the inner city areas, large concentrations of casual and unskilled labour had given rise to persistent and noisome slums and, over the second half of the nineteenth century, the State sought strenuously, though sporadically, to resolve this problem by passing copious amounts of health and housing legislation in an attempt to upgrade living conditions in the cores of the large cities. Two pieces of legislation stand out as being of particular importance in this context. First, the Torrens Act of 1868 enabled local authorities to compel owners of insanitary premises either to demolish them, or to repair them at their own expense. Second, the Cross Act of 1875 gave local authorities powers to purchase and clear tracts of slum housing and then to sell or lease the land at a discount to such groups as private builders, the Model Dwellings Associations, or other semiphilanthropic organizations willing to put up new housing on the cleared land. As Ashworth (1954) has written, both the Torrens Act and the Cross Act were designed to help sustain an adequate standard of working-class housing in urban areas, although neither really succeeded fully in its aims. Under the Torrens Act local authorities could intervene only on a strung-out house-by-house basis, and the net results of the Act turned out to be fairly negligible in practice. The Cross Act had more widely ranging potentialities, for it was one of the first major efforts in Britain at something approaching comprehensive urban planning over extended tracts of land. However, while the Cross Act on balance helped significantly to improve housing conditions at the cores of the large cities

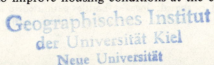

Table 10.1. Summary of principal British Housing Acts and related legislation, 1851–1919. Source: Rose (1978).

Act	Provisions
1851 Common Lodging Houses Act (Shaftesbury Act)	vestries and boroughs given supervisory public health powers over 'common lodging houses' for the very poor and transients
1851 Labouring Classes Lodging Houses Act (Shaftesbury Act)	vestries and boroughs permitted to raise money on local rates or from Public Works Loan Commissioners for building lodging houses for single *working* people
1853 Common Lodging Houses Act	police given powers of entry to inspect conditions in common lodging houses
1855 Dwelling Houses for the Working Classes (Scotland) Act; Labourers' Dwellings Act	facilitated investment by private capital in philanthropic housing by encouraging formation of companies for the erection of dwellings
1855 Metropolis Local Management Act	established Metropolitan Board of Works in London, with wide powers for street building, etc; ordered appointments of Medical Officers of Health
1855 Nuisances Removal Act	established minimum standards of housing conditions, gave local authorities duty to close houses 'unfit for human habitation'
1866 Labouring Classes Dwelling Houses Act	Public Works Loan Commissioners empowered to make loans to private companies and local authorities for the erection of labourers' dwellings in populous towns
1866 Sanitary Act	'overcrowding' made a statutory nuisance; adoptive powers given to local authorities to make public health regulations and control standards
1868 Artisans' and Labourers' Dwellings Act (Torrens Act)	boroughs and vestries given powers for compulsory purchase of insanitary premises for demolition or improvement
1874 Building Societies Act	building societies given limited company status, establishment of 'Permanent' societies providing investment for savings independent of house purchase
1875 Artisans' and Labourers' Dwellings Improvement Act (Cross Act)	Metropolitan Board of Works and boroughs with population over 25000 given powers to purchase and clear large tracts of insanitary property and to lease it to bodies willing to build housing
1875 Public Health Act (extends Nuisances Removal Act)	established conditions under which local authorities should take action to purchase premises for clearance purposes
1879 Artisans' and Labourers' Dwellings Act (1868) Amendment Act	provisions of compensation to owners of condemned houses added; rebuilding and rehousing clauses reinstated
1879 Artisans' and Labourers' Dwellings Improvement Act (1875) Amendment Act	limited amount of compensation claimable by owners of slum property to value of house after overcrowding abated; local authorities permitted to rehouse on alternative sites and let cleared land for commercial use

Table 10.1 (continued)

Act	Provisions
1882 Artisans' Dwellings Act	obligation to rehouse under Cross and Torrens Acts reduced to 50% of those displaced
1883 Cheap Trains Act	railway companies in London area made subject to Board of Trade orders to introduce workmen's trains and fares on lines where working-class housing had been built, in return for remission of passenger duty paid to Board of Trade
1885 Housing of the Working Classes Act	consolidated and amended Shaftesbury, Torrens, and Cross Acts; lodging houses redefined to include separate dwellings for labouring classes; interest rates for Public Works Loan Board lowered; severe limitation of compensation to slum owners
1888 Local Government Act	Metropolitan Board of Works abolished; London County Council established; provincial county councils with elected members and salaried officers introduced
1890 Public Health Act	extended 1875 Act; local authorities given powers to strengthen sanitary regulations for private houses
1890 Housing of the Working Classes Act	further consolidation of previous housing legislation; removal of obligation to rehouse displaced tenants in provincial cities; local authorities allowed to build houses for working class (for disposal within ten years)
1894 Housing of the Working Classes Act	local authority borrowing powers under 1890 Act extended
1899 Small Dwellings (Acquisitions) Act	local authorities empowered to advance money for purchase of small dwellings by their occupiers
1899 London Government Act	abolished vestries and district boards; created twenty-eight London Boroughs with powers to build housing
1900 Housing of the Working Classes Act	amended 1890 Act; local authorities given powers to purchase land outside their own jurisdiction for new house building in addition to building on cleared sites
1903 Housing of the Working Classes Act	amended 1890 Act; extended period of loan repayment from sixty to eighty years; limitations on borrowing reduced
1909 Housing and Town Planning Act	obligation on local authorities to sell their housing stock removed; Local Government Board given powers to enforce local authorities to build housing; powers for slum clearance strengthened
1915 Increased Rent and Mortgage Interest (War Restrictions) Act	rents of private houses with rateable values not exceeding £35 in London (£30 in Scotland, £26 elsewhere) fixed at prewar level (extended to more expensive houses after the war)
1919 Housing and Town Planning Act (Addison Act)	imposed duties on local authorities to survey housing needs in their districts and to carry out building schemes as needed, with approval of Ministry of Health; all losses in excess of a penny rate to be borne by local authority

by eliminating many of the more pestilential slums, it was not an unqualified success. Its implementation created difficult and unresolved problems of rehousing families displaced by large-scale slum clearances, and it contributed to the creation of new slums elsewhere as evicted families crowded into other areas of the inner city. These problems grew in intensity after 1879 when much of the land cleared under the Cross Act was now permitted to be used for commercial and other nonresidential purposes. Like the urban renewal programme in the United States almost a century later, the provisions of the Cross Act were eventually made to serve the immediate purposes of accumulation at the expense of reproduction (cf Rose, 1978); and their translation into active collective intervention provoked virtually as many new problems as were resolved.

In suburban areas, there was a particularly rapid growth of population throughout the second half of the nineteenth century. A series of major improvements in urban transport systems linking the suburbs with the urban core made possible the outward migration of population on a large scale "as a most desirable means of curing great cities of their dreadful congestion and their soaring rents" (Ashworth, 1954, page 148). It was also a means of accommodating those families—especially families belonging to the labour aristocracy—made homeless in London and the large provincial towns in the 1850s and 1860s as a result of housing clearances to make way for the railways, and, later, as a result of the extensive slum demolitions under the Cross Act. Government policy with regard to suburbanization was above all concentrated on methods of encouraging the development of cheap rapid transport between the centre and the periphery, on the correct supposition that private builders would then jump into the breach and spontaneously set about the production of suburban housing in large quantities. In the 1860s statutory requirements were imposed on several London suburban lines to provide special daily trains at cheap fares for working men. In 1883, the Cheap Trains Act was passed. This Act called for the extension of cheap commuter services up to 8.00 a.m. along railway lines which already served working-class suburbs. In addition, the London County Council began in the 1890s to municipalize tramway lines and to subsidize fares. The gradual extension of cheap metropolitan train services and other officially encouraged (and subsidized) urban transport services caused a vast outward expansion of working-class suburbia around the large English cities (cf table 10.2). By the end of the nineteenth century, suburbanization was firmly established as a continuing process of urban expansion, and the foundations were now irrevocably laid for the suburban life and culture that were at this stage beginning to emerge as definite elements of the urban scene.

Both in the core areas of the large cities and in the suburbs these efforts of the government to improve the reproductive potential of the urban environment were being underpinned by a continuing careful watch over sanitary conditions in the large towns and by an extensive effort to provide and preserve open spaces and parks for health and recreation purposes. This latter effort was echoed in the United States by the urban parks movement and the work of Frederick Law Olmstead. British State intervention in the reproduction process culminated in the Housing Acts of 1890, 1894, 1900, and 1903, and in the great Housing and Town Planning Act of 1909 in which comprehensive town planning first received statutory encouragement (see table 10.1). By the early decades of the twentieth century, State intervention in the formation and domestication of the urban labour force was an established and unalterable fact.

Over the second half of the nineteenth century, a series of complex private-public interactions in the urban land nexus laid the foundations for the city that we know today. The city that emerged in 1900 now set the scene for the characteristic problems of the urban land nexus in the twentieth century: the accelerating dynamic of outward peripheral expansion, the intensive overdevelopment of commercial land use in central business district areas, the ever augmenting problems of urban transport, and, eventually, the critical deterioration of the inner city as a place to live and work. Furthermore, just as the emergence of the primitive industrial town at the beginning of the nineteenth century constituted an undecided and nondecidable historical process, so this new urban form was one (as Roweis, 1975, has written) that no one desired or anticipated and that no one had actually planned in any meaningful sense of the term. This new urban form, too, now began to throw out an entirely fresh and perplexing collection of problems and predicaments.

Table 10.2. Growth of workmen's train facilities and population in the London suburbs of Edmonton and Walthamstow. Source: Royal Commission on London Traffic (1905, page 14).

Year	Edmonton		Walthamstow	
	daily workmen's trains	population	daily workmen's trains	population
1851		9708		4959
1861		10930		7137
1871	just started	13860	just started	11092
1881		23463		21715
1883	3		3	
1891	5	36351	6	46346
1901	7	61892	8	95131

10.3 Baron Haussmann and the reconstruction of central Paris

Gaillard (1977, page 9) writes of the massive physical and spatial transformation of central Paris that was carried out in the second half of the nineteenth century under the administrative tutelage of Baron Haussmann:

"The great works of Haussmann were not simply born out of an abstract will to grandeur ... they were born out of the urban crisis itself.
  The urban crisis, structural in nature, effectively manifested itself in the piling up of population in the central districts of the capital ... ."

In 1850, Paris was still, in its physical form and constitution, essentially a medieval city composed very largely out of notoriously densely populated assemblages of tenement housing interlaced by a nearly impenetrable network of narrow winding streets and alleys (cf Pinkney, 1958). Much of central Paris was a congested mass of slum dwellings and a multitude of small-scale workshops, industries, commercial premises, and markets. From a population of about half a million at the beginning of the nineteenth century, the city had grown to over a million inhabitants by the middle of the century, though without benefit of any corresponding reconstruction of the internal physical space of the city. In the old slums on the right bank, population densities attained levels of 850 persons per hectare and upwards. Here were to be found the very worst cases of fetid, cholera-ridden alleys and courtyards combined with the social decay and instability that so frequently go hand-in-hand with such conditions. Since the time of the French Revolution, the inhabitants of these slums had given frequent evidence of a disconcerting willingness to descend into the streets at the least provocation.

But Paris was also the burgeoning metropolis of a country whose industrial and commercial expansion was beginning to accelerate markedly. The rapid growth of Paris in relation to this overall pattern of national economic expansion was finally entrenched after the late 1830s when the railway system began to emerge with its insistent geographical focus on the capital city. Paris in the mid-nineteenth century was thus on the threshold of great economic changes if only the physical barrier of its congested and depreciated central space could somehow or other be overcome. The imperative of bringing Paris firmly into the current of the nineteenth century by means of various urban renovation programmes was thus becoming increasingly forceful. It was becoming ever more urgently necessary to transform the pattern of internal circulation and to make traffic flow reasonably smooth and efficient; to create new space for commercial and business activities as well as to ensure the continued penetration of the railway system that converged on the metropolis; to make available an adequate and uncontaminated supply of water; to make provision for the disposal of waste and excrement by constructing an extensive underground system of sewers; to renew many of the structures housing the administrative apparatus of the State; and last, but by no means least, to quell and discipline the hordes of restless slum dwellers; in brief, to transform on a massive and hitherto unprecedented scale the infrastructural bases of the life and work of the entire city. This was a project that was to serve handsomely the immanent purposes of capital, and yet it was also a project that could never be accomplished in its entirety by the individual agents of capital as such. Capitalists possessed no direct control over the political, legal, and administrative instruments that might enable them to expropriate massive tracts of land while at the same time quelling the opposition that such expropriation would inevitably engender. Nor did capitalists have sufficient practical and operational means to redevelop the land on the requisite grand scale and in conformity with some reasonably coherent overall plan. Civil society, that is, could transcend neither its fundamental roots in private property, nor its own practical and operational limits. Only the State could even begin to hope to marshall the degree of social momentum and coordination necessary for a concerted attack on the problem of transforming the spatial bases of central Paris, and to unleash the energetic private entrepreneurial activity by which this task was ultimately mediated. Even so, it was a task that seemed at times to be beyond even the capacities of so powerful and centralized a regime as that which superintended the development of France during the Second Empire.

Figure 10.2. Property demolition in Paris: public works in the Place Saint-Germain-des-Prés to make way for the Rue de Rennes. Reproduced by permission of the Viollet Collection.

Before about 1850, desultory and on the whole ineffective public efforts to improve the functionality of the space of central Paris had been attempted on several occasions. However, it required the exceptionally strong and stable government of Napoleon III, and the financial effervescence set off by the *coup d'État* of 1851 to bring matters to a head. Thus, in the early 1850s, and in response to the multiple and overpowering imperative to modernize central Paris and thus to release its full potential for growth and development, the French State, in the guise of the specific *personae* of Louis Napoleon and his agent Baron Haussmann, set about a programme of massive urban renewal and public works—a programme whose linchpin and central motor was a vast project involving the multiple piercing of the mass of central Paris to make way for a network of *grands boulevards* (see figures 10.2 and 10.3). The land necessary for the construction of these boulevards was acquired under a decree of 1848 which enabled the State to make compulsory purchases of all parcels of land which lay along and to the side of any projected public thoroughfare. In implementing this decree the State was able not only to acquire the land necessary for the construction of the boulevards themselves, but also to acquire a large surplus reserve of land whose value was invariably vastly enhanced after completion of the adjacent improvements. In regard to this surplus land, Pisani (1977, page 79) writes that the collectivity

"... then sold it after having drawn up a strictly designed plan of subdivision. The sales contracts were at once an occasion to assure a harmonious implantation of buildings, a coherent structure of the urban fabric, and a relative architectural unity. They also helped to finance the public works by making the collectivity the principal beneficiary of all increments in land prices."

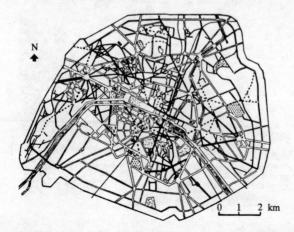

Figure 10.3. Paris: new thoroughfares of the Second Empire. Source: Lavedan (1960, page 93).

Significantly, however, in 1858, the landowning bourgeoisie secured the passage of a major legislative amendment to the legal procedure by which Haussmann had hitherto been able to expropriate land and in part to refinance his programme of public works. In 1858 the Council of State decreed that the collectivity could no longer expropriate properties except those that lay along the immediate alignment of any projected new thoroughfare. Hence, any individual who owned a parcel of land which encroached onto a projected new street alignment could still be dispossessed (after generous indemnification); but he was now allowed to retain any portion of his land not incorporated into the public highway. In this manner, as Malet (1973) has clearly indicated, the collectivity after 1858 lost to private landowners virtually the whole fiscal benefit of its public works programme. If the bourgeoisie was more than ready to accept the multiple advantages of Haussmann's urban policies, it was not prepared to envisage anything but the minimum amount of public intervention necessary for the procurement of those advantages. Haussmann was thus forced into increasingly unconventional methods of financing his programme of public works. Long before the development of Keynesian economics, he discovered the merits of deficit budgeting and its theoretical justification in the notion of 'productive expenses'.

In spite of frequent political obstacles to his work, Haussmann effectively reconstituted the entire infrastructural framework of central Paris during his prefectoral administration from 1853 to 1869. He cleared slum property on a massive scale, while hemming in those slum areas that remained, by means of an extensive network of wide thoroughfares (thus, by the same token, making it finally possible to police and control the slums of Paris). He opened up the centre of Paris to efficient traffic circulation, and further underpinned the functional success of the network of boulevards that he had constructed by building and restoring many bridges across the River Seine. He completely renewed the water supply system of Paris while at the same time building over 450 kilometres of new sewers, and as a consequence of these improvements there was a marked reduction in the number of epidemics in central Paris after the 1850s. He established many new parks, and between 1863 and 1869 he constructed no fewer than twenty-four squares (modelled on the pattern of the typical eighteenth-century London square) thereby helping further to let light and air into the heart of the city. He constructed and renovated many public edifices: churches, barracks, hospitals, local town halls, municipal theatres, a deservedly celebrated opera house designed in 'Napoleon III style' by Charles Garnier, the central law courts, and many purely decorative monuments. In all of these gestures there is not simply a strong utilitarian significance, but also a compulsive urge to embellish the city and to proclaim a political message. Through his reconstruction of the space of central Paris, Haussmann secured at once an improvement in the functional bases of urban civil society, an extension of the material foundations of the political collectivity, and a vigorous affirmation through architecture of the power, presence, and prestige of the Imperial State. As a result of Haussmann's manifold interventions, land prices, always a faithful reflection of the degree of vitality of the urban system, rose with extraordinary rapidity in central Paris in the 1850s and 1860s (see figure 10.4). In the words of Pisani (1977, page 81)

"The enrichment of the bourgeoisie, the extension and the prosperity of business, the growth of population brought about by the great works and reconstruction, provoked a fantastic rise in the value of built property, a substantial rise in rents, and an unimaginable increase in the price of building sites. The phenomenon ... had at the time a sudden and unforeseen quality, and it caused many difficulties."

Among the many difficulties caused by the imposition of a new spatial order in the centre of Paris in the second half of the nineteenth century was an ever growing spatial disorder on the periphery. Large numbers of slum dwellers displaced by Haussmann's programme of renovations now migrated out to new subdivisions being rapidly but haphazardly opened up around the fringes of the city. Attracted by the accelerating pace of metropolitan growth, many new factories sought to establish themselves in the Paris area, and they too for the most part found it necessary to take up locations in the urban fringe where land was plentiful and cheap. This pattern of peripheral development had already begun to manifest itself prior to Haussmann's interventions in central Paris; however, the major public works programme carried out in the centre after 1853 provoked a system of side effects that definitely set the seal on the characteristic Parisian version of suburban growth and development. The expansion of the suburbs of Paris in the second half of the nineteenth century was both vigorous and disorganized. It frequently comprised an anarchical intercalation of housing and factories, and new subdivisions often remained for decades inadequately serviced with even the most rudimentary forms of infrastructure. The whole suburbanization process was further perturbed by the periodic bursts of speculative activity on the fringes of the city that broke out as the reconstruction of central Paris proceeded. In this way, the foundations were established of the main geographical pattern

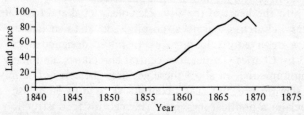

Figure 10.4. Average land prices in Paris in francs per square metre. Redrawn from Gaillard (1977, page 129).

that has marked the evolution of the Paris metropolitan region ever since: on the one hand, a central area, rich in infrastructural endowments, increasingly monopolized by commercial and residential activities with exceptionally high rent-paying abilities, and tending persistently to highly inflated land prices and congestion; on the other hand, as Bastié (1964) shows, an outer ring of working-class suburbs characterized by marked spatial disorder, inferior local services (both public and private), inadequate transport connections, and an accentuated propensity to vote Left (whence the designation *ceinture rouge* for the urban periphery). The problems and predicaments of contemporary Paris are comprehensible only in the light of this general historical and geographical process.

Even though many urban historians seem to treat the renovation of central Paris after 1853 as a mere psychological caprice ultimately ascribable to Napoleon III, it was, rather, an outcome of deeply rooted social and urban imperatives. The point is rendered all the more emphatic by the observation that various versions of haussmannism were a decided feature not only of many provincial French towns, but also of very many old European capital cities such as Brussels, London, Madrid, Rome, Stockholm, and Vienna. In every case, the common goal accomplished was the emancipation of the city from oppressive inherited physical constraints, thereby discharging new rounds of rapid accumulation of capital and urban growth.

10.4 The origins and consequences of land-use zoning in North American municipalities

By the early decades of the twentieth century, the vigorous expansion of the North American capitalist system was beginning to provoke a decided increase in the pace of urban growth, and, as a consequence of this growth, a series of refractory conflicts over the use of urban land. In the context of the largely unbridled nature of private land-use transactions in North American cities at this time, the rapid development and redevelopment of urban space was beginning to induce very severe problems involving the persistent juxtaposition of incompatible types of land uses. The problem was rendered all the more pressing by a rapid evolution of the technical division of labour (and hence an increasing differentiation of productive land uses) and by the growing imperative of smooth and effective reproduction. As it was, industrial, commercial, and residential land uses tended to intermingle freely with one another in many parts of the city thus giving rise to a complex system of negative spillover effects. These spillover effects threatened to compromise the functional efficiency of the city, to impede the upward ascension of property values, and ultimately to perturb the foundations of municipal taxation. This was a situation that was individually and socially undesirable, and to be rectified, if possible.

An early semipolitical response to the problem of land-use dissonances and incompatibilities in North American cities at the end of the nineteenth century had already emerged in the guise of the City Beautiful Movement, which in turn grew out of the Columbian Exposition held in Chicago in 1893. The City Beautiful Movement, however, set forth, at best, an extremely shallow analysis of the problem, and in the light of its rather precious rhetoric on Art and Culture, its ultimate demise as a programme of practical urban reform was more than assured. It was succeeded in 1912 by the more pragmatic and realistic City Efficient Movement, which accurately analyzed the outstanding current problems of North American cities in terms of their interrelated need for the segregation of land uses into functionally homogeneous districts (that is, land-use zoning) and for a workable and extensive transport system.

Accordingly, in the period immediately following 1916, when comprehensive zoning was first introduced in the city of New York, zoning emerged as an archetypical and, in its own immediate terms, extraordinarily successful collective solution to the universal problem of discordant land uses in North American municipalities. In the 1920s, zoning procedures diffused with remarkable rapidity across North America, so that by the end of the decade, more than 800 US towns and cities had adopted comprehensive zoning ordinances of one sort or another. Babcock (1966, page 5) describes the simple but effective qualities of these early zoning ordinances in the following terms:

"The typical ordinance of the 1920s divided the city into three zones—Single-Family, Commercial, and Industrial. If the community was sufficiently urbanized, an apartment district might be included .... It was a simple matter to draw lines on the municipal street map showing the boundaries of the districts: six pages took care of the simple requirements for permitted uses, yards, and maximum heights."

With the passage of time, of course, zoning procedures have become considerably more complex and convoluted than this, though their essential function and purpose remains unchanged: to rationalize the land-development process by segregating types of land uses that are incompatible with one another, thus reducing negative spillover effects. By encouraging the formation of homogeneous land-use districts, zoning helps to streamline the processes of production and reproduction in capitalist cities just as it helps to make more efficient the provision of such public services as transport, utilities, fire protection, and so on. As Hason (1977) has suggested, zoning not only performs the function of reordering the urban land market in the immediate present, it also reduces potential future uncertainties by giving property owners some assurance about the likely course of urban development. Zoning ensures that residential districts are relatively free from massive interferences in the working out of the reproduction process, that commercial areas are able to the maximum degree to capitalize upon their internally generated agglomeration effects, and that a reasonably adequate supply of land is permanently earmarked for industrial purposes. As a consequence of these benefits, the introduction of zoning into North American municipalities in the 1920s triggered off a new and more advanced stage of urbanization that resulted in still greater increases in land rents and property values than had hitherto been the case. It is hardly surprising, then, that the institutionalization of zoning was widely supported by such normally antiplanning groups as real estate agents and developers, chambers of commerce, financial institutions, and the rest.

Yet if land-use zoning had a positive and even, in certain senses, a progressive side, it also had, and continues to have, a negative and regressive side. Hence, zoning cleared the way for the unhindered takeover by business and commercial activities of central business districts and this then set the scene for the massive and dysfunctional vertical development of downtown areas. But more importantly, perhaps, zoning has been widely applied in North American municipalities as a specifically discriminatory and exclusionary device. In the United States, zoning powers are typically delegated to local governments and, given the prior tendency for a ring of independent middle-class suburban communities to appear around the cores of large American cities, it was more or less inevitable that these communities would begin to make use of zoning procedures in order to exclude socially incompatible neighbours. This exclusionary tendency became all the more urgent in view of the rapidly increasing possibilities of personal mobility for blue-collar individuals throughout the urban system. Obviously any major incursion of working-class or ethnic families into middle-class suburban communities would at once have threatened to throw a major burden on the local tax system, to cause a deterioration in the quality and effectiveness of local schools, to inject into the locality an atmosphere of disunity and disassociation; in brief, to mar forever those communities as efficient centres for the reproduction and domestication of white-collar and managerial social fractions. For these reasons, working-class and ethnic families have for decades been systematically excluded from many middle-class communities by means of discriminatory zoning ordinances. This includes zoning for large lots, thus maintaining a minimum threshold on the price of any property, and zoning for single-family residences, thus preventing low-income families from clubbing together on individual residential lots so as to reduce rental payments per family. The extremely widespread application of these devices in North American cities is testimony to the inability of a free residential land market effectively to secure the (socially functional) segregation of white-collar and blue-collar families in urban space. Moreover, the exclusionary qualities of much contemporary residential zoning are underpinned in many municipalities by subdivision regulations which require that roads and sidewalks conform to minimum width standards, or that developers donate land to the community for public use. Such regulations all have the final effect of raising local property prices.

In these ways, then, zoning practices in North American cities have contributed significantly to the maintenance of a situation in which the poor and the disadvantaged are faced constantly with a limited range of housing opportunities. In the United States, and possibly to a somewhat lesser degree in Canada, exclusionary zoning has helped maintain a very marked spatial pattern of social and racial segregation. Hemmed in by institutionalized restrictions, the poorest and most disadvantaged neighbourhoods frequently start to develop within themselves distinctive subcultures, elements of which (for example, crime, drugs, prostitution) proceed to perturb the rest of urban society. These neighbourhoods also give signs of such chronic pathologies as decayed infrastructure, physical blight, deteriorated schools, and so on: the very converse of urban and social conditions in the independent, inviolable, and prosperous middle-class communities. In the late 1960s, this contrast and the resentment that it engendered among many poor and blacks helped to ignite, or at least to fan the flames of, open riots across major US cities. In part as a response to these problems, two very distinctive but predicament-laden courses of collective action began to emerge. First, since the late 1960s, the busing of school children across community boundaries has been widespread in the United States in a highly controversial attempt to mitigate some of the educational problems resulting from residential segregation. Second, there is now much pressure from within government itself and from groups of concerned citizens to test in the courts and in various political forums the constitutional validity of discriminatory zoning procedures, though with what ultimate consequences (on reproduction practices, social order, and urban form) remains largely unknown. Zoning as a collective solution to one set of problems in capitalist cities succeeds also in setting in motion complex series of derivative social problems.

10.5 The US urban renewal programme, 1949–1961

Neither master planning nor the widespread application of zoning procedures could stem the tide of inner city decay in the United States in the years following World War II. As firms and households migrated in ever augmenting surges outwards from the core of the city to the suburbs, so the core began to fall bit by bit into decline and dilapidation. This process fed further upon itself: waves of blight spread outwards from the epicentres of decay, and as the local blue-collar employment base became progressively more attenuated there was a corresponding increase in poverty and unemployment in working-class central city neighbourhoods. Caught in this self-fuelling vicious circle, property owners could do little more than to boost the whole dynamic of inner city deterioration by refraining from making unproductive new investments in blighted neighbourhoods, and by milking their properties for maximum short-run gains. The overall consequence was an increasingly inefficient allocation of inner city land resources, a diminishing municipal tax base, and massive negative spillover effects emanating out of central city slums and threatening to perturb the whole established order of urban life.

In view of the seriously compromised functional rationality of inner city areas in the United States in the immediate post-World War II period, some form of collective intervention was virtually a foregone conclusion. Above all, it was essential collectively to redirect the decisions of private developers into more socially productive channels, and to coordinate private action in such a way as to break the vicious circle of blight and decay. Something of the nature of this imperative was captured by the President's Task Force on Urban Renewal (1970, page 3), which identified the renewal process as one way of counteracting the persistent failure of the market to generate efficient land-use patterns, and in almost embarrassingly revealing terms, the report affirms that

> "Since urban renewal is an instrument for planning, assembling, and redistributing underused and misused urban land, a primary objective is to achieve desirable land uses not otherwise attainable .... While the free enterprise system is capable of serving many of these needs without aid, special circumstances will warrant exercising the power of eminent domain for land assembly and may also justify a writedown of land costs."

The report goes on to describe in detail some of the "special circumstances" that may justify such abrogation of the free enterprise system, namely, (a) where a local redevelopment plan requires major changes in the layout of streets and public utilities, (b) where the costs of redevelopment are so great that it is not possible to form private financial syndicates of sufficient size to carry it out, (c) where individual landowners withhold parcels of land that are essential for the redevelopment of any specified area so that it is impossible to complete land assembly by means of voluntary transactions, and (d) where financial risks are high so that it is essential to provide some incentive to individual developers to encourage them to participate in the renewal process. In the more analytical terms of Davis and Whinston (1966) urban renewal is a rational collective response to free-rider situations where individual action does not or cannot result in redevelopment, but where coordinated redevelopment would nonetheless produce an outcome whose overall benefits exceed the costs. As the argument below unfolds, it will be shown in what precise and concrete terms the benefits from the urban renewal programme set in motion by the United States government after the Second World War exceeded the costs. Generally, urban renewal can be seen as a collective attempt to stimulate the performance of the urban land market so that it does indeed begin to allocate land to something approximating its highest and best use (in terms of capitalistic economic calculation, that is). In so doing, urban renewal also has extremely beneficial effects on property taxes and hence on municipal finances.

Accordingly, in 1949 a Federal Housing Act was passed which made special provision for the renewal of inner city areas. Under Title I of the Act, local renewal agencies were granted special funds and power of eminent domain to assist them in carrying through the urban renovation process. They were thus enabled to acquire central city slum properties, to clear the land, and subsequently to sell the cleared land at a discount to private developers. Under a formula established by the Act, the federal contribution to local renewal agencies consisted of a two-thirds capital grant on all approved projects. Originally, Title I required that redevelopment projects consist predominantly of residential structures. This provision was modified, however, under the 1954 Housing Act, which now permitted 10% of federal urban renewal funds to be used for nonresidential redevelopment. At a later stage, this percentage was increased to 30%.

While much of the 1949 housing legislation (especially its provisions regarding public housing) was strenuously opposed by business interests, the Title I provision, by contrast, was warmly welcomed by business in general and by the real estate lobby in particular. The reason is dramatically revealed in a description by Bellush and Hausknecht (1967, page 12) as to just how the Title I provisions worked out in one specific renewal project:

"Just south of Washington Square in New York in the late nineteen forties was an area of deteriorated industrial and commercial loft buildings interspersed with a handful of sound residential structures. This blighted area ... was designated as a redevelopment area. Under Title I the costs incidental to planning the redevelopment of the area were defrayed by a federal loan to the city out of a fund specially set up for this purpose. After the plan was approved by the federal government the city purchased this valuable land for forty-one million dollars, and then resold it to private interests for twenty million dollars. Two-thirds of the twenty-one million dollar difference between what the city paid and the price it received for the land, the 'write-down', was recovered in the form of a federal grant to the city. The other third, or seven million dollars of the costs were borne by the city. In other words, Title 1 subsidized the purchase of prime land by private entrepreneurs, with the federal government paying the lion's share of the subsidy."

Small wonder that, throughout the 1950s, private developers cooperated enthusiastically with the urban renewal programme. By December 1964 as many as 970 different redevelopment projects throughout the United States had been officially approved, and these projects accounted for a total of 36400 acres of inner city land (Slayton, 1966). Everywhere, the renewal programme operated by demolishing rundown properties which were then replaced by more prestigious land uses such as middle- and high-income housing, schools, libraries, parks, and so on. Slayton indicates that on average assessed property values rose by as much as 400% or 500% after renewal. Undoubtedly, in addition, renewal generated widespread positive spillover effects that greatly enhanced property values in surrounding neighbourhoods. In all of these various ways, then, it is clear that urban renewal responded to a real and urgent call for collective intervention in US cities, and that it secured major benefits and rewards for the American capitalist system at large.

As Gans (1967) points out, however, only one-half of 1% of all federal expenditures on urban renewal between 1949 and 1964 was spent on relocating families displaced by renewal. Despite the ideological rhetoric that surrounded the urban renewal programme—a rhetoric that depicted the programme as a major public drive to improve urban housing conditions—renewal was never concerned with housing for the poor (Castells, 1970). In fact, in the 1950s, so oblivious was the programme to this latter question that it resolutely neglected, in all but token ways, to alleviate the predicament of slum families rendered homeless by renewal. In this respect there is a striking resemblance between the US urban renewal programme (in its early phases, at least), and the mass housing clearances in London and Paris that occurred in the latter half of the nineteenth century (see sections 10.2 and 10.3 above). Notwithstanding some half-hearted official attempts to manage and coordinate the relocation of families dislodged by renewal, these families were almost wholly left to their own devices. Their problems were yet further intensified, first, by the circumstance that they consisted largely of low-income and black families (80% of all households made homeless by renewal were black) and, second, by the fact that the land they were forced to vacate was then converted to uses that in most cases excluded housing for such families. Hartman (1964), for example, shows that in the case of Boston's West End urban renewal area, a neighbourhood covering forty-eight acres and sheltering some 7500 persons (in this instance, mainly blue-collar workers of Italian descent) was demolished to make way for a luxury apartment complex which effectively barred the original inhabitants from returning once the renewal process was completed.

Evidently, urban renewal in US cities in the 1950s brought with it a number of powerful beneficial effects from the standpoint of capitalist rationality, but it also produced a variety of quite irrational side effects. Displaced slum families encountered severe difficulties in finding alternative low-rent accommodation. Thrown as they were onto an already tight low-income housing market, many of them experienced considerable hardship before a suitable replacement for their original homes could be found. Moreover, the housing market in the 1950s was made yet more tight as a consequence of the depredations of the federal highway programme, which also eliminated much existing urban housing stock and displaced additional large numbers of low-income families. Urban renewal itself destroyed in short order organic and tightly knit communities that had evolved slowly over the decades and could not simply be instantly recreated elsewhere.

The families expelled from these communities tended to move into adjoining neighbourhoods which then rapidly began to evince signs of overcrowding, congestion, and instability. In this way, urban renewal created nonfunctional slum neighbourhoods out of functional, or at least quasi-functional, slum neighbourhoods. As ousted slum families invaded substitute neighbourhoods that had been spared the bulldozer, so the preexisting residents of those neighbourhoods began to express their resentment and concern over the increasing perturbation of the character and stability of their established residential patterns. In many neighbourhoods, racial 'tipping' occurred as displaced black families moved *en masse* into formerly white communities. This phenomenon aggravated racial tensions and conflicts, and contributed very significantly to the racial unrest in US cities in the 1950s and 1960s. At the same time, as whites fled from neighbourhoods invaded by black families displaced by renewal, so they in turn irrupted into other neighbourhoods, re-creating there the very uncertainty and instability from which they, in part, had sought to escape.

On balance, urban renewal no doubt helped to some degree to arrest, though by no means to reverse, the deterioration of inner city areas in the United States in the 1950s. It is clear, too, that renewal benefitted business at the expense of underprivileged inner city residents, and that it improved housing conditions for upper-income groups at the cost of a decline in housing standards for lower-income groups. Nonetheless, even in terms of the capitalist rationality, of which urban renewal was a fairly clear expression, the programme was a decided failure overall. At the outset, of course, urban renewal did not even try to resolve the problem to which it was nominally addressed: slums, inferior housing conditions, poverty, helplessness. But, in addition, in view of its emasculated operational qualities, nor could it possibly hope to resolve the real problem to which it was addressed in subterfuge: the structural misallocation (in capitalistic terms) of inner city land resources and the progressive decline in the differential locational advantages of the central city relative to the locational advantages of the suburbs. In a *ceteris paribus* world urban renewal may conceivably have triggered off a significant revitalization of inner city areas. As it was, the potential success of the urban renewal programme was shackled from the start by the overriding process of vigorous outward urban expansion fuelled by the highway programme, unstinting public expenditure on local *in situ* infrastructure in the suburbs, generous mortgage arrangements for middle-class households, and the powerful ideology of suburban bliss. Something considerably more powerful than the provisions of Title I was needed to turn the tide in favour of the inner cities. Indeed, there is some merit to the hypothesis that urban renewal in the end hastened rather than delayed the demise of the inner cities, for by reducing the net population of the inner cities (as of March 1961 126000 dwelling units had been demolished and about 28000 new ones built), urban renewal effectively reduced yet further the overall differential locational advantages of central city areas.

By the early 1960s, the urban renewal programme had inevitably attracted to itself a swelling current of political controversy and community resistance as slum dwellers became increasingly sensitive to its negative effects on their living arrangements and as they learned from the experience of others how to resist renewal and protect their meagre patrimony. The provisions of the 1961 Federal Housing Act sought to blunt and divert political attacks on the programme by putting more emphasis on the rehabilitation of property rather than on the crude bulldozer approach, and by encouraging more construction of public housing. After 1961, then, urban renewal continued apace in American cities, but now within a considerably modified frame of reference. However, it is clear from a recent study by Harvey (1977) that the implementation of US federal housing policy in the 1960s was associated with just as many problems, conflicts, and failures as it had been in the 1950s. Federal housing policy in the 1960s re-created precisely the same predicament-laden logic that is evident throughout the urban renewal programme of the 1950s: in attempting to resolve one set of problems, it simply discharged another set elsewhere. Need it be added that the urban renewal programme in the United States in the 1950s is an object lesson, if ever there was one, in the irrelevance of the Pareto criterion as a putative guide to the understanding of public policy?

10.6 Transport problems and policies in Metropolitan Toronto from 1953 to the mid-1970s

Much current thinking on the nature of urban transport problems and policies seems to take the transport system itself as a kind of exogenously given object whose principle quality is that it unidirectionally mediates 'plans' into 'impacts'. This conception is, of course, imperfect. The urban transport system is contained as an intermediate functional element within the structure of the capitalist city as a whole: it is a partial determinant of the structural logic that governs the working of the city, but it is also itself enveloped within that same logic. Above all, urban transport is called into being as the necessary foundation of the effective circulation of commodities and labour within the city. In securing this process, the transport system contributes markedly to the determination of urban form and structure, for as the transport system is readjusted in response to changes in the urban environment, so these readjustments also give rise, via the market responses of firms and households, to new configurations of the urban environment. In addition, as a highly capital-intensive and naturally monopolizable infrastructural service, modern urban transport is for the most part managed by the State, which supplies in the noncommodity form such differentiated outputs as expressways, local street networks, subways, bus service, and so on. By thus guaranteeing what private capital in and of itself can never guarantee—the unhindered circulation of commodities and labour within the city—the State ensures the continued functional coherence of the urban land nexus. This activity of the State, however, is fraught with innumerable problematical consequences, and, in what follows, some of these consequences will be elucidated for the specific case of transport development in Metropolitan Toronto over the last couple of decades.

The Municipality of Metropolitan Toronto was formed in 1953 in considerable part as a response to the need for more effective area-wide urban (including transport) planning. At the present time, the metropolitan federation consists of the central City of Toronto together with the five peripheral boroughs of East York, Etobicoke, North York, Scarborough, and York (see figure 10.5). Within the geographical area covered by the federation, public responsibility for transport matters is unequally divided between the three different levels of government comprising (a) the individual municipalities, (b) Metropolitan Toronto, and (c) the Province of Ontario. The City and the boroughs severally control the local roads within their respective jurisdictions. The metropolitan government manages the main arterial road network and certain expressways (namely, the Don Valley Parkway, the F G Gardiner Expressway, and the Spadina Expressway), and it also supplies, through the Toronto Transit Commission (TTC), an integrated system of subway, bus, streetcar, and trolley service. The Province has overall responsibility for all remaining expressways and for a rapidly growing express commuter rail and bus service (known as the GO system) connecting the outlying communities of the greater Toronto region to the core of the city. Further, the provincial administration has, since about 1971, played a very significant role in subsidizing TTC operations. In practice, it would seem that even the metropolitan federation is too small both as a spatial and as a fiscal entity to provide an adequate

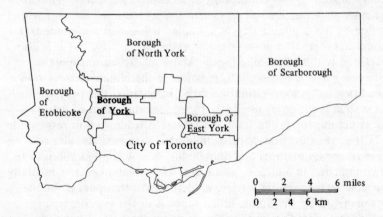

Figure 10.5. The municipal federation of Metropolitan Toronto.

framework for the administration of transport services in the whole urban region, and, as the region grows, so the Province is called upon to intervene to an ever augmenting degree in the process of urban transport development.

In the period between the mid-1950s and the mid-1970s the transport system of Metropolitan Toronto has undergone constant expansion and infilling, and this process may be described by means of a brief account of the spatial structure of urban transport in the metropolis in each of the years 1954, 1964, and 1974.

In 1954, the main basis of the overall transport system of Metropolitan Toronto comprised the three radial expressways directed from the west, north, and east towards the core of the city, as shown in figure 10.6(a). These expressways then fed in to a dense network of arterial and local roads covering the whole metropolitan area, and they were, in addition, interconnected by a further expressway (Highway 401) which passed through a tier of intermediate suburban communities. Also in 1954, the first segment of the Toronto subway system was opened. This segment was $4 \cdot 5$ miles in length, and ran from north to south along one of the most densely utilized movement corridors in the whole metropolitan area.

By 1964, the expressway system, now enlarged by various incremental projects over the preceding ten years, penetrated to the very centre of the city from the west (via the F G Gardiner Expressway) and from the northeast (via the soon to be completed Don Valley Parkway) [cf figure 10.6(b)]. In addition, the subway system had now been extended by a further $2 \cdot 4$ miles to form an open loop within the core of the city.

In 1974, the expressway system retained essentially the same configuration that it had possessed in 1964, whereas a very pronounced expansion of the subway had now occurred by comparison with the situation as it was in 1964 [cf figure 10.6(c)]. By 1974, there had come into being a major east-west branch of the subway system together with a $5 \cdot 4$ mile northward extension of the north-south line. These developments were later supplemented in 1978 by a major expansion of subway service towards the northwest. In addition, a rapid commuter rail service (the GO system) linking the suburban communities lying along the lake shore was now in operation, and this service was further augmented by several express bus lines.

Besides these various main developments over the twenty-year period stretching from 1954 to 1974, local public transport by surface vehicles throughout the metropolitan area has been continuously expanded; and there has been a constant upgrading and improvement of the system of local and arterial roads.

This general expansion of the urban transport system of Metropolitan Toronto has been intimately bound up as both effect and cause with the growth and spread of population and employment in the metropolitan area. Thus, while population in the City of Toronto declined by $5 \cdot 2\%$ in the period from 1956 to 1976, population in the rest of the metropolitan area grew by $216 \cdot 0\%$ in the same period. Similarly, while total employment in the City grew by 10·0% from 1956 to 1975, total employment in the rest of the metropolitan area grew by 234·4%. In spite of this outward spread of population and jobs, however, the core area still remains by far the predominant focus of employment in the whole metropolitan region. The urban geography of Toronto over the last couple of decades has thus been characterized by a dual spatial process involving the continued but, in relative terms, diminishing concentration of employment opportunities

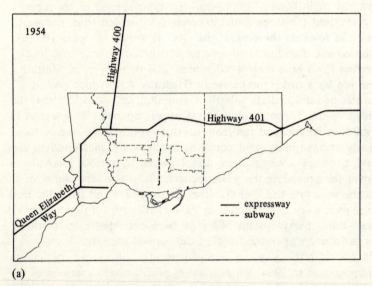

(a)

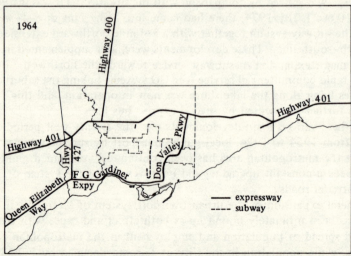

(b)

Figure 10.6. Major transport facilities in Metropolitan Toronto, 1954, 1964, and 1974.

in the core combined with rapid expansion of the suburban fringe [though as Goldberg (1977) has indicated, this outward expansion has been rather less forceful in Canadian cities than it has been in the United States]. Accordingly, the changing pattern of transport development as revealed in figure 10.6 can in part be seen as a response to general circulation needs in a context where home places and work places are separated by a constantly widening gap. Moreover, as a consequence of the steady growth of the low-density fringe areas, the current pattern of urban development in the Toronto region today is one that is most effectively and efficiently serviced by means of the private car supplemented by mass transit in the most heavily utilized movement corridors. It is, however, precisely in the domain of the powerful mutual interactions between the continued peripheral expansion of the urban area and the use of (and need for) the private car, that transport planners in Toronto over the last ten or fifteen years have encountered some of the most perplexing and difficult problems.

The general geographical expression of transport planning practices in Metropolitan Toronto between about 1953 and the mid-1970s has been descriptively outlined in figure 10.6. A somewhat more analytical comprehension of these policies can be derived from a scrutiny of figure 10.7, which identifies total capital expenditures (provincial plus metropolitan capital expenditures) on roads and expressways and on public transport in the Metropolitan Municipality from 1954 to 1975. Throughout the 1950s and 1960s, capital expenditures on roads and expressways were clearly very strongly on the rise. In the 1950s and in the early part of the 1960s, capital expenditures on public transport also

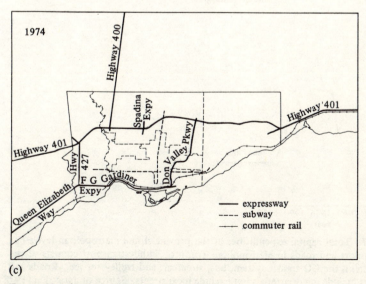

Figure 10.6 (continued)

increased rapidly as the first segment of the new subway system was opened and as the system was subsequently extended to the east and the west. After 1965, however, with the completion of the most economically efficient potential subway alignments, further expansion of the subway system was brought temporarily to a halt, so that capital expenditures on public transport now began to decline; by contrast, expenditures on roads and expressways continued to move upwards, reaching a peak in 1968. This relative emphasis on road development in the 1950s and 1960s was in large degree concomitant upon the massive expansion of the suburban fringe of Toronto and the corresponding increase in the use of the private car. Suburban expansion itself was fuelled to a significant extent by the provisions of the National Housing Act of 1954 and subsequent amendments which strongly promoted white-collar homeownership. Both in public policy statements and in planning practice, expressways linking the burgeoning suburbs and the core of the city were seen as the rational dominant response to the overall circulation needs of the metropolis, and a necessary guarantee of the continued viability of economic and residential activity in the city. More accurately, perhaps, it might be said that the committed patterns and structures of the metropolis—themselves engendered by the urban processes and policy decisions that had obtained in the 1930s and the 1940s—made it indispensable in the 1950s and the 1960s to provide for an extensive network of radial expressways and arterial roads connecting the centre to the periphery. The spirit of urban transport planning in Toronto in the early 1960s is caught in a report of the

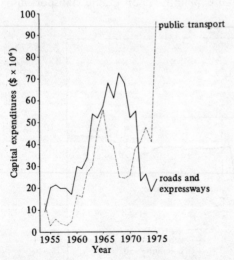

Figure 10.7. Total capital expenditures at the provincial and metropolitan levels on public transport and roads in Metropolitan Toronto. Public transport consists of the subway system, the GO transit system, bus, streetcar, and trolley service. Roads and expressways include major arterials but exclude local streets. Source of data: Lai (1978).

Metropolitan Toronto Planning Board (1964, page 17), which, while calling for a 'balanced' transport system, makes no bones about its conviction that this system will consist of a network catering primarily to the needs of the private car:

> "By 1980 it is expected that there will be some 540,000 person trips in the Planning Area at peak hour, an increase of about 85% over the 1961 figure of 290,000. Perhaps 365,000 of these trips will be by private automobile, involving—at the current rate of car occupancy—about 265,000 vehicle trips at rush hour, or about double the number in 1961. Combined with an expected slight increase in average trip length, it is estimated that the road system will have to accommodate nearly 3 million vehicle miles, or about 150% more than in 1961. At the same time, the public transportation system is expected to handle about 50% more rush hour trips than was the case in 1961. These projections, taken together, establish the general dimensions of the transportation system which will have to be provided to support the anticipated growth and development of the area over the next 15 to 20 years."

Despite these exuberant prognostications of a greatly enlarged road transport system by 1980, the existing system was already, in the mid-1960s, beginning to encounter serious barriers to its further expansion as it progressively set off a series of complicated and highly contentious negative externality effects. In the first place, as the expressway system grew more extensive, so more and more traffic began to pour into the downtown area, creating problems of congestion, noise, and air pollution, and provoking a minor crisis of parking accommodation. Many of these problems spilled over into the residential neighbourhoods that surrounded the central business district. In the second place, the dramatically improving differential locational advantages of the central business district as a result of expressway development helped to spark off and to sustain a building boom in the core of the city, and this phenomenon in turn provoked deleterious incursions of business and commercial premises into inner city neighbourhoods. And, in the third place, many residential communities within the central city lay across the alignments of proposed new expressways, so that they found themselves menaced with destruction of significant portions of their housing stock and with severe disruption of their residential functions. Accordingly, a powerful coalition of concerned citizens' groups representing various white-collar and blue-collar inner city neighbourhoods began to make its appearance towards the end of the 1960s, and to make vociferous demands for the cessation of all further expansion of the expressway network. A major structurally rooted conflict now emerged between central city residents who wanted to stop all expressway development, and various suburban communities (together with general business interests) which predominantly wanted continued expansion of the expressway system.

These conflicts found their institutional expression in clashes over urban transport policy between the respective councils of the City and the Metropolitan Municipality.

These differences between central city and suburban residents over the issue of continued expressway development in the 1960s erupted into a major political confrontation over one specific case: the proposed Spadina Expressway which was intended to link the northern suburban communities with the central core. The project had been first suggested as early as 1953, and an initial small section of the expressway was actually built in 1966 [cf figure 10.6(c)]. Before construction could proceed any further, however, a growing groundswell of opposition, rooted in the central city neighbourhoods, provoked a temporary halt to work on the project. Indeed, the momentum of the opposition grew steadily to such impressive proportions that in 1971, the provincial government cancelled the Spadina Expressway project outright. Fortified by this victory, and carried off by a surge of reformist zeal, the City elected a new council in 1972 that pushed strongly for public transport as the only tolerable alternative to expressways. There was, in brief, a growing commitment at all levels of government in the early 1970s to public transport at the expense of expressways. Public transport was now seen as the most politically acceptable response to Toronto's transport needs, and, in further confirmation of this trend, several pending expressway projects, in addition to the Spadina project, were abandoned at this time. Hence, if reference is made once more to figure 10.7, it will be seen that, after about 1970, capital expenditures on public transport began to accelerate markedly while capital expenditures on roads declined in reciprocity. These turnabouts in the main thrust of transport planning in the metropolitan area greatly mollified inner city residents, but left many suburban residents inadequately serviced with transport access to the rest of the area. Despite the enormous expansion of public transport services that had taken place in the early and mid-1970s—including major expansion of the GO system and the completion in 1978 of a major extension of the subway towards the northwest—much of suburbia remained virtually untouched by these developments. Moreover, as the public transport system was enlarged, so it began to show signs of massive diseconomies of scale. In 1971, for example, the TTC operated with the relatively negligible deficit of $2·9 million, whereas by 1976, the deficit had grown to as much as $49·0 million. In the same period, TTC ridership per head of metropolitan population increased by only 17·9% from 138·0 to 162·7. Many suburban communities in Metropolitan Toronto are now pressing, and with an increasingly persuasive case given the growing disenchantment with the fiscal performance of the extended public transport system, for some reactivation of expressway proposals that had been successively put aside in the early 1970s. Already, and in spite of earlier assurances to the contrary on the part of the Province, the Spadina Expressway (around which so much political energy was generated in the late 1960s and early 1970s) has now been extended southwards to a point just short of those inner city neighbourhoods which had so vigorously opposed it at an earlier time; and some further resuscitation of selected new expressway projects is not entirely beyond the limits of the possible as the imperatives of efficient urban circulation begin to reassert their supremacy within the total urban complex (cf Goldrick, 1978).

As it enters the 1980s, Toronto is in an uncertain transitional phase. It has now left behind the recent period of turbulent political conflicts over the actual and anticipated impacts of expressways on the environment of the inner city, and it is moving into a new stage of development in part guided and coordinated by the new core area plan which was officially approved, in its essentials, in 1978. This plan is in large part an outcome of the turbulence and conflicts of the late 1960s and early 1970s. It provides for continued active growth of the central business district of Toronto while simultaneously limiting all really intensive growth of commercial premises to a restricted innermost area. The plan also provides guarantees against the further destruction of inner city residential neighbourhoods, and, indeed, seeks to promote much new residential construction in the downtown area. On the assumption that more and more white-collar workers will migrate into central city areas, this promotion of new residential construction downtown will no doubt help to reduce some of the pent-up demand for extensions to the intraurban arterial road and expressway systems. Further, the new plan seeks to encourage the development of outlying subcentres of commercial and business activity in the west (in Mississauga), north (in North York), and east (in Scarborough) in order to channel much new economic activity away from the central business district, and to relieve some of the stresses and strains contingent upon land-use intensification in the core. Clearly, however, some upgrading of the transport infrastructure serving these subcentres will be necessary before they can effectively accomplish this goal. In these different respects, the new plan seems likely to help dissolve away many of the pressure points that in the past have contributed so strongly to the creation of a highly organized citizens' movement resolutely opposed to downtown redevelopment in general and to new expressway construction in particular.

Whatever the specific details of the future evolution of the transport system of Metropolitan Toronto, we may expect any new rounds of transport planning to differ significantly in style of execution and in broad aims from those of the past. For one thing, transport planning in the future is likely to be more sensitive to issues of cost effectiveness and social and environmental impacts. For another thing, it will now have to cater to the needs of an urban system characterized not only by a functionally powerful centre but also—in all likelihood—by three active and decentralized subcentres of development. But any new rounds of urban transport planning will also quite certainly be structured by the same basic dynamic that has characterized the public provision of urban transport services in Toronto in the past: notwithstanding its checkered history in detail, transport planning in Metropolitan Toronto since 1953 has responded above all to the single and surpassing need to assure the unhindered movement of commodities and labour through the urban system, that is, to maintain high levels of accessibility in relation to the ever changing locations of firms and households in urban space. In practice, this has meant for the most part attempting to keep the suburbs effectively tied in to employment activities in the central business district, and, to a lesser extent, to employment activities in suburban districts. In spite of occasional setbacks, this need is continually reaffirmed within the structure of the city as a whole. Or rather, if recent experience is anything to go by, it seeks to accommodate itself, without changing its essential nature, to the specific practical and political difficulties that make their appearance at any given instant in the evolution of the urban land nexus. In fact, transport planning in Metropolitan Toronto between 1953 and the mid-1970s has been reactive *par excellence*, and it provokes subsidiary urban effects (urban peripheral expansion, land-use intensification at the core, and so on) which in turn give rise to additional rounds of reactive planning. In this regard, the history of transport planning in Metropolitan Toronto over the last couple of decades exemplifies yet another specific element of the general theory of planning described in earlier pages: while each individual planning project (such as a new expressway alignment, a street-widening project, or an extension of the subway system) is invariably planned with meticulous care and high levels of technical rationality, the set of all planning endeavours, taken as an aggregate over time, is caught up within a structure of social relationships that renders it incoherent as a whole, and immune to reasoned social decisionmaking. This phenomenon reflects very faithfully the Sisyphean nature of urban planning in capitalist society where palliative and piecemeal public decisions made at one moment in time lead onward to new problems and predicaments at later moments in time.

10.7 Reprise

The few and highly selected case studies examined above, all illustrate the single central point that urban planning in capitalist social formations emanates directly out of the various imbroglios that develop in the urban land nexus as it moves forward through time. Despite the disparate nature of these cases, they do not simply constitute a random collection of disjointed events; they are linked together conceptually by a structural logic that runs through every case. Hence, as the urban land nexus evolves historically, so it gives rise to various manifestations of that central contradiction, as described in earlier chapters, between the mutually contradictory imperatives of private and collective action in urban space.

On the one hand, the social and property relations of capitalism give rise to a historically specific system of private decisionmaking in urban space that engenders its own self-paralysis. On the other hand, the capitalist State is then obliged to intervene when the problems and predicaments produced by this self-paralysis begin to threaten the overall viability of the urban land nexus. However, as a consequence of the specific limits that society puts around collective action, the interventionist strategies of the State in the urban land nexus are confined to perennially palliative measures. This is as true of late capitalist society today as it was true of early capitalist society formerly. Thus, in seeking to redress one set of problems, the State invariably sets in motion (via the responses of urban civil society) a yet further sequence of problems. In this way, the fundamental contradiction in the urban land nexus between the imperatives of private and collective action is continually re-created at successively higher levels of complexity, and the contradiction thus feeds on itself in a never ending spiral of escalations. With due allowances made for its specific empirical content at any given moment in time, and for the particular political struggles and conflicts that coalesce around it, it is *this* structural logic, as it works its way through the locational system of the urban land nexus that is the mainspring of the historical and geographical development of cities under the capitalist mode of production.

Planning ideologies

Quand on s'explique mal un événement,
on se convainc facilement qu'il est "voulu"
  Le Monde 27-28 November, 1977

In this penultimate chapter, a critical analysis of mainstream planning theory is undertaken. The purpose here is to demonstrate, on the basis of the entire preceding discussion, the ways in which much contemporary discourse about urban planning obstructs the attainment of a clear (and critical) view of the historical significance of the interventions of the capitalist State in the urban land nexus. To the degree that this discourse does indeed derange comprehension of the planning process, it can properly be designated an ideology (or, rather, a system of ideologies). In the present chapter the ideologies that constitute a currently dominant discourse about the nature and purposes of planning are treated in precisely the same manner as that in which the phenomena of private and public action in the urban land nexus were themselves treated at an earlier stage in the proceedings: as definite social events to be explained and accounted for in terms of their roots and development, and as outgrowths of some wider social process. In any case, for reasons that will by now be abundantly clear, no attempt is made here to treat these ideologies as autonomous systems of ideas to be accepted or rejected merely on the basis of their own internal logic. Accordingly, a critique of current planning ideologies is developed in four main steps as follows. First, a simple description is undertaken of a mainstream body of planning theory that grows out of an eclectic functional-structural analytic framework. Second, this body of theory is shown to be irredeemably divorced from any real substantive content so that it persistently fades off into metaphysical abstractions. Third, a second and minor theoretical stream is identified and is shown to be (like manipulated-city theory) nothing more than an internal critique of the mainstream from within the latter's universe of discourse. Fourth and lastly, an attempt is made to highlight and to criticize a major epistemological flaw in conventional planning theory, that is, its idealist-utopian origins, and it is shown how this leads to the self-defeat of conventional theory as both a scientific programme and a basis for action.

Despite the fact that in earlier chapters of this book cautionary observations have several times been made as to the essential unity of the phenomena of urbanization and planning, the present critique of urban planning theory is effectively cut off from the critique of urban theory that was accomplished in chapter 5. But this apparent anomaly is only a direct echo of the circumstance that the mainstream itself maintains a massive and artificial rupture between the theories of urbanization and the theories of urban planning that it puts forward.

11.1 The foundations and biases of mainstream planning theory
A brief description of mainstream planning theory

Many current theories of urban planning seek to distill the essence of the planning process by reducing it to a twofold functional-structural system whose main characteristics are (a) that it is purposive and goal-seeking in function, and (b) that it consists of administrative/procedural structures designed to sustain this general function. There exists in the literature an immense variety of formulations of this general bipartite theme, though the essentials remain more or less constant from case to case: the function of planning is to achieve 'preferred states', 'desired goals', 'specified objectives', etc, via some structured apparatus whose internal logic identifies the main essence of the planning system. In the last instance, this apparatus can be conceptualized as a broad methodological procedure such as mathematical programming, organization theory, or systems analysis.

In general, the functional tasks that mainstream theory ascribes to urban planning are formulated in terms of some decisionmaking or problemsolving calculus, itself expressed at high levels of abstraction. Much of the flavour of this propensity of modern planning theory is captured in the following statement (part of which has already been quoted in the preceding chapter) where Davidoff and Reiner (1962, page 103) describe planning as

> "... a process for determining appropriate future action through a sequence of choices .... Since appropriate implies a criterion of making judgements about preferred states, it follows that planning incorporates a notion of goals. *Action* embodies specifics, and so we face the question of relating general ends and particular means. We further note from the definition that *action* is the eventual outcome of planning efforts, and, thus, a theory of planning must be directed to the problem of effectuation.
>
> The choices which constitute the planning process are made at three levels: first, the selection of ends and criteria; second, the identification of a set of alternatives consistent with these general prescriptives, and the selection of a desired alternative; and third, guidance of action toward determined ends."

Observe, however, that this passage evades all reference to the concrete social conditions and conjunctures within which urban planning comes into existence and takes on specific content. On the contrary, Davidoff and Reiner simply bypass this crucial issue by identifying planning as a substantively empty system of organizational rules and goals. In other words, and in conventional theory generally, the function of planning is seen as being geared to the solution of problems, but in an entirely indeterminate and abstract manner. Conventional planning theory condenses the tasks of urban planning into such general goal-seeking processes as promoting human growth, securing the public interest, maximizing social welfare, guiding action towards determined ends, and so on, without, however, any corresponding effort to make specific and to problematize *within* the theory of planning the notions of human growth, the public interest, etc. Such questions are by and large dismissed on the assumption that planning theory is not properly a component of social theory, but stands apart as a domain of discourse bound by quite special criteria of evaluation (cf Harris, 1978). Unlike ordinary social theory which, at least in part, is judged in relation to corresponding empirical situations, the validity of planning theory is, evidently, to be assessed uniquely on the basis of its internal analytical coherence, and this means in particular its coherence as a series of socially disembodied decisionmaking routines. Concomitantly, much of the weight of contemporary planning theory is thrown into an attempt to situate goal-seeking administrative behaviour within a broad structural framework which defines the crucial decision points (and their interconnections) in any universalized planning process.

In much of the recent literature on planning theory, this concern for the identification of a structural framework for planning is frequently (though not necessarily always) operationalized in terms of the preexisting calculus of general systems theory. This theory is especially suited to the task of accommodating mainstream conceptions of the planning process by reason of the highly adaptable, and yet coherent, structural logic of the general systems model. Any cursory glance at the literature immediately brings to light a score of systems-theoretic descriptions of urban planning. A simple but entirely representative case taken from Reif (1973) is shown in figure 11.1. This exemplary case incorporates most of the usual features of the classic systems model of the planning process: 'review and understanding', 'problem formulation', 'evaluation', and so on, combined with assorted appropriate feedback loops. Where the model seems inadequate or deficient, it is capable of infinite extension and modification in any conceivable direction by opening up new elemental categories and new structural connections. Then, the *planning system* in this specifically

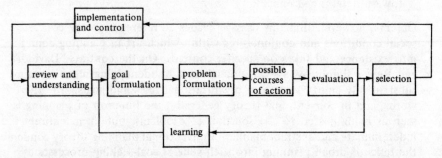

Figure 11.1. A systems view of the planning process. Redrawn from Reif (1973, page 44).

structural sense, and as animated by some overall objective function, becomes a universal control system superimposed upon and intersecting with human society, itself conceived as a hierarchy of systems within systems. The point is succinctly expressed by Wilson (1968, page 250), who writes

> "Cities and regions can be usefully considered to consist of systems .... Most systems have features which can be controlled to greater or lesser degrees by the decisions and acts of planners, and these can be called planned systems (even though the control may be partial). The set of planners, however, is itself a system which can be called the planning system."

Given the insistence in the literature upon a theory of planning *qua* a theory of general control systems, it is small wonder that the literature is so overwhelmingly concerned with questions of methodology and procedure. This concern has recently expressed itself in a very explicit call by Harris (1978) simply to assimilate planning theory into the theory of mathematical programming. And, in a similar vein, one of the most elaborate recent statements on the theory of planning (Faludi, 1973) insists on the identification of planning theory with a broad attempt to establish an operating model of a planning bureaucracy.

The failure of mainstream planning theory

This empirically empty and transhistorical conception of planning as a general control system undoubtedly represents the main theoretical view of urban planning in the contemporary (English-language) literature. However, this view immediately poses a number of serious difficulties, most of them pivoting in one way or another around its fallacious insistence that the administrative and methodological structures that are built up around the activity of planning constitute the essence of planning. In the following argument, an attempt will be made to show that this insistence leads mainstream theory into three major interrelated errors and misconceptions. These are (1) its indeterminacy in concrete social terms, (2) its failure to address the real question, namely, the genesis of urban policy, and (3) its self-defeating refusal to problematize urban planning as an activity of the capitalist State. At a later stage in the discussion it will be shown that all of these difficulties can ultimately be traced back to the idealist–utopian foundations of contemporary planning theory. Let us, for the present, expand upon the three major points identified above.

First, then, mainstream planning theory takes as an *a priori* category that which is socially and historically determined—collective intervention in the urban land nexus. Mainstream theory, that is, seeks to go beyond the realized history of urban planning as a socially embedded human practice, and to posit itself as an analytical *concept* representative of goal-seeking decisionmaking in general. But precisely because it denies to urban planning any definite empirical content, mainstream theory falls into *indeterminate abstraction* and circularity. Then, within its own terms of reference, mainstream theory emerges as a series of statements that are not so much incorrect as they are simply trivially true. Hence, assertions that the planning process involves goal formulation, evaluation, implementation and control, learning, and all the rest, are certainly formally correct, but they are also plainly vacuous. This is not a vacuity that emerges from a lack of complexity in the basic systems model as such, but from a fundamental failure to go beyond abstract logical formalizations and to discover the real social forces that drive the planning system forward. Quite simply, and to put the matter in Popperian terms, mainstream planning theory is structured for minimum rather than maximum refutability. This is because it consistently refrains from ascribing anything but the most vapid social content to its basic units of analysis (goal formulation, evaluation, etc). Thus, just at the point where mainstream theory stops short, the really important and puzzling analytical tasks of a truly scientific theory begin. As a result of its indeterminate abstraction, immunizing it against refutability, mainstream planning theory tends to impede critical scrutiny of the real world of urban planning, and consequently to license false consciousness and cognitive myopia. In testimony to this point, a recent questionnaire survey of Canadian planners (Page and Lang, 1977) has shown that there exists a pervasive chasm between the kinds of planning theories that individual planners espouse on the one hand, and their perceptions as to the realities of practical planning on the other hand. As will be shown at a later stage, any attempt to explain away this discrepancy on the grounds that planning theory is by its nature normative in intent, is only to compound the problem.

Second, the attempt on the part of mainstream theory to reduce planning to a series of procedural models misses much of the point: it assigns a privileged analytical status to the ephemeral administrative media through which the basic political imperatives of urban society are eventually expressed, while neglecting to pay attention to the social substance of those imperatives. However, in the world of actual urban planning, neither the inputs (particular problems) nor the outputs (political decisions) to and from the planning system are *essentially* dependent upon the specific administrative arrangements of that system. Hence, in city after city in North America today, and despite wide variations in local planning systems and bureaucracies, we observe the same fundamental urban problems (blight, slums, traffic congestion, central city decay, urban sprawl, etc) succeeded everywhere by fundamentally similar kinds of practical and political responses. It is not intended here to suggest that the structure of the planning system has *no* influence on the course of urban planning in any given situation, but only that the planning system as such seems to exist as a highly flexible intermediary relation that is structured around the central main events of planning as a concrete social phenomenon. More explicitly, the deeply rooted logic of urban planning in practice cannot possibly be understood in terms of its ephemeral bureaucratic manifestations at the local level, or, for that matter, in terms of its constantly changing preoccupation with administrative methodologies. On the contrary, *the planning system*—like the individual planner—is itself a derivative phenomenon emanating out of a social process that in the end is nothing less than the evolutionary pattern of the whole capitalist system. Rondinelli (1970, page 45) effectively touches upon the critical point that is at issue here when he writes that "the irony of planning theory is ... [that] it has never described accurately *how* urban and regional development policy is made". In this sense, mainstream planning theory fails dramatically to confront the central issues that must be tackled in any really viable theory.

Third, and as a concomitant of the above point, mainstream planning theory treats the activity of planning itself as being entirely non-problematical. That is, it treats planning as a *datum* rather than as an *explicandum*. Then, having taken this step, the mainstream seeks to transcend all that is historically specific and politically significant in urban planning by equating planning with general abstract rationality, and, more specifically, with normative action 'in theory' and the calculus of meliorative problemsolving. It must be stressed, once more, that there is no hidden intent in these latter remarks to question the practical usefulness of planning techniques within the overall apparatus of planning; the intention here is only to affirm that any attempt to theorize the activity of planning in terms of methodological procedures is to lose sight entirely of the essential content and meaning of planning as a specific system of collective political action *in capitalism*. Worse, because it evades and conceals this crucial social relation, mainstream planning theory establishes itself as an *ideology*; in brief, it deforms in thought the origins and character of urban planning by transforming planning into the semblance of a purely administrative matter carried out in conformity with general and disinterested rules of urban decisionmaking and management. Mainstream planning theory, then functions in such a way as effectively to depoliticize the planning process and, by the same token, to legitimate collective political intervention as a presumed expression of purely rational decisions and imperatives. Similarly, the admitted shortcomings of urban planning in practice become (when seen through the lenses of mainstream theory) simple human, administrative, or technical miscarriages as opposed to what they fundamentally are: the necessary failures of collective action within a system of capitalist social and property relations.

From each of these different points of criticism and evaluation of mainstream urban planning theory, a single dominant conclusion emerges. The character of mainstream theory can only be seen as serving the ideological and apologetic functions that must inevitably be called into being in a society whose social and property relations are such that (a) they give rise to the imperative of ever escalating planning intervention on the one hand, and (b) they result in a form of State intervention that by its very nature produces massive systematic biases of various sorts in the distribution and redistribution of the rewards and penalties of urban life.

11.2 The imperfect negation

Of course, in recent years, there has been a very considerable criticism in the planning literature of the methodological and procedural biases of current planning theory. Much of this criticism, however, seems to have taken mainstream theory on its own terms: it tends not to see this theory simply as a mask, or a mystification, but as a living social force whose thorough-going commitment to technical rationality has automatically nudged planners into increasing despoliation of the urban environment. This view fallaciously ascribes to mainstream planning theory a power that it simply does not and cannot possess, for the methodological preoccupations of that theory are merely the concomitants, and not the causes, of publicly induced dislocations in the urban land nexus. At the same time, much of the existing critique of mainstream planning theory has been frequently accompanied by explicit claims as to the intrinsically political, or at least conflictual, character of urban planning. But insofar as this critique is yet again unself-conscious about the fundamental structures of commodity-producing society, it, too, is mystified and self-limited. To these degrees, many of the attacks on current planning theory constitute an imperfect negation of the mainstream, and they remain part of the mainstream as a purely internal gloss. There appear to be two principle variations on this critical line of analysis within the mainstream, the one being advocacy planning and the other being contingent upon the question of citizens' participation.

Thus, many planning analysts have queried the supposedly monolithic role of planning in the context of a society where a plethora of different and competing sociocultural groups abounds. Davidoff (1965), for example, has suggested that individual planners should respond to the marked social heterogeneity of North American cities by becoming advocates on behalf of those people or groups whose interests and attitudes most conform to their own. Such advocacy is then supposed to secure the general public interest, for, by acting in this way, the planner becomes an agent serving the surpassing social purpose of securing "full participatory democracy in planning" (Porteous, 1977). We will return to this latter point below.

The planning literature has also in recent years been much given over to the issue of citizens' participation. The citizens' movement has in practice been a response to the very real frustrations, conflicts, and uncertainties of urban life, particularly in inner city areas. But simultaneously, it has also given rise to a sort of conceptual effluvium that has entered the general domain of planning theory. In particular, much of the theoretical literature that is derivative in one way or another out of the citizens' participation movement has been especially concerned (like advocacy planning) to identify and to remove barriers to a wholly democratic decisionmaking process in matters of urban planning. This approach has been especially notable for its critical attacks on entrenched planning bureaucracies, variously condemning them as conscious or unconscious agents of different sorts of elite groups. The point is made with some clarity in a recently published textbook by Porteous (1977, page 317):

"In many cities, the political process is manipulated by power elites each consisting of influential upper class persons who are able to achieve consensus and make their opinions felt among the elected decision makers. The latter are frequently persons strongly connected with real estate development .... The power elite exerts continuous pressure for its own ends through overlapping representation on school boards, planning commissions and boards of university governors, through the direction of banks, construction firms, mortgage companies, and the media, and through membership of prominent clubs, charities, and other cultural and civic organizations .... An examination of membership structures of such bodies frequently reveals a recurring list of names, a small group of people who are 'the real planners' of the urban environment."

This sort of theoretical viewpoint has already been criticized in chapter 5 under the rubric of 'manipulated-city theory'. All that remains to be said of it here is that this approach is questionable, not because power elites do not exist as an empirical fact—they obviously do exist—but because this sort of characterization of the planning process fails entirely to pose the critical problem as to what specific logic structures the decisions and behaviour of dominant groups within society. By failing in a fundamental way to penetrate down to the level of the encompassing social dynamics that are the mainspring of all collective intervention in the urban land nexus, simple power-elite theories of the planning process lead directly into an intellectual impasse.

Precisely because advocacy planning and the kinds of theories that have grown up around the citizens' participation movement are indeed oblivious to the deeply rooted bases of political action in contemporary society, their predominant conclusion that the urban planning issue *par excellence* is the issue of securing and extending popular participation in planning decisions is shallow and unduly credulous. This is not, of course, to suggest that the goal of democratic participation is a worthless goal; on the contrary, it is both important and commendable. But it must also be made clear that even perfect popular participation in all collective decisions provides no guarantee that the social and property relations that call for collective decisions and that imbue those decisions with specific content will in any sense be fundamentally modified. This same point was underscored by Marx (1870; 1948 edition, page 50) when he observed that one thing in particular was proved by the Paris Commune, viz that "the working class cannot simply lay hold of the ready-made State machinery, and wield it for its own purposes". The subjugation of the power of the State, in short, does not simply consist in shuffling around the individuals within a specific apparatus, but in attempts to reform the stubborn social relationships which surround and define that apparatus. Because the internal critique of mainstream planning theory fails to appreciate the full implications of the powerful structural impediments to *real* democratic control over the urban environment, it cannot see that its simple advocacies evade the fundamental problem. In this way, the internal critique establishes itself as being in the end basically in agreement with the mainstream: in both cases, the abstractly meliorative potential of urban planning is seen as being effectively unlimited.

11.3 The idealist-utopian origins of mainstream planning theory

The various preceding arguments all now seem to point strongly in the direction of a basic sophism at the core of conventional planning theory, whether of the procedural functional-structural variety discussed earlier or of the modestly critical variety discussed immediately above. This sophism consists of a pervasive *idealist-utopian* epistemology underlying virtually the whole of the mainstream. This epistemology is only dimly apprehended by conventional theorists themselves, though its basic nature is insistently revealed for what it is in the context of a paradox that appears repeatedly in the literature on planning theory. In this literature there is a recurrent split between planners' conceptions of the nature of the real world of practical urban intervention on the one hand, and their idealized view of a rational world of planning theory on the other hand. The domain of practical urban intervention is seen as being full of apparent unreason and disarray, while the domain of planning theory is seen as being the quintessence of order and harmony (especially in its common manifestation as the ideology of rational-comprehensive planning). Mainstream theorists then set about the task of resolving this mismatch between reality and theory by interjecting the idea that planning theory is in any case not so much an attempt to describe the world as it *is*, but as it *ought* to be. While engaging in this perilous manoeuvre, however, mainstream theorists typically fail to enumerate the necessary and sufficient conditions under which any given normative statement may be considered to be meaningful and workable in practice. In the light of this failure, mainstream theorists persistently adduce models of the planning process which, as Roweis (1975) has written, may conceivably be descriptions of planning somewhere, someday, but are definitely not descriptions of planning in contemporary capitalism. Thus, in refusing to confront urban planning as a concrete social phenomenon to be problematized and explained *as given*, much current planning theory condemns itself to the dead end of idealist-utopian discourse. It is idealist in the specific sense that it takes simple disembodied normative conceptions (human growth, the public interest, rational-comprehensiveness, etc) as the authentic guidelines of social change. It is utopian in the sense that it sees human society as being endlessly renegotiable via the proclamation of 'good ideas'. There is little surprise in the discovery, then, that conventional planning theorists constantly and one-sidedly conclude that the various failings of practical urban planning are predominantly the result of failings in the power of human thought.

The earlier discussion has already established the groundwork of a critique of these positions. At this stage, only three brief points need to be made clear. In the first place, the world as it is certainly presents innumerable *opportunities* for intentional human action and choice. However, these opportunities are objectively given; they are neither invented in the minds of planners nor created by astute normative theorizing; they may simply be revealed for that they are or are not. As Hason (1977) has remarked in this respect, it is not planners who define urban problems in need of a solution; it is urban problems threatening institutional stability that call for collective intervention and that thus define the roles that planners play *or may choose to play*. In the second place, planning ideas as *realizable* ideas-in-practice (that is, operational norms) are born within and are organically related to ongoing social situations and conjunctures. For example, new towns planning (in the manner of the first generation of British new towns planning) makes its appearance as a working system of ideas only in the aftermath of the emergence of a process of massive suburban development; in any case, new towns planning is most certainly not the result of the entirely secondary and indeed historically fortuitous circumstance that one Ebeneezer Howard happened, at the outset, to write a widely circulated tract on the supposed merits of life in garden cities. In the third place, the real, as opposed to the metaphysical imperatives of urban planning today are intertwined with and given definite meaning by the concrete political conflicts and issues that run through capitalist society as a whole. It is within the structure of this society that the material and antiutopian point of departure for a truly scientific (and emancipatory) theory of urban planning is to be found. This is a theory, as has been shown, that has no need of free-floating universal norms.

In spite of the rather obvious deficiencies of the idealist–utopian problematic, many recent restatements of planning theory have in fact responded even more decidedly to its siren call. These restatements have seemed to carry to its extreme and inevitable conclusion the notion that planning progresses out of the naked mind. On the one hand, they tend to insist ever more strongly [as in the case of a recent paper by Papageorgiou (1977)] on deriving a theory of planning out of decisionmaking methodologies and the general analytics of allocative action. On the other hand, many of these restatements have attempted to discover the ultimate

roots of planning somewhere in human psychology. In regard to this
latter tendency, several recent pronouncements on the matter of planning
theory have not only invoked psychology in the ordinary sense, but have
also called upon oriental mysticism (Friedmann, 1973) and even paranormal
mental powers (Michaels, 1974) as basic inputs to a reformulated theory
of planning. More generally, there has been a pervasive, if now perceptibly
waning, discussion of such issues as dialogue, empathy, community spirit,
and so on as definite possible foundations for an approach to the solution
of urban problems and fixes. The recent study by Friedmann (1973)
exemplifies well this latter kind of discussion.

In line with all the previous arguments put forward in this book, these
ultimate forms of idealist-utopian planning theory can only be passing
ephemera. They constitute neither a viable science on the one hand nor a
viable system of human practices on the other hand, for they are vitiated
right from the start by their abstraction of human intentions away from
real historical contexts. Moreover, when disembodied ideas, whether in
the form of logicomathematical formalizations, or in the form of states of
consciousness, are erroneously transformed into the autonomic motor of
social change, the result is a sort of Manichaeism that seems to haunt the
recent literature on the theory of urban planning. The result, in brief, is
the genesis of both innocence and despair; namely, on the one hand the
innocent belief that somehow the world's ills can and will be put to rights
by a process of technical or moral transformation; and, on the other hand,
the concomitant backlash of despair when it is realized that human society
remains curiously and inexplicably immune either to abstract reason or to
uplifting emotions and beliefs.

11.4 The impasse of mainstream planning theory
Mainstream planning theory presents itself to the world as a system of
ideas that is no doubt internally coherent and logical. However, it fails
dramatically to reflect and explain an underlying historical reality. On
the contrary, it interposes identifiable barriers to a global understanding
of the real universe of urbanization and urban planning. It is, in the fullest
sense of the term, an ideology. And we all pay the price that must always
be paid when the daily experiences of life and their ideological reflections
become disconnected. We are thrown into that eternal alternation between
a purely subjective optimism, as we put our faith in the ideology, and a
purely subjective pessimism, as we put our faith in the naked facts, that
forever blind us to the real opportunities for meaningful intellectual work
and practical social reform that lie before us.

Urban problems and urban planning today

The major thematic concern of this book has been to elucidate the dynamics of the urban land nexus as a web of spatial relationships embedded in the capitalist mode of production. One of the outstanding features of this web of relationships is the way in which it grows out of a series of locational responses and counterresponses by individual firms and households on the one hand, and by the State on the other hand. This phenomenon is decipherable in terms of the dialectic of private and public action as described in chapters 8 and 9. Directly as a consequence of this phenomenon, however, the State is drawn ever more insistently into the domain of urban life, and urban planners begin to encounter more and more conflict and controversy as they set about the endless task of attempting to reequilibrate the endemic breakdowns of the urban land nexus. Just as the State as a whole in capitalism is faced with a mounting crisis of legitimacy, so urban planning participates in and contributes to this selfsame crisis. In the urban sphere, it is a crisis that has its roots in the powerful evolutionary dynamic which leads the State on to continually escalating rounds of land-use intervention and control. By its very nature, urban planning in capitalism engenders its own eventual repoliticization.

This process of the broad repoliticization of collective action in contemporary society contrasts markedly with the situation that existed in the early *laissez-faire* period of capitalist development. In early capitalist society, the pervasive market institution of exchange of monetary equivalents affirmed itself as a universal principle of social organization and legitimacy. Adam Smith's invisible hand seemed to dispense largesse or penury in conformity with an entirely naturalistic finality, and in this sense, the outcomes of free market exchanges in commodities and factors of production *appeared* to be quite beyond and above all merely personal, factional, and class interests. Market society seemed, on the surface, to be nothing more than an agglomeration of free, equal, atomistic individuals confronting each other in the neutral roles of buyers and sellers in the process of open exchange. Accordingly, exchange of equivalents, and the market arrangements that made such exchange possible were fetichized into self-legitimating principles of social integration and fair play. So long as the processes of commodity production and exchange proceeded reasonably smoothly their apparently naturalistic operation was turned into a subtle and powerful ideology that served to mask the real nature of capitalist society, and, in particular, its concrete realization as a dominant bourgeoisie and a subordinate proletariat. Thus, in early capitalist society, the impersonality of contractual relations and the naturalistic operation of free market exchanges functioned in such a way as effectively to depoliticize class relations in general, and the social and political hegemony of the bourgeoisie in particular. Thus, the continued legitimation of the capitalist order of things depended in large degree upon the continued smooth operation of the mechanisms of commodity production and exchange.

Manifestly, however, the progress of capitalist commodity production and exchange has been far from smooth. Internally generated threats to the stability of the established order have been remarkably persistent throughout the development of capitalist society, and, as society has evolved, the State has found itself compelled to intervene ever more insistently in the workings of the entire system. As a result, contemporary life has been invaded in virtually all its aspects by this eminently *visible hand*. In particular, the State itself has become a significant circuit of exchange and appropriation, to the degree that in many cases it now supercedes and overrides the 'natural' circuit of the market. Nowhere is this visible hand more apparent today than in the urban land nexus, and all the evidence seems to point rather clearly in the direction of its becoming yet more so. Moreover, as a consequence of its urban planning interventions, the State induces massive shifts in the underlying urban structures through which life chances and expectations along with monetary and psychic incomes are in part appropriated. In these circumstances, increasing social friction over urban planning issues is virtually assured.

The contemporary phenomenon of the repoliticization of collective action is thus deeply intertwined with the structured evolution of the capitalist system. Habermas (1976, page 376) discusses this phenomenon in terms that starkly reveal its contradictory nature:

"Thus the State apparatus is confronted with two tasks at once. On the one hand it must collect the necessary sum in taxes by skimming off profits and income, and put it to such *rational* use that critical disturbances in growth can be avoided. And on the other hand, the selective raising of taxes, the recognizable scale of priorities according to which they are employed, and the administrative procedure, must be such that the need for *legitimation* which here arises may be satisfied. If the State fails in the fulfilment of the first of these tasks there arises a deficit in administrative rationality; if it fails with regard to the second task there arises a deficit in legitimation."

Further, precisely because the modern allocative and redistributive functions of the capitalist State are *seen* to be an outcome of bureaucratic decisions, and precisely because these decisions cannot be explained away in terms of some transcendent logical principle of social rationality (despite the heroic efforts of mainstream planning theory and such cognate ideologies as welfare economics, systems analysis, and the like) the planning process inevitably and openly becomes the focus of political controversy, and the implementation of planning decisions becomes increasingly fraught with complex conflicts. As urban planning continues to penetrate steadily more deeply into the sphere of urban life—and recall that our earlier analysis suggests that it must—then we can surely expect as a corollary, heightened social divisions over the issues of urban development, combined with and in part growing out of increasing difficulties in establishing the legitimacy of public planning decisions. One likely side effect of this emerging process of the repoliticization of planning is the final explosion of many of the myths and fables propagated by mainstream urban planning theory as the manifest impossibility of setting up a universally approvable objective function for planning becomes increasingly clear in practice.

At the same time, the complexity and society-wide significance of the problems of modern cities are likely to encourage national (as opposed to local) governments to become more and more involved in urban policy questions. This trend, however, is likely to accentuate yet further the repoliticization problem by projecting urban issues into the domain of national politics. Therefore, simultaneously, and in apparent contradiction to this centralizing impulse, the State is also likely to begin to seek out ways of devolving executive responsibility for urban planning decisions onto whatever organs of local government can be made to bear them. In brief, while urban policy is currently being increasingly initiated at the top, there are strong countervailing pressures on the State to attempt actively to *de*politicize its urban involvements by transforming them, at least in part, into the semblance of matters of strictly local concern. The effective devolution and depoliticization of urban (and regional) policy is evident in virtually all the major capitalist societies today and these trends are being reinforced by the proliferation of programmes of public consultation and sounding, and by an administratively encouraged widening of the bases of popular participation in urban planning decisions. In these ways, among others (including its incessant ideological discourse about its own purposes), the State is likely more and more to seek to deflect public opposition to its urban planning activities, and to attempt to legitimate its pervasive intervention throughout the urban land nexus.

Despite the manipulative implications of these latter trends, they also correspond to a genuine and liberalizing search for increased public participation in urban planning decisions of the part of the citizenry at large. If this participation is to be authentic, however—as opposed to being merely an administratively managed method of smoothing out the bureaucratic process of decisionmaking—it must, at the outset, be informed by a real understanding of the current urban situation as well as by an effective conception of its own role and functions. Furthermore, these essential prerequisites to fruitful popular participation in urban planning decisions are contained within a more global political issue. As the problems of the urban land nexus become steadily more complex and pervasive, and as urban planning itself becomes more and more overtly politicized, so the endemic conflicts and controversies in capitalist society make definite shifts in their locus and conformation. The central structural conflict in capitalist society around the capital-labour relation now becomes to an ever augmenting degree overlaid and intersected by derivative territorial conflicts around such issues as reproduction, the quality of community life, spatial biases in the provision of urban public goods, and so on. Hitherto these two domains of social conflict have tended to remain sealed off from one another (in North America, at least), even though they are only in the end different facets of the single fundamental question as to the human meaning and purposes of a society whose central motor is the capitalist system of production and accumulation. As Harvey (1976, page 295) has written of these two types of social conflict:

> "They are not mirror images of one another, but distorted representations mediated by many intervening forces and circumstances, which mystify and render opaque the fundamental class antagonism upon which the capitalist mode of production is founded. And it is of course the task of science to render clear through analysis what is mystified and opaque in daily life."

In line with these observations, it may well be that the steady repoliticization of urban life generally in late capitalist society will encourage the formation of a broadly based consciousness of the structural interconnections between exploitation and inequality in society at large, and disparities and dislocations in the urban environment. In this regard, there would seem to exist enormous possibilities for mutually beneficial alliances between progressive social movements of all kinds (including citizens' organizations), and for the development of a coherent programme capable of forging these into a common front. Certainly, a disciplined and coherent programme would help to make larger sense out of each specific conjunctural issue; and it would help to build up a reasonably steady political momentum, as opposed to the usual experience in North America where disjointed individual movements grow up around ephemeral problems, and then predictably collapse as those problems change their outer form. Paradoxically, the great danger is that the repoliticization of urban life may induce yet more social fractionation, and that augmented doses of State intervention in the urban land nexus will simply intensify intergroup and intercommunity antagonisms as different sections of society start to compete with one another for politically decided benefits. This is an area, however, in which meaningful analysis and education have a definite potential role to play in the development of strategies leading to real urban reform, and hence to the ushering in of a more rational and humanly significant urban environment.

The theoretical perspective on urbanization and planning that has been developed in this book has sought to reveal for what they are the tensions and dilemmas of urban life within a system of capitalist social and property relations. The analysis has disclosed a fundamental historical pattern at the core of the capitalist urbanization process, namely, the constant rearticulation at ever higher levels of complexity of the contradictory imperatives of private and public action in the urban land nexus. For structural reasons, this historical pattern evolves steadily in the direction of less privatization and more socialization of the urban land nexus, and this in turn induces the concomitant phenomenon of the repoliticization of modern urban planning. Part of the task that has also been faced up to in this book has been to lay down some of the groundwork for a critique of mainstream theories of urbanization and planning and to identify their unspoken ideological tendencies. Further, and in contradistinction to mainstream arguments, the analysis developed here purports to show that urbanization and planning do *not* constitute self-constitutive entities (and hence are not decipherable as independent units of analysis), but are secondary and derivative social relations embedded in the total structure of capitalism at large. For these reasons, the innumerable problems and predicaments of the contemporary city cannot be seen as simple, localized, quasi-mechanical failures that begin and end at the level of the land-use system; rather, they are surface symptoms of a stubborn contradictory social logic that reaches down to the very inner core of capitalist society. In the same way, the very real practical deficiencies of urban planning today can never be explained away as simple technical miscarriages; these deficiencies are the observable counterpart of the Sisyphean character of urban planning in capitalism, for in spite of its necessary historical emergence, planning remains permanently repressed and restricted by the very social relationships that call it into being at the outset.

This analysis, then (if correct), eliminates a few common delusions about the phenomena of urbanization and planning, and it simultaneously opens the way to a definite reexamination of these phenomena as concrete socially rooted occurrences. Most importantly of all, however, this analysis provides a basic framework for a thorough reevaluation of the urban question and for a critical reconsideration of the course of current urban policy.

References

AFTRP, undated *Les Zones d'Aménagement Différé* (Agence Foncière et Technique de la Région Parisienne, Paris)

Alonso W, 1965 *Location and Land Use* (Harvard University Press, Cambridge, Mass)

Althusser L, Balibar E, 1973 *Lire le Capital* (François Maspero, Paris) two volumes

Amin S, 1977 *La Loi de la Valeur et le Matérialisme Historique* (Minuit, Paris)

Ashworth W, 1954 *The Genesis of Modern British Town Planning* (Routledge and Kegan Paul, London)

Babcock R F, 1966 *The Zoning Game* (University of Wisconsin Press, Madison)

Banfield E C, 1973 *The Unheavenly City* (Little, Brown, Boston)

Barker G, Penny J, Seccombe W, 1973 *Highrise and Superprofits* (Dumont Press Graphix, Kitchener, Ontario)

Bastié J, 1964 *La Croissance de la Banlieue Parisienne* (Presses Universitaires de France, Paris)

Bator F M, 1958 "The anatomy of market failure" *Quarterly Journal of Economics* **72** 351-379

Baumol W J, 1952 *Welfare Economics and the Theory of the State* (Harvard University Press, Cambridge, Mass)

Bellush J, Hausknecht M (Eds), 1967 *Urban Renewal: People, Politics, and Planning* (Doubleday, Garden City, NY)

Benevolo L, 1967 *The Origins of Modern Town Planning* (Routledge and Kegan Paul, London)

Berry B J L, 1963 *Commercial Structure and Commercial Blight* RP-85, Department of Geography, University of Chicago (University of Chicago Press, Chicago)

Berry B J L, 1967 *Geography of Market Centers and Retail Distribution* (Prentice-Hall, Englewood Cliffs, NJ)

Burgess E W, 1925 "The growth of the city: an introduction to a research project" in *The City* by R E Park, E W Burgess, R D McKenzie (University of Chicago Press, Chicago) pp 47-62

Cameron G C, 1973 "Intraurban location and the new plant" *Papers of the Regional Science Association* **31** 125-143

Castells M, 1968 "Y-a-t-il une sociologie urbaine?" *Sociologie du Travail* **1** 72-90

Castells M, 1970 "La rénovation urbaine aux Etats-Unis: Synthèse et interprétation des données actuelles" *Espaces et Sociétés* **1** 107-136

Castells M, 1977 "Towards a political urban sociology" in *Captive Cities* Ed. M Harloe (John Wiley, Chichester, Sussex) pp 61-78

Castells M, Godard F, 1974 *Monopolville* (Mouton, Paris)

City of Toronto Core Area Task Force, 1974 *Report and Recommendations* (City of Toronto Planning Board, Toronto, Ontario)

Clark C, 1951 "Urban population densities" *Journal of the Royal Statistical Society, Series A* **114** 490-496

Clark C, 1968 *Population Growth and Land Use* (Macmillan, London)

Daniels P W, 1975 *Office Location* (G Bell, London)

Daniels P W, 1977 "Office location in British conurbations: trends and strategies" *Urban Studies* **14** 261-274

Davidoff P, 1965 "Advocacy and pluralism in planning" *Journal of the American Institute of Planners* **31** 331-338

Davidoff P, Reiner T A, 1962 "A choice theory of planning" *Journal of the American Institute of Planners* **28** 103-115

Davis O A, Whinston A B, 1966 "The economics of urban renewal" in *Urban Renewal: The Record and the Controversy* Ed. J Q Wilson (MIT Press, Cambridge, Mass) pp 50-67

Engels F, 1845; 1969 edition *The Condition of the Working Class in England* (Panther Books, London)

Engels F, 1872; 1970 edition *The Housing Question* (Progress, Moscow)
Fales R L, Moses L N, 1972 "Land use theory and the spatial structure of the nineteenth century city" *Papers of the Regional Science Association* **28** 49-80
Faludi A, 1973 *Planning Theory* (Pergamon Press, Oxford)
Flink J J, 1975 *The Car Culture* (MIT Press, Cambridge, Mass)
Foreman-Peck J S, Gripaios P A, 1977 "Inner city problems and inner city policies" *Regional Studies* **11** 401-412
Frankena F, 1973 "Income distributional effects of urban transit subsidies" *Journal of Transport Economics and Policy* **7** 1-16
Friedmann J, 1973 *Retracking America: A Theory of Transactive Planning* (Anchor Press/Doubleday, Garden City, NY)
Gaillard J, 1977 *Paris, La Ville, 1852-1870* (Honoré Champion, Paris)
Gale S, Moore E G (Eds), 1975 *The Manipulated City* (Maaroufa Press, Chicago)
Gans H J, 1967 "The failure of urban renewal: a critique and some proposals" in *Urban Renewal: People, Politics, and Planning* Eds J Bellush, M Hausknecht (Doubleday, Garden City, NY) pp 465-484
Goddard J B, 1973 "Office linkages and location" *Progress in Planning* **1** 109-232
Goldberg M A, 1977 "Housing and land prices in Canada and the U.S." in *Public Property?* Eds L B Smith, M Walker (Fraser Institute, Vancouver) pp 207-254
Goldrick M, 1978 "The anatomy of urban reform in Toronto" *City Magazine* **3** (4/5) 29-39
Gripaios P A, 1977 "Industrial decline in London: an examination of its causes" *Urban Studies* **14** 181-189
Habermas J, 1976 "Problems of legitimation in late capitalism" in *Critical Sociology* Ed. P Connerton (Penguin Books, Harmondsworth, Middx) pp 363-387
Harris B, 1978 "A note on planning theory" *Environment and Planning A* **10** 221-224
Harris C D, Ullman E L, 1945 "The nature of cities" *Annals of the American Academy of Political and Social Science* **242** 7-17
Hartman C W, 1964 "The housing of relocated families" *Journal of the American Institute of Planners* **30** 266-286
Harvey D, 1976 "Labour, capital, and class struggle around the built environment in advanced capitalist societies" *Politics and Society* **6** 265-295
Harvey D, 1977 "Government policies, financial institutions and neighbourhood change in United States cities" in *Captive Cities* Ed. M Harloe (John Wiley, Chichester, Sussex) pp 123-139
Harvey D, 1978 "The urban process under capitalism: a framework for analysis" *International Journal of Urban and Regional Research* **2** 101-131
Hason N, 1977 "The emergence and development of zoning controls in North American municipalities: a critical analysis" Papers on Planning and Design 13, Department of Urban and Regional Planning, University of Toronto, Toronto
Hindess B, Hirst P Q, 1975 *Pre-Capitalist Modes of Production* (Routledge and Kegan Paul, London)
Hindess B, Hirst P Q, 1977 *Mode of Production and Social Formation* (MacMillan, London)
Hirsch J, 1976 "Remarques théoriques sur l'état bourgeois et sa crise" in *La Crise de l'État* Ed. N Poulantzas (Presses Universitaires de France, Paris) pp 103-129
Holloway J, Picciotto S, 1977 "Capital, the State and European integration" in *Sur l'État* Association pour la Critique des Sciences Économiques et Sociales (Contradictions, Brussels) pp 23-65
Hoover E M, Vernon R, 1959 *Anatomy of a Metropolis* (Harvard University Press, Cambridge, Mass)
Hotelling H, 1929 "Stability in competition" *The Economic Journal* **39** 41-57

Hoyt H, 1939 *The Structure and Growth of Residential Neighborhoods in American Cities* (US Federal Housing Administration, Washington, DC)
Isard W, 1956 *Location and Space-Economy* (MIT Press, Cambridge, Mass)
Kohn M L, 1969; 1977 edition *Class and Conformity* (University of Chicago Press, Chicago)
Koopmans T C, Beckmann M J, 1957 "Assignment problems and the location of economic activities" *Econometrica* **25** 53-76
Krampen M, 1979 *Meaning in the Urban Environment* (Pion, London)
Lai J, 1978 *Urban Transport Financing, Planning and Policies in Metropolitan Toronto, 1954-76* unpublished MSc (P1) paper, Department of Urban and Regional Planning, University of Toronto, Toronto
Lavedan P, 1960 *Histoire de Paris* (Presses Universitaires de France, Paris)
Leclercq Y, 1977 *Théories de l'État* (Arthropos, Paris)
Lipietz A, 1974 *Le Tribut Foncier Urbain* (François Maspero, Paris)
Lipietz A, 1977 *Le Capital et son Espace* (François Maspero, Paris)
Lojkine J, 1977 *Le Marxisme, l'État et la Question Urbaine* (Presses Universitaires de France, Paris)
Lorimer J, 1976 "Canada's urban experts: smoking out the liberals" in *The City Book* Eds J Lorimer, E Ross (James Lorimer, Toronto, Ontario) pp 97-103
Malet H, 1973 *Le Baron Haussmann et la Rénovation de Paris* (Les Éditions Municipales, Paris)
Mandel E, 1975 *Late Capitalism* (New Left Books, London)
Marx K, 1859; 1970 edition *A Contribution to the Critique of Political Economy* (International, New York)
Marx K, 1870; 1948 edition *The Civil War in France* (Progress, Moscow)
Massey D, Catalano A, 1978 *Capital and Land* (Edward Arnold, London)
Massey D, Meegan R A, 1978 "Industrial restructuring versus the cities" *Urban Studies* **15** 273-288
McKenzie R D, 1925 "The ecological approach to the study of the human community" in *The City* Eds R E Park, E W Burgess, R D McKenzie (University of Chicago Press, Chicago) pp 63-79
Mearns A, 1883; 1976 edition "The bitter cry of outcast London" in *Into Unknown England, 1866-1913* Ed. P Keating (Fontana/Collins, London) pp 91-111
Metropolitan Toronto Planning Board, 1964 *Report on the Metropolitan Toronto Transportation Plan* (Metropolitan Toronto Planning Board, Toronto, Ontario)
Michaels D N, 1974 "Speculations on future planning process theory" in *Planning in America: Learning from Turbulence* Ed. D G Godschalk (American Institute of Planners, Washington, DC) pp 35-61
Michelson W H, 1970 *Man and His Urban Environment: A Sociological Approach* (Addison-Wesley, Reading, Mass)
Mill J S, 1848; 1920 edition *Principles of Political Economy* (Longmans, Green, London)
Mills E S, 1972 *Studies in the Structure of the Urban Economy* (Johns Hopkins University Press, Baltimore)
Moffitt R, 1977 "Metropolitan decentralization and city-suburb wage differentials" *International Regional Science Review* **2** 103-111
Moroney J R, Walker J M, 1966 "A regional test of the Heckscher-Ohlin hypothesis" *Journal of Political Economy* **74** 573-586
Moses L N, 1958 "Location and the theory of production" *Quarterly Journal of Economics* **73** 259-272
Moses L N, 1962 "Towards a theory of intra-urban wage differentials and their influence on travel patterns" *Papers of the Regional Science Association* **9** 53-63

References

Moses L N, Williamson H F, 1967 "The location of economic activity in cities" *The American Economic Review* **57** 211-222

Murdie R A, 1969 *Factorial Ecology of Metropolitan Toronto, 1951-1961* RP-116, Department of Geography, University of Chicago (University of Chicago Press, Chicago)

Muth R F, 1969 *Cities and Housing* (University of Chicago Press, Chicago)

Nowlan D M, 1977 "The land market: how it works" in *Public Property?* Eds L B Smith, M Walker (Fraser Institute, Vancouver) pp 3-37

Olson M, 1965 *The Logic of Collective Action* (Harvard University Press, Cambridge, Mass)

Page J, Lang R, 1977 *Canadian Planners in Profile* Faculty of Environmental Studies, York University, Downsview, Ontario, Canada (unpublished report presented to the annual conference of the Canadian Institute of Planners, 1977)

Papageorgiou G J, 1977 "Fundamental problems of theoretical planning" *Environment and Planning A* **9** 1329-1356

Park R E, 1936 "Human ecology" *The American Journal of Sociology* **42** 1-15

Pašukanis E B, 1970 *La Théorie Générale du Droit et le Marxisme* (Études et Documentation Internationales, Paris) translated from the original Russian edition of 1924

Pinkney D H, 1958 *Napoleon III and the Rebuilding of Paris* (Princeton University Press, Princeton, NJ)

Pisani E, 1977 *Utopie Foncière* (Gallimard, Paris)

Pollard S, 1965 *The Genesis of Modern Management* (Edward Arnold, London)

Porteous J D, 1977 *Environment and Behavior: Planning and Everyday Life* (Addison-Wesley, Reading, Mass)

Poulantzas N, 1974 *Les Classes Sociales dans le Capitalisme d'Aujourd'hui* (Seuil, Paris)

President's Task Force on Urban Renewal, 1970 *Urban Renewal: One Tool Among Many* (US Government Printing Office, Washington, DC)

President's Urban and Regional Policy Group, 1978 *A New Partnership to Conserve America's Communities: A National Urban Policy* report HUD-S-297, US Department of Housing and Urban Development, Washington, DC

Preteceille E, 1973 *La Production des Grands Ensembles* (Mouton, Paris)

Pye R, 1977 "Office location and the cost of maintaining contact" *Environment and Planning A* **9** 149-168

Rees A, Shultz G P, 1970 *Workers and Wages in an Urban Labor Market* (University of Chicago Press, Chicago)

Reich W, 1933; 1975 edition *The Mass Psychology of Fascism* (Penguin Books, Harmondsworth, Middx)

Reif B, 1973 *Models in Urban and Regional Planning* (Leonard Hill, Aylesbury, Bucks)

Rhodes J, Kan A, 1971 *Office Dispersal and Regional Policy* (Cambridge University Press, London)

Richardson H W, 1977 *The New Urban Economics: And Alternatives* (Pion, London)

Rondinelli D A, 1970 *Urban and Regional Development Planning: Policy and Administration* (Cornell University Press, Ithaca, NY)

Rose D, 1978 *Housing Policy, Urbanisation and the Reproduction of Labour-power in Mid-to-late Nineteenth Century Britain: A Conceptual Appraisal* unpublished MA paper, Department of Geography, University of Toronto, Toronto

Roweis S T, 1975 "Urban planning in early and late capitalist societies: outline of a theoretical perspective" Papers on Planning and Design 7, Department of Urban and Regional Planning, University of Toronto, Toronto

Roweis S T, Scott A J, 1978 "The urban land question" in *Urbanization and Conflict in Market Societies* Ed. K Cox (Maaroufa Press, Chicago) pp 38-73

Royal Commission on London Traffic, 1905 *Report of the Royal Commission Appointed to Inquire into and Report upon the Means of Locomotion and Transport in London* command 2597 (HMSO, London)

Samuelson P A, 1959 "A modern treatment of the Ricardian economy: I, The pricing of goods and of labor and land services" *The Quarterly Journal of Economics* **73** 1-35

Schwirian K, 1974 *Comparative Urban Structure* (D C Heath, Lexington, Mass)

Scott A J, 1975 "Discrete dynamic locational systems: notes on a structural framework" in *Dynamic Allocation of Urban Space* Eds A Karlquist, L Lundqvist, F Snickars, J W Weibull (Saxon House, Teakfield, Farnborough, Hants) pp 121-158

Scott A J, 1976 "Land and land rent: an interpretative review of the French literature" in *Progress in Geography, Volume 9* Eds C Board, R J Chorley, P Haggett, D R Stoddart (Edward Arnold, London) pp 103-145

Scott A J, Roweis S T, 1977 "Urban planning in theory and practice: a reappraisal" *Environment and Planning A* **9** 1097-1119

Scott A J, Roweis S T, 1978 "A note on planning theory: a response to Britton Harris" *Environment and Planning A* **10** 229-231

Slayton W L, 1966 "The operation and achievements of the urban renewal program" in *Urban Renewal: The Record and the Controversy* Ed. J Q Wilson (MIT Press, Cambridge, Mass) pp 189-229

Smith L B, Walker M (Eds) 1977 *Public Property?* (The Fraser Institute, Vancouver)

Solow R M, 1973 "On equilibrium models of urban location" in *Essays in Modern Economics* Ed. M Parkin (Longman, London) pp 2-16

Sraffa P, 1960 *Production of Commodities by Means of Commodities* (Cambridge University Press, Cambridge)

Steed G P F, 1976 "Standardization, scale, incubation, and inertia: Montreal and Toronto clothing industries" *Canadian Geographer* **20** 298-309

Steedman I, 1977 *Marx after Sraffa* (New Left Books, London)

Stewart C, 1952 *A Prospect of Cities* (Longmans, Green, New York)

Stone D N, 1974 *Industrial Location in Metropolitan Areas* (Praeger, New York)

Struyk R J, James F J, 1975 *Intrametropolitan Industrial Location* (D C Heath, Lexington, Mass)

Teitz M B, 1968 "Toward a theory of urban public facility location" *Papers of the Regional Science Association* **21** 35-51

Thompson W R, 1965 *A Preface to Urban Economics* (Johns Hopkins University Press, Baltimore)

Topalov C, 1973 *Capital et Propriété Foncière* (Centre de Sociologie Urbaine, Paris)

Topalov C, 1974 *Expropriation et Préemption Publique en France 1950-1973* (Centre de Sociologie Urbaine, Paris)

Touraine A, 1973 *Production de la Société* (Seuil, Paris)

Walker R A, 1978 "The transformation of urban structure in the nineteenth century and the beginnings of suburbanization" in *Urbanization and Conflict in Market Societies* Ed. K Cox (Maaroufa Press, Chicago) pp 165-212

Webber M M, 1963 "The prospects for policies planning" in *The Urban Condition* Ed. L J Duhl (Basic Books, New York) pp 319-330

Wilson A G, 1968 "Models in urban planning: a synoptic review of recent literature" *Urban Studies* **5** 249-276

Wingo L, 1961 *Transportation and Urban Land* (Resources for the Future, Washington, DC)

Wirth L, 1938 "Urbanism as a way of life" *American Journal of Sociology* **44** 1-24

Appendix

The main empirical test performed in section 6.3 is based upon two major sets of data for each of the census metropolitan areas of Montreal, Toronto, and Vancouver, namely, (1) industrial production in the central city and in the total census metropolitan area for two-digit major industrial groups, and (2) estimated metropolitan capital–labour ratios for the same industrial groups. The following are notes on these data.

1 Industrial output is measured in terms of total dollar value of shipments.
2 Changes in the standard industrial classification in 1960 mean that designated industrial groups in 1956–1959 differ from designated industrial groups in 1961–1964 and 1971–1974.
3 Statistics Canada confidentiality regulations result in the nondisclosure of pertinent data from time to time. This explains why it is that the number of observations used in calculating the correlation coefficients in table 6.2 differs from case to case. In addition, data for primary metal industries are deleted from the analysis for 1961–1964 owing to a significant change in the official definition of this category between 1961 and 1964; as a result, statistics for primary metal industries are not comparable for the years 1961 and 1964.
4 The three time intervals 1956–1959, 1961–1964, and 1971–1974 were chosen so as to eliminate data inconsistencies due to (a) changes in the standard industrial classification in 1960 and 1970, (b) changes in the boundaries of the census metropolitan areas of Montreal, Toronto, and Vancouver, and (c) the failure of Statistics Canada to publish the basic data source *Manufacturing Industries of Canada: Geographical Distribution* in certain years in the late 1960s and early 1970s. Disaggregated data on industrial production in census metropolitan areas in Canada first became publicly available in 1956.
5 Metropolitan capital–labour ratios $(K_{i\tau}/W_{i\tau})$ for major industrial groups in each of the years 1956, 1959, 1961, 1964, 1971, 1974 were computed as follows: (a) $K_{i\tau} = k_{i\tau}^1 + k_{i\tau}^2 + k_{i\tau}^3$, where $k_{i\tau}^1$ is estimated total annual fixed capital depreciation (see next paragraph), $k_{i\tau}^2$ is total annual expenditures on fuel and electricity, and $k_{i\tau}^3$ is the total annual cost of material supplies (plus goods for resale); (b) $W_{i\tau}$ is defined as total wages and salaries in the ith branch at time τ.
6 Fixed capital depreciation, $k_{i\tau}^1$, was estimated thus: calculate depreciation $(k_{i\tau}^{1n})$ in the ith branch of production *in Canada as a whole* at time τ as equal to the midyear gross stock of fixed capital (physical plant and equipment) minus the midyear net stock of fixed capital in that branch. Compute $\kappa_{i\tau} = k_{i\tau}^{1n}/X_{i\tau}$, where $X_{i\tau}$ is the total dollar value of output in branch i in Canada as a whole at time τ. Then, for each branch in each census metropolitan area, it is assumed that each dollar's worth of output at time τ contains a depreciation factor equal precisely to $\kappa_{i\tau}$, the national coefficient. Now estimate total depreciation in each branch in each metropolitan area accordingly.

7 Notwithstanding the attempt described above to combine fixed capital with commensurable units of circulating capital, it is by no means certain that this has been achieved. In the absence of specific measures of velocity of turnover of individual capital items, error-free determination of aggregate capital inputs is, of course, impossible. As it is, the method described above for calculating the overall measure of capital, K_{ir}, undoubtedly introduces a bias by exaggerating the capital intensity of labour-intensive branches of production that are characterized by a high velocity of turnover of circulating capital. This bias, however, at least has the merit of reducing rather than increasing the probability that the main statistical test undertaken in chapter 6 will be successful.

8 It need hardly be pointed out that the method described in paragraph 6 for calculating metropolitan capital-labour ratios is rough and ready. However, since the census metropolitan areas of Montreal, Toronto, and Vancouver account collectively for a third to a half and upwards of the total Canadian output in any sector, the amount of inconsistency introduced into the analysis as a result of this method of calculation is probably not so great as may at first appear to be the case. At the same time, an attempt was made to calculate separate capital-labour ratios for central city areas and suburban rings by means of the method described above. However, it was felt that this procedure significantly overestimates capital inputs in central city areas (where much old plant tends to be reused) and significantly underestimates capital inputs in suburban ring areas (where much of the existing plant and equipment is comparatively new). As a consequence, this line of attack was abandoned.

Index

Absolute rent 38
Abstract rationality 233
Accessibility 94, 114-115
Accumulation 18, 25, 180
Ackroyden 122
Advocacy planning 234-236
AFTRP (Agence Foncière et Technique de la Région Parisienne) 156
Agglomeration effects 107-108, 210
Alonso W 73, 77
Althusser L 10
Amin S 19
Ashworth W 195, 199, 202

Babcock R F 210
Balibar E 10
Banfield E C 62, 72
Barker G et al 83
Bastié J 209
Bator F M 79, 149
Baumol W J 171
Beckmann M J 165
Bellush J 214
Benevolo L 196
Berry B J L 115
Bid-rent curves 74
Blacks 212, 216
Blight 159, 213-217
Blue-collar neighbourhoods 126-127
Boddy M preface
Boston 93, 215
Bourgeois conspiracy 182
Bourneville 122, 197
Broadbent T A preface
Brussels 209
Bureaucracy 231, 233
Burgess E W 67, 68
Busing 212

Cadbury G 197
Cambridge School 16
Cameron G C 101
Capitalism 15-23
Capitalist mode of production 15-18
Capitalist State (see also State, urban planning) 23-27, 180-183
Capital-labour ratio 89, 102-106, 111, 112, 249-250
Capital-labour relation 24, 183, 184, 191, 241
Capital-labour substitution 99-100
Carter Administration 1
Castells M preface, 5, 7, 140, 215

Catalano A 13, 30, 31
Ceinture rouge 209
Central business district (see also inner city, urban core) 58, 116, 211, 223
Cheap Trains Act 202
Chicago 67, 68, 69, 92, 96, 117
Chicago School (see also urban sociology) 66-73, 137
Child rearing 125
C.i.f. prices 34
Circulation space (see also transport planning, urban transport) 128-133, 217-227)
Citizens' groups 152, 223-224
Citizens' participation 234-236, 241-242
City Beautiful Movement 55-56, 124, 210
City Efficient Movement 210
City of Toronto Core Area Task Force 111
Civil society 23-26, 180, 189
Clark C 117
Class 10-15, 184
Class conflict 16, 24-25, 241-242
Class conspiracies 27
Clothing industry 106-108
Collective action and decisionmaking (see also State, urban planning) 24-27, 139-140, 175-192, 186
Commodity production 15-18, 88
Commodity production and land use 28-54
Community 66-73
Community Land Act 65
Company towns 122-123
Competitive locational logic 166-167
Composite commodity 21
Consciousness 14, 238
Consumer choice behaviour 75, 76
Consumer sovereighty 77
Consumption 146-147
Critical approaches to urban analysis 7-9
Cross Act 199, 202

Daniels P W 110, 113
Davidoff P 176, 229, 234
Davis O A 213
Decentralization 56, 97-109, 113-114
Democratic decisionmaking 234-235
Depoliticization 241
Development policy 64
Devalorization 181
Development timing (see also land development, land-use conversion) 161-165

Devolution 241
Differential locational advantages 136, 161
Differential rent 35-41
Discriminatory zoning 211-212
Distribution (of surplus) (see also income shares) 16, 21, 30, 130-131
Don Valley Parkway 218, 219
Dynamic locational systems 166-168

East York 218
Edmonton 203
Empiricist approaches to urban analysis 7-9
Engels F 84, 121, 194, 196
Environmental psychology 72
Equalization programmes 180
Ethnicity 119-120
Etobicoke 218
Excess profit 36-37, 43-53
Exchange of equivalents 26-27, 239
Exclusionary zoning 211-212
Expressways 58, 59, 217-227
Expropriation 155
Extensive land-use change 47-51
Externalities (see also spillover effects) 80, 148-155

Face-to-face contact 110, 112
Factorial ecology 72, 119
Factory system 121, 196
Fales R L 91, 96
Falling rate of profit 182
Faludi A 176, 231
Familism 119-120
Federal housing acts 214, 217
Fiscal crisis 60, 153-154
Fiscal policy 61-63
Fixed costs 144-145
Flink J J 122
F.o.b. prices 34
Forces of production 10-12
Ford H 122
Foreman-Peck J S 109
Fourier C 197
Fourierism 178
Frankena M 132
Free public transport 132
Free-rider problem 158-159, 197, 213
French Revolution 204
Friedmann J 238
Gaillard J 204, 208
Gale S 82

Gans H J 215
F G Gardiner Expressway 218, 219
Garnier C 207
General systems theory 230
Geographical space 28-54
Glasgow 195
GO transit 218, 219, 224
Goals in planning 229-234
Godard F 140
Goddard J B 114
Goldberg M A 59n, 220
Goldrick M 225
Grand bourgeoisie 182-183, 184
Grands boulevards 206
Gripaios P A 108, 109
Gross income 17
Growth 180

Habermas J 185, 240
Harris B 172n, 230, 231
Harris C D 68
Hartman C W 215
Harvey D preface, 123, 160, 217, 242
Hason N 82, 210, 237
Hausknecht M 214
Baron Haussmann 193, 204-209
Heckscher-Ohlin theorem 88, 89, 98, 101, 102-108
Hegel G W F 77
High-rise development 59-60
Highway programme 215, 216
Hindess B 8, 10, 11, 194
Hirsch J 185
Hirst P Q 8, 10, 11, 194
Historical materialism 8, 11
Holloway J 26
Hoover E M 90, 93, 98, 101, 108
Horizontal plant lay-out 89
Hotelling H 165
Housing 215
Housing and Town Planning Act of 1909 203
Housing clearances 188, 199
Housing legislation 199-203, 214, 217
Howard E 237
Hoyt H 68
Hygiene 188

Idealist-utopian epistemologies 236-238
Ideology 228-243
Income shares (see also distribution) 130-131
Incubation hypothesis 101-102

Index

Indeterminate abstraction 232
Industrial activities 88–109
Industrial complexes 96–97
Industrial decentralization 89–90, 97–108
Industrial location 96–109
Industrial towns 194–203
Infrastructure (see also urban equipment) 57, 64, 160, 207, 217–227
Inner city (see also central business district, urban core) 109, 199–202, 212–217
Input–output model 19, 33
Intensive land-use change 42–47, 59, 172–173
Intentionality 13–14
Intervening opportunities 94
Intraurban wage rate surface 93
Invisible hand 239
Isard W 28

James F J 99, 101
Journey-to-work 92–95, 111–112

Kan A 113
Keynesian economics 207
Kohn M L 125
Koopmans T C 165
Krampen M 126

Labour 92–95
Labourer 11–12
Labour-intensive industry 96–97
Labour market (see also local labour market) 197
Labour theory of value 19, 22, 182
Lai J 222
Laissez-faire 78, 239
Land 28–31, 78, 81, 136
Land banking 155–158
Land contingency 2–3, 7, 136, 169, 184, 190
Land-contingent goods and services 145–147
Land development (see also development timing, land-use conversion, redevelopment) 136–137
Land development bottlenecks 155–158
Land hoarding 59
Land market 213
Landowners 13, 30–31, 33
Landownership 155–158
Land regulation policy 63–64

Land rent (see also absolute rent, differential rent, scarcity rent) 28–54
Land use (see also extensive land-use change, intensive land-use change) 28–54
Land-use conflict 55–61, 140
Land-use conversion (see also development timing, land development) 161–165
Land-use dynamics 41–54
Land-use problems 148–168
Land-use systems (see also urban land nexus) 28–54
Land-use zoning (see also zoning) 193, 209–212
Lang R 232
Lavedan P 206
Leapfrogging 168
Leclercq Y 181
Legitimate violence 25, 141
Legitimation 180, 239–240
Legitimation crisis 133, 191
Le Monde 228
Lever W H 197
Lipietz A 76, 140
Local labour market (see also labour market) 92–95
Locational logic 4
Locational myopia 165–168
Lojkine J 140, 183
London 110, 113, 114, 202, 209, 215
Lorimer J 83

Macroeconomic model of capitalist production relations 18–23
Madrid 209
Mainstream planning theory 229–234
Mainstream urban theory 66–85
Malet H 207
Manchester 194
Mandel E 131
Manipulated-city theory 82–85, 228, 235
Manufacturing towns 194–203
Marginal producer 36
Market failure (see also externalities, free-rider problem, land development bottlenecks, locational myopia, monopolies, noncommodity, slow-convertibility problem) 79, 148–168
Market mechanism 22, 73–82
Market norms 78, 239–240
Market prices 22–23
Market society 239–240

Marx K 10, 235
Marxian theory of the State 181
Massey D 13, 30, 31, 101
Materials-intensive industry 96
Mathematical programming 231
McKenzie R D 71
Mearns A 121
Meegan R A 101
Metropolitan Toronto 217-227
Metropolitan Toronto Planning Board 223
Michaels D N 238
Michelson W H 72
Middle-class communities 211
Mill J S 78
Mills E S 77
Mississauga 225
Model Dwellings Associations 199
Mode of production 10-15
Moffitt R 93
Monopolies 143-145
Montreal 102-108, 249, 250
Moore E G 82
Moroney J R 89
Moses L N 91, 93, 96, 99
Municipal finance 154, 189
Municipal government 153-154
Murdie R A 119
Muth R F 77

Napoleon III 206, 209
National Housing Act of 1954 222
Negative exponential density function 117
Negative spillovers 149-153
Neighbourhoods 124-128, 151-153
Neoclassical theory 16, 23, 73-82,
  117-118, 127, 138-139, 144, 151
Net income 17, 19-23, 33
Net present value 162-163
New Harmony 196
New Lanark 122, 197
New towns 57
New York 56, 93, 210, 214
North York 218, 225
Noncommodity 140
Nonlabourer 11-12
Normative theory 176, 178, 236-238
Nowlan D M 78n, 163, 164

Office activities 109-114
Olmstead F L 203
Olson M 171
Ontario, province of 218, 219
Overaccumulation 181-182

Oriental mysticism 238
Owen R 196, 197

Page J 232
Papageorgiou G J 237
Paranormal mental powers 238
Pareto-optimality 78, 79, 81, 82, 142,
  171, 178, 217
Paris 156, 193, 204-209, 215
Paris Commune 236
Park R E 69, 71
Participatory democracy 234-235
Pašukanis E B 26
Peripheral expansion (see also
  suburbanization) 56, 57, 60, 168, 208
Picciotto S 26
Pinkney D H 204
Pisani E 206, 208
Planned locations 167
Planning education 189
Planning history 187
Planning ideologies 228-243
Planning legislation 200-201
Planning system 230, 233
Planning theory 176-179, 228-243
Political conflict 130, 241-242
Political economy 16
Pollard S 196, 197
Population density 117
Porteous J D 234, 235
Port Sunlight 122, 197
Poulantzas N 13
Power elite 183, 235
President's Task Force on Urban Renewal
  213
President's Urban and Regional Policy
  Group 1
Preteceille E 140
Price system 20-23
Private action and decisionmaking 24-27,
  138-139, 186
Private locators 137, 168
Private-public interface 128-129,
  189-191
Production prices 20-23
Production space 86-116
Production techniques 42-54
Profits 16, 17, 19-23
Property tax 62
Proudonism 84
Public transport 222
Pullman G 197
Public goods 129, 143-147, 155

Public policy 142
Pye R 112

Racial tipping 216
Range of a good 115
Rate of profit 20, 87
Reactive planning 61, 226
Redevelopment 213-214
Rees A 92
Refutability criterion 232
Rehabilitation 217
Reich W 14
Reif B 230
Reiner T 176, 229
Rent (see also land rent) 28-31
Rent control 62
Repoliticization 189, 239-243
Reproduction 146-147, 194-203
Reproduction space 117-128, 151-153
Residential land use 54, 117-128
Residential rent 75
Residential segregation (see also spatial segregation) 212
Retail activities 114-116
Rhodes J 113
Richardson H W preface, 73
Roads 222
Road transport technology 91
Rome 209
Rondinelli D A 233
Rose D 200, 202
Roweis S T preface, 15, 18, 172n, 191, 203, 236
Royal Commission on London Traffic 203

Salt, Sir Titus 122, 197
Saltaire 122, 197, 198
Samuelson P A 38
Scarborough 218, 225
Scarcity rent 38-39
Schools 125
Schwirian K 72, 119
Scott A J preface, 38, 167, 172n
Seattle 59n
Second Empire 205-206
Service activities 114-116
Sex ratios in manufacturing 94
Shultz G P 92
Slayton W L 214
Slow-convertibility problem 160
Slums 159, 194-203, 205, 207, 213-217
Smith A 239
Smith L B 80, 170

Social Darwinism 69, 71
Social formation 11-12
Socialization 121-128, 147, 194-203
Social networks 126
Social optimum 163, 165, 167
Social rank 119-120, 126
Social relations of production 10-12
Solow R M 75
Spadina Expressway 218, 224
Spatial segregation (see also residential segregation) 211
Spillover effects (see also externalities) 148-155, 209, 210, 212-213, 223
Sraffa P 16, 18, 90
Sraffa model 18-23
Sraffa-von Thünen system 31-41, 53
Standardization 106-107, 111-112
State (see also capitalist State, urban planning) 16, 23-27, 81-82, 128-130, 135-174, 175-192, 217, 218, 227, 236, 239-240
State monopoly capitalism 181-183
Steed G P F 106, 107
Steedman I 18, 19, 22, 182
Stewart C 122
Stockholm 209
Stone D N 93
Streetcar suburbs 56
Struyk R J 99, 101
Suburban communities 223-224
Suburbanization (see also peripheral expansion) 57, 58, 202-203
Suburban solution 123
Subway system 218, 222
Surplus 10-12
Surplus labour 11, 15, 17, 22, 30
Supply and demand 22-23
Switching of techniques 42, 46, 50, 53, 89
Systems theory 230-231, 240

Tastes and preferences 75, 76, 77
Taxes 130-131
Teitz M B 166
Theory of production 99
Thompson W R 181
Threshold 115
von Thünen model 31-41, 160
Topalov C 136, 155
Toronto 93-94, 102-108, 110, 111, 152, 173, 193, 217-227, 249, 250
Toronto Transit Commission 218, 224
Torrens Act 199

Touraine A 183
Transport costs 33-35, 74-75, 91
Transport planning 217-227
Transport problems and policies 217-227
Travel costs 114-115
Truck transport 97

Ullman E L 68
Urban conflict 241-242
Urban core (see also inner city, central business district) 113-114
Urban ecology 66-73
Urban equipment (see also infrastructure) 143-144
Urban general plan 154, 188
Urban government 153-154
Urban growth 187
Urbanism 70
Urbanization and planning 55-65
Urbanization process (see also urban land nexus) 86, 135-136
Urban land nexus (see also land-use conflict, urbanization process, urban planning, urban problems) preface, 2-7, 64-65, 135-174, 185, 189-190, 203, 226, 227, 240-241, 243
Urban planning (see also State, urban policy) 5-6, 27, 140, 147-148, 154, 170-174, 175-192
Urban policy (see also fiscal policy, land regulation policy, development policy, urban planning) 61-65
Urban problems 55-61, 186-187
Urban question 4-9, 135, 243
Urban reformers 195-203
Urban renewal 58, 159, 212-217
Urban sociology (see also Chicago School) 66-73

Urban transport 59, 128-133, 217-227
Utility function 73-74
Utility-maximizing behaviour 73-82
Utopianism 178, 190, 196-197, 236-238
Utopian reformers 86

Vancouver 59n, 102-106, 249, 250
Vernon R 90, 93, 98, 101, 108
Vienna 209
Viollet Collection 205

Wages 16, 17, 19-23, 92-95, 111, 113, 145-146
Walker M 80
Walker R A 123
Walrasian theory of rent 38
Walthamstow 203
Webber M M 176
Weber M 25, 141
Welfare economics 142, 181, 240
Welfare-Statism 25-26
Whinston A B 213
White collar neighbourhoods 126-127
Williamson H F 96
Wilson A G 231
Wingo L 92
Wirth L 70, 71
Working classes 194-203

York 218

ZAC (zone d'aménagement concerté) 156-157
ZAD (zone d'aménagement différé) 156-157
Zoning (see also discriminatory zoning, exclusionary zoning, land-use zoning) 56, 63, 153, 154, 188, 189, 193, 209-212